YOUR LIVING TRUST

How to Protec...

from Probate, ... rs

GORDON K. WILLIAMSON, J.D.,

M.B.A., M.S., C.F.P., CLU, ChFC

A PERIGEE BOOK
NEW YORK

To my beloved agent, Julie Castiglia. She is talented, patient, loyal, dependable and very supportive. I am fortunate to have her representing me.

I would like to thank my close friend Helen Ide Nicoll for proofreading and setting up the index for this book. Her skills and work are greatly appreciated.

Perigee Books
are published by
The Putnam Publishing Group
200 Madison Avenue
New York, NY 10016

Williamson, Gordon, 1940-
   Your living trust / Gordon Williamson.
      p.   cm.
   Includes index.
   ISBN 0-399-51739-1 : price
   1. Living trusts—United States—Popular works.   2. Estate
planning—United States—Popular works.   I. Title.
KF734.Z9W55   1992
346.7305'2—dc20   92-7305 CIP
[347.30652]

Cover design by Dorothy Wachtenheim

Printed in the United States of America

1 2 3 4 5 6 7 8 9 10

This book is printed on acid-free paper.

CONTENTS

PART IV

INTRODUCTION

YOU MAY NOT know it, but you have an estate plan. If you do not plan your estate, the government will do it for you. *Without consulting you or anyone else in your family,* Uncle Sam will decide (1) who your heirs are, (2) what each one will get, (3) when they will get it and (4) how much of your estate will be eaten away by taxes, probate, administrative fees, and legal costs. The courts may also end up making decisions on your behalf *while you are still alive* and without your consent. Fortunately, you can take control of your destiny and that of your estate's.

The reason why you should plan your estate is to save money and to obtain peace of mind. No one likes to be taken advantage of. Take advantage of the laws; do not let them take advantage of you.

By the time you have read just a few chapters in this book, you will be convinced that becoming an active participant in the planning of your estate just makes common sense. I make such a bold statement because over the past dozen years, I have yet to come across a client who did not share this sentiment once he or she *even began* to explore the benefits *and* simplicity of estate planning. You will also see that not only can strategic estate planning be simple, it does not have to be a drawn-out process.

Your objective should be to plan now so you and your family have little or no future involvement or need for lawyers, the courts, administrators, conservators, and the IRS. A great many of these objectives can be accomplished with something known as a revocable living trust. In addition to a living trust you will find that there are other simple documents that, when combined with a trust, can help you and your family.

A living trust, *combined with other documents,* offers the following advantages:

1. Avoids probate.
2. Allows you to maintain control during *and* after your life.
3. Decides who will inherit your property and at what ages.
4. Provides for family members who may be physically or mentally incapacitated.
5. Determines what type of health- and nursing-home care you will later receive.
6. Reduces or eliminates estate taxes.
7. Can be changed at any time.

8. Provides a quick and inexpensive estate settlement.
9. Saves income taxes for your surviving spouse.
10. Lessens the likelihood of having your will contested.
11. Does away with the need for a court-appointed conservatorship.
12. Avoids guardianships.
13. Eliminates the need for a lawyer or court intervention.
14. Minimizes emotional stress.
15. Eliminates ongoing fees or expenses.
16. Maintains privacy.
17. Creates an effective prenuptial agreement.
18. Can take you off life support if your situation is terminal.

Our law firm calls this package "The Great Estate." Other firms around the nation either have their own names for these combined documents or provide similar services. Later chapters in the book will detail how these ancillary documents can enhance the benefits of a living trust. Keep in mind that you can either do these things for yourself, with or without the aid of an attorney, or you can let the government make all of the decisions.

Each of these 18 benefits is discussed briefly below. Later chapters will cover several of them in much greater detail.

Probate: Going to Court

Probate means "proving the will." It is a process that often occurs after someone has died. It is the only way to have property listed in your will retitled in the name of the beneficiaries. If you do not have a will, then probate is still necessary to dispose of your separate property and assets owned as community property or tenancy in common. Without this formal change in title, your heirs will never be able to sell, gift, or transfer their inheritance.

The person who settles your estate has little say as to how your property is transferred or titled. Your estate will go through probate

unless proper estate planning was done before death. As you will see in the second chapter, probate is a court proceeding that can be very costly, unfair, time-consuming, and frustrating.

Control: During Your Lifetime and From the Grave

Since a living trust is something created for the well-being of you and/or your spouse, it is only proper that you determine how your assets are to be handled while you are alive. What may surprise you is that this power and control can continue long after your death.

A trust includes a set of instructions for managing and/or distributing your possessions. Even if you are physically or mentally incapacitated, the trust continues, just as you had set it up originally.

Inheritances: Who and When

One of the problems that joint tenancy and a will share is that you cannot control when the beneficiary will inherit the asset. At death, the new owner receives the property outright. Your intended beneficiaries may be either too young or too immature at this time. A trust is the only way to pass property to someone when the person reaches a specific age or accomplishes a certain task.

Handicapped Family Members: Special Provisions and Protection

There may be a member of your family who is physically or mentally incapacitated. You may want to ensure that this person is taken care of. A living trust can describe, in detail, what type of care is to be provided and/or how much is to be spent. Another document within the living trust package can designate what person is to oversee such help.

Health Care and Nursing Homes: Only the Best

There may come a time when you need special attention. If you are unable to make your own decisions, someone will have to make them for you. Unfortunately, this decision-maker may be a selfish heir who wants to keep the estate as large as possible by sacrificing on the quality of your care. A living trust can include provisions mandating what kind of care you will receive, who will administer it, and at what location.

Estate Taxes: Reduced or Eliminated

Upon death, estate taxes may be due. Estate-tax liability begins at 37% and can be as high as 55%. A later chapter will show you how to reduce or eliminate such taxes. This same chapter includes information that will help your spouse and protect the inheritance of your children.

Flexibility: Can Be Changed at Any Time

The name *revocable* living trust means that this is something you can add to or change at any time before incompetency or death. You can alter your trust at any time without having to answer to anyone. Parties listed in a trust have no voice in the control, management, or disposition of your estate. No court approval or legal help is required. As the trust creator, only you and/or your spouse have the power to change or revoke the trust.

Estate Settlement: Quick and Easy

As you will see in the second chapter, two of the disadvantages of an estate that goes through probate are cost and delay. As an example, in California the typical probate lasts well over a year and costs several thousand dollars. If you have a living trust, your estate can be settled in a matter of days, not months or years.

Income Taxes: Savings Ahead for Your Spouse

Living trusts are often called "income-tax neutral" in that they do not increase or decrease your income or property taxes. However, most people do not know that certain types of living trusts can actually save your surviving spouse income taxes. These trusts, known as A-B and A-B-C Trusts, are described in detail later in the book.

Contesting Your Will and Wishes: Now Less Likely

We often hear about heirs, or people who *thought* they should have been heirs, contesting the decedent's will. This may not only be unfair to the legitimate beneficiaries, but it is also unfair to you. Oftentimes, people come forward claiming that they should have been named in a will when in fact they know that there was no such intent. A living trust makes such a scene less likely and less profitable for illegitimate heirs, whether they are your children, relatives, friends, or former spouse.

Court-Appointed Conservators: Not Needed

When most people think of a living trust, they have a tendency to believe that such a document is only beneficial for heirs. This is simply not true. There are several provisions of a trust that can aid you while you are alive. We are living longer. If you reach age 65, chances are that you will live another 15 years, 18 years in the case of women. Since we are living longer, the chances that something will happen to you physically or mentally are increased. If you are unable to make decisions or are declared incompetent by a court, you can make sure that the person making decisions for your health and financial well-being is your choice, not the court's.

Guardianships: Protect Your Children and Grandchildren

The law recognizes that minor children lack the experience, maturity, and capacity to make informed decisions. Courts also realize that sometimes a parent, sibling, or other relative may not have the child's best interest at heart when it comes to money. It is for these reasons that the court will intervene in the event that both of the minor's parents die. Intervention may also occur if a single parent has legal custody of the child and that parent dies before the child becomes an adult.

The court-appointed guardian may not end

up being the same person you would have chosen. A document included as part of your living trust package can make sure that your wishes about the child are carried out, even if you are no longer able to speak. This is also comforting to a grandparent who wants to ensure that an inheritance or gift benefits its intended donee.

Lawyers and Courts: How They Can Be Avoided

One of the reasons that living trusts have not become popular until recently is that the legal community did not adequately promote trusts. The avoidance of probate can mean that the estate is not paying hefty legal fees or court costs. Once you have a living trust, there is a good chance that as far as your estate is concerned, you and your future heirs will never have to deal with an attorney or court of law.

Emotional Distress: Minimized

Estate settlement that is drawn out is not only frustrating, it is also emotional. If your family is subjected to probate, they will be reminded of their loss every time a document is filed or a court appearance is made. You can save them this added grief and frustration by having a living trust.

Ongoing Fees and Expenses: None

A living trust never becomes outdated. The trust you set up today may be valid 100 years from now. Trusts are valid in all 50 states; if you move to another state it is still valid. Therefore, there are no ongoing fees or costs. The rules and regulations that govern living trusts have not changed in years. Many of our local and national lawmakers have living trusts; they understand the benefits these things provide. It is not likely that trust laws will change in the future.

Privacy: Complete

If your estate is probated, certain notices are mailed and published. In some ways, your life now becomes an open book. These court records are open to the public, including your neighbors, ex-spouse(s) and former business competitors. We know that Natalie Wood owned seven fur coats because her estate was probated—she did not have a living trust. On the other hand, we know nothing about Bing Crosby's estate because he had a living trust. A living trust keeps your affairs completely confidential and private. There are no court records.

Prenuptial Protection: Better Than Prenuptial Agreements

Prenuptial agreements are frequently shot down or contested when there is a divorce or death. A living trust is usually a better alternative since it is an effective way to segregate all property acquired before marriage, no matter what state you were married in or currently reside in.

Terminally Ill: Dying with Dignity and Reducing Medical Costs

You or your spouse may get in a serious car or plane accident or one of you may contract some type of terminal disease or condition. A document that can be included with your living trust can intercede and stop life-sustaining treatment if it is determined by doctors that the condition is hopeless. Without your wishes being known beforehand, the hospital is morally and legally required to keep you alive, no matter how much it drains your family's pocketbook.

Summary

So far you have been given a capsule view of what a living trust is and its accompanying benefits. This is a document that may not end up replacing a will, but it does provide many features not found in a will or in other estate-planning devices. As you can now see, a living trust is useful while you are alive.

There are several ways in which assets are owned and titled; living trusts are just one form.Chapter 1 shows you the different forms of ownership. You may be surprised to learn that the biggest financial mistake a great number of people make is incorrect ownership.

PART I

CHAPTER 1

How Property Is Titled

How you own real estate and personal property can cost or save you thousands of dollars; for some people, tens of thousands of dollars. It might even cost you the property itself. There are important legal and tax consequences associated with every form of ownership. This chapter will show you all of the different ways you can own something; the advantages and disadvantages of each are discussed. After you have finished this chapter, most of you will want to change the title to one or more of your holdings. As you will see, the changing of a title is simple, quick, and usually free; in the case of real estate, your county recorder's office will charge a fee in the neighborhood of $20 for such a "transfer."

Titled property includes real estate, automobiles, mobile homes, boats, bank accounts, mutual funds, individual securities, and brokerage firm accounts. Title to these assets can be held in one of the following ways: (1) separate, (2) tenancy in common, (3) joint tenancy with rights of survivorship, (4) community property, (5) tenancy by the entirety, (6) custodian, (7) partnership, (8) corporation, or (9) in trust. You cannot hold title to the same asset in different ways; you must choose one and only one. Each of these forms of ownership is described below.

Separate

Separate property includes all of those things you acquire while single. It consists of those items earned or acquired after legal separation or divorce. It also includes those things that you receive by gift or inheritance during marriage. Separate property maintains its identity unless it is transferred by the owner to some form of joint ownership or gifted to another person.

As the sole owner of separate property, only you can decide if and when the asset is to be sold or given to someone else. No other person, including your spouse, can transfer, buy, sell, or give away any of your separate property unless you give them permission.

Since only one name appears on the title, it is easy to transfer, sell, or refinance real estate or personal property. The owner simply signs his or her name to the document.

Tenancy in Common

Tenancy in common is a form of joint or co-ownership. As a "co-tenant" you own the asset with one or more other people or entities (a corporation, trust, or partnership). You can sell, transfer, gift, or bequeath (leave in your will or trust) your interest to anyone without the permission of the other co-owners. If the entire asset is being disposed of, all of the people listed on the title must sign off.

Joint Tenancy with Rights of Survivorship (JTWROS)

The most common form of co-ownership is joint tenancy with rights of survivorship, often abbreviated as "jtwros." Like tenancy in common, jtwros means that two or more individuals or entities own the asset and any co-owners are free to dispose of their share in any manner while they are alive. And, just like tenancy in common, everyone shown on the title as owner must sign his or her name before the item can be transferred. However, unlike any other form of ownership, upon the death of one of the co-owners under jtwros, the decedent's share automatically passes on to the surviving tenants. Joint tenancy takes precedence over any will or trust. Thus, even if you try to give jtwros property to someone else in your will, it will have no effect.

People own assets as joint tenants for one of three reasons: (1) their real-estate broker or title company either suggested or pointed out that most people take ownership in this form, (2) in order to avoid probate, or (3) out of ignorance. As you will see, there are numerous problems with joint tenancy.

Most married couples own property in joint tenancy. When the first spouse dies, the surviving spouse inherits the property outright. The decedent's name is taken off the title as soon as the survivor retitles the property. Retitling requires a certified copy of the death certificate and a letter of instruction from the survivor. This often only *postpones* probate. Unless the surviving spouse later adds a new joint tenant (i.e., a child, friend, or new spouse), the asset might be subject to probate.

Adding another person onto the title is common. However, this creates other problems. First, this new "partner" automatically inherits the property when the second spouse dies, regardless of what a will or trust might say to the contrary.

You can list as many co-tenants as you want, but each of them will now be co-owner. The property cannot be transferred unless all sign the conveyance. If you have children who move around or are married to troublesome or greedy in-laws, getting everyone to sign may be difficult. Multiple ownership, however, poses a far greater problem.

Since a joint tenant is an owner, the property is subject to the claims of creditors and lawsuits of every owner. Whether or not the co-owner is your child, friend, or other relative, if they are successfully sued, there may be a forced sale or lien on the asset. The suit may later be settled or won and the asset still sold to pay for legal expenses; it is very rare for the defendant or plaintiff ever to recover legal expenses, no matter how "right" they were. Listing anyone as a joint tenant who drives a car, is a professional, or owns a business greatly increases the odds that the asset may be lost. The chances of such an occurrence are even greater if the co-tenant is married. You would also have to be concerned about that spouse being subjected to a lawsuit.

Another problem with joint tenancy has to do with protecting your beneficiaries. If you are married and have children from a previous marriage, a joint tenancy with your spouse means that he or she gets the property when you die. This surviving spouse has no duty or obligation to pass it on to your children later. If the survivor has children of his or her own or later remarries, there is a good chance that the ultimate heir will be someone you may not have even met.

With rising health-care costs and people living longer, you may be hospitalized for an extended period or kept alive. If this situation arises and you can no longer sign your name due to a physical or mental impairment, then it may be difficult for your loved ones to raise needed cash to live on or pay your bills. More important, with the exception of your personal residence, these assets may have to be disposed of before there is any financial assistance from the state or federal government.

Joint tenancy increases the chances of a conservatorship. If any co-owner becomes incapacitated, a conservatorship must be established.

Up to now, all of the negative things associated with joint tenancy are from events and circumstances that may or may not arise. But the worst part about joint tenancy is a certainty. This has to do with the sale or gifting of the asset.

Anytime a sale, transfer, gift, or inheritance of an asset is contemplated, always consider any potential income, gift, or estate tax. When you acquire an asset, such as a home, business interest, stock, or bond, you take on what is known as a "cost basis." This "basis" is important if the asset is ever disposed of; any and all profits or losses are determined based on the asset's basis. The cost, or basis, is the purchase price minus any depreciation or plus any additions (fix-up expenses, additional contributions, etc.).

When personal property (stocks, bonds, cars, boats, jewelry, furniture, etc.) or real estate is sold for more than the purchase price, a taxable event can occur. The profit, referred to as gain, is determined by subtracting the purchase price (adjusted for any depreciation or fix-up costs claimed) from the *net* sales price (the selling price minus any costs, fees, or commissions). As an example, if you paid $20,000 for a car, spent $5,000 fixing it up, depreciated $6,000 of it as a business expense, and then paid someone $1,000 to sell it for you for $22,000, the tax consequences would look like this:

	$20,000	purchase price
+	5,000	fix-up costs
−	6,000	depreciation
=	19,000	adjusted-cost basis
−	22,000	selling price
=	3,000	gross profit
−	1,000	selling commission
=	2,000	net (taxable) profit

This net figure results in a taxable event unless the final figure is zero or a negative number or the asset being sold is somehow sheltered (within a retirement plan, part of an annuity, or a tax-free exchange). One of the goals of estate and financial planning is to lower, eliminate, or defer, whenever possible, any tax event.

Unless somehow sheltered, assets sold while you are *alive* are fully taxable if a net profit results. Assets sold for a loss may result in a tax loss that can be used to offset gains. You can also use a "tax loss" to offset earned income such as your salary. Death of an owner or co-owner can change the tax consequences because of what is known as a "step-up in basis."

A Step-up in Basis

A "stepped-up" basis means that, in the eyes of the IRS, the asset being sold or transferred now costs more than it originally did. This means that any resulting profit will be reduced or eliminated. A step-up in basis occurs only upon the death of a sole owner or co-tenant in the case of community property or joint tenancy with rights of survivorship. The best way to show how a new basis is calculated is by example.

Suppose that you were the *sole owner* of some stocks, bonds, personal property, or real estate that originally cost you $100,000. For sake of illustration, let us assume that the cost basis is not altered due to any depreciation, additional contributions, or fix-up costs. The asset is now worth $300,000 and you decide to sell it. If the asset was sold for $300,000 you would have a $200,000 profit. Unless somehow sheltered, taxes on the $200,000 gain would be due for the year in which the asset was sold.

Change the set of facts slightly and assume that just before the sale occurred, you died. Your heir(s) would receive a step-up in basis equal to the fair market value of the asset as of the date of your death ($300,000 in this example). If the heirs later sold the asset, any profit or loss would be determined based on the new cost basis. If, in our example, the property you paid $100,000 for was worth $300,000 at your death, and the heirs later sold it for $300,000, there would be no taxable gain. This is because the new basis is $300,000; your heir(s) received a 100% step-up in basis. This is one of the few ways in which income taxes can be avoided, but death must occur to get this tax advantage.

Let us change the facts again. Now assume that you and someone else own the property as joint tenants with rights of survivorship (jtwros). If a sale occurred *while both of you were alive*, there would be a taxable gain of $200,000; just like what happened if you owned the asset as separate property. If, however, either tenant died before the sale, there would be an adjustment in the cost basis of the decedent's share. *Half* of the property would get a step-up in basis equal to *that share's* value at the date of death.

In our example, upon the death of a joint owner his or her share is now considered to have an "original purchase price" of $150,000 (one-half the fair market value at death), even though they only paid $50,000 for that interest. Any profit or loss is now based on the new cost basis. In this case, the new cost basis is the decedent's share, adjusted upward to $150,000. The surviving tenant's original cost of $50,000, or other half of the original purchase price, does not change. Taxes are based on an *adjusted basis* of $200,000. If the property were sold for $300,000 the surviving tenant would pay taxes on a gain of $100,000 (unless there was some exclusion, tax-free exchange, or the sold asset was part of a qualified retirement plan or annuity).

Let us change the facts one last time. Assume everything is the same except this couple is married, they live in a community-property state, and the asset is titled as community property (e.g., "Nathan and Ina Baty, c/p"). Upon the death of either spouse the property will receive a 100% step-up in basis *on both halves*, even though only one spouse has died. If the property had been sold while both spouses were alive, there would have

been a potential taxable gain of $200,000 (the $300,000 sales price minus the $100,000 purchase price). However, in this particular example, wherein one or both spouses have died, there is no taxable event since the property has a new cost basis of $300,000. Any profit or loss is based on the new basis, $300,000, being subtracted from the sales price. In our example where the sales price is assumed to also be $300,000, there are no taxes due since $300,000 minus $300,000 results in a gain of zero. Community property is discussed in the next section.

Keep in mind the following points concerning community property and a step-up in basis: (1) the property must be titled as "community property" *prior to* the sale and death of either spouse (living in a community-property state is not enough), (2) death must occur to receive the stepped-up basis, and (3) this 100% step-up in basis also occurs if both spouses die at the same time. All items titled as community property will receive a 100% step-up in basis upon the death of either the husband or wife, even though such items have been retitled under the name of the trust.

Most people in community-property states take title to their home, savings accounts, and securities as jtwros with their spouse. As you can now see, this may be the biggest mistake you have ever made. Fortunately, you can go out and retitle the asset tomorrow for little or no cost. You do not need a lawyer or court order to make such a change. Simply contact the savings institution, brokerage firm, or county recorder's office and find out what form they require.

Community Property

There are seven community-property states: Arizona, California, Idaho, Nevada, New Mexico, Texas, and Washington. All other states, except Louisiana and the District of Columbia, are classified as "common-law" states. Common-law states are also referred to as separate-property states. Wisconsin is a common-law state but has adopted marital-property laws that are similar to community-property jurisdictions. The distinction between community and common-law states is important whenever death or divorce occur.

Community property (c/p) includes everything that you acquire while you are married and reside in one of the seven community-property states. It includes all assets, income, salary, personal possessions, and real estate of both spouses.

Marriage in a community-property state means that assets earned or obtained by *either* spouse are owned equally by both spouses. Items acquired by gift or inheritance are considered the separate property of that spouse. Gifts and bequests retain their separate-property identity unless the person receiving the gift, known as the donee, decides to make a "gift" of the asset to the other spouse or to the community.

As you saw under the section titled "A Step-up in Basis," community property offers a tremendous tax advantage not found with other forms of ownership; but this benefit comes at a cost. Under community-property laws, either spouse can sell, transfer, bequest, or gift his or her share without the permission of the other spouse. You may own an asset as community property with your spouse and discover that upon that spouse's death his or her share has been left to someone other than you (a child, neighbor, friend, etc.). In a community-property state the decedent's will may say that a secret boyfriend is to receive her share of the community property.

Tenancy by the Entirety

Tenancy by the entirety is a form of joint ownership except that it involves a husband and wife. It can be terminated only by the joint agreement of both spouses. This form of co-ownership is often used by married couples in separate-property states (*see "Community Property" above to determine if you live in a separate-property state*).

Custodian (FBO)

Accounts set up for minor children or mentally incapacitated persons must name a cus-todian. This is because these categories of people are not considered to have "legal capacity" and therefore cannot normally enter into a binding contract. Only the custodian can trade, buy, or sell assets in the custodial account. Title to these accounts is usually taken as "Mary Smith, custodian for the benefit of (abbreviated as FBO) Jeff Jones." Even though Jeff Jones is the owner, he lacks legal capacity, owing either to age or mental condition. It is for this reason that only Mary Smith, the custodian listed on the account, can make decisions concerning the asset.

Custodians are similar to trustees in that they are overseeing an account, asset, or property for the benefit of another individual, group, or entity. In the case of a trust, the trustee is also often the trustor (the person who created the trust).

Custodial accounts are most frequently found with minor children. Once a child becomes an adult, the custodian's name is dropped from the account and the 18-year-old (age 21 in some states) is free to do whatever he or she wants with the account. Custodian accounts are usually part of a guardianship or conservatorship.

Partnership

Any two or more adults may enter into a partnership. A partnership has some common business goal. There are two types of partners: general and limited. A general partner is responsible for the day-to-day operations of the partnership. A general partner is fully liable for any claims against the partnership.

Limited partners have limited rights and therefore limited liability. A limited partner is not liable for the losses, debts, or lawsuits incurred by the partnership. Limited partners can lose their entire investment in the partnership, but no more. The only way a limited partner may be liable for more than his or her contribution to the partnership is if he or she signed a note or obtained a letter of credit. Sometimes a limited partner is found to have been so active in the partnership that he or she is deemed to be a general partner.

Corporation

A corporation can be created by one or more individuals. Corporations are usually formed to limit one's liability. It is commonly believed that in the event of a lawsuit or claim, only the assets of the corporation are at risk. This is often not true. A corporation will not protect the personal assets of a corporate officer or employee who is accused of fraud or an intentional act such as slander or bodily harm. Furthermore, the "corporate veil" will not protect someone who uses the corporation as an alter ego. It is not very common that a court will protect the personal assets of someone just because he or she has a personal corporation.

Until a few years ago, corporate tax brackets used to be lower than individual rates. This has all changed; corporate rates are now higher than individual. For the privilege of being a corporation, franchise tax fees must be paid annually and corporate tax returns filed each year for the state and the federal government. Accounting and tax-preparation fees are usually higher than those charged for individuals and couples. This is yet another reason why the corporate status should be avoided by most people.

Trust

Accounts and property that are part of a trust must name one or more trustee(s). Only the trustee or trustees have the right to manage, buy, or sell assets within the trust. Trust accounts are easy to identify; title to the account is something like "Ursel Jones, trustee of the Jones Family Trust." The person who creates the trust, known as the trustor or "trust maker," can change trustees at any time. People who create trusts usually name themselves as trustee.

Assets placed within a trust maintain their original identity; all separate property remains under the sole ownership of one person. Jointly held property (tenancy in common, jtwros, c/p, tenancy by the entirety) also keeps its co-owner status. These distinctions are normally important only if there is a divorce or death.

Future chapters will detail how a trust is set up and handled during your lifetime and after your demise. The next chapter deals exclusively with probate. When you finish this chapter, you will know more about probate than most attorneys. Better still, the chapter is laid out in a way that is easy to understand.

It is important for you to have a good understanding as to how probate works. After reading this one chapter you will probably be convinced that a living trust is something that you should have if for no other reason than to avoid probate. You may be thinking that probate is not something you will ever go through. Think again. There is something called a "living probate" that you may be subjected to if you, your spouse, or a relative becomes mentally or physically incapacitated. Furthermore, you may be the victim of the probate process if you are the heir of an estate that was not properly planned.

Summary

There are several ways to own property. How your assets are titled can cost or save you a great deal of money in the event of a divorce or death. The amount of income-tax liability is dependent upon four things: (1) if there was a death before the sale, (2) how the property was titled just before it was sold, (3) the selling price, and (4) the adjusted basis (cost) of the asset. When computing estate taxes, the title of the asset and its fair market value on the date of death are the two deciding factors.

Before you go out and retitle your assets into community property or joint tenancy, bear in mind two points. First, any name change will have a bearing only if the property is sold after death, for estate tax purposes, and in the event of a divorce. Second, the potential tax savings may be small in comparison to what would happen if there were a divorce. That is, there is little satisfaction in minimizing taxes if you now own only part of the asset because of a divorce settlement or death. Therefore, a name change from separate property to some form of co-ownership or from joint tenancy to community property should be considered only if you completely trust your mate.

Checklist of Things to Do

1. Review how all of the property you own is titled.
2. Retitle assets held as jtwros with your spouse to community property (c/p).
3. Consider changing the title on your separate property to c/p.
4. If you are incorporated, rethink the actual benefits vs. ongoing costs.

CHAPTER 2

PROBATE

PROBATE MEANS "PROVING the will" through a court proceeding. As a practical matter, it is the way in which your final bills are paid and your property is distributed. Your estate can still be subject to probate even if you do not have a will. Probate is the only way to transfer title to real estate or personal property when the person listed as the owner cannot sign his or her own name due to death, incompetency, or because that person is a minor.

What may surprise you is that the probate court may end up getting involved in your affairs twice: while you are alive *and* after death. Without proper estate planning, the court can end up taking control of your personal and financial affairs if you are unable to; this control will last until there is recovery, death, or the child becomes an adult.

Probate was created to protect the interests of you and your family. It has been in existence for hundreds of years. Over the years it has provided an orderly means of paying the decedent's bills and transferring real estate and personal property. The probate court was also designed to manage the finances of an incompetent person or minor child.

Technically, probate is a court proceeding wherein a will is introduced and proven to be valid. If there is no valid will, the court then determines who the deceased's heirs are, using that state's rules of "intestate succession" (discussed in another chapter).

A will may be offered for probate by anyone interested in the estate. An "interested party" would include the named executor, a beneficiary, an intestate heir (who might be hoping to get something), or a creditor of the estate. In several states, the will must be offered for probate within 3 years after the decedent's death; if this does not happen, then, as far as the law is concerned, the deceased died intestate. You can be liable to the beneficiaries named in the will if you possess the decedent's will and do not present it to the probate court within a specified period. In some states, you may also be criminally liable.

After the will is admitted to probate, or the heirs are established by the court, a personal representative is appointed. If the will names an executor, then the court gives its blessing to this selection. If no executor is named, or the person chosen refuses to accept or is unable to carry out the required duties, the court appoints what is known as an administrator. In either case, this person is called a personal representative.

At this point, the administration of the estate begins. Estate administration includes the gathering and inventory of the decedent's assets; debts and claims are settled and the remaining assets are distributed according to the terms of the will or intestate succession if no valid will exists.

Strictly speaking, you *probate* the deceased's will and *administer* his or her estate. For many years, the word "probate" has been used by lawyers and laypersons alike to refer to all steps of estate administration. The steps listed below are involved in probating a decedent's estate in all 50 states. The exact procedures will vary somewhat from state to state.

Primary probate jurisdiction is in the decedent's state of domicile at the time of death. Actual estate administration usually takes place in the county of the decedent's domicile when death occurred. If you own property in another state, there is an ancillary probate in each and every one of those states. An ancillary probate can also take place in any county where a debtor of the decedent resides (one more reason to have a living trust).

In the case of real estate located in another state, ancillary probate and administration are necessary to clear title to the property. Without such a "clearance," the heirs (beneficiaries) will not ever be able to sell the real estate. Procedurally what happens is the "ancillary administrator" takes possession of the property within his or her jurisdiction, makes sure any claims and taxes within the state are satisfied, and then distributes whatever remains to the *principal* executor or administrator.

Let us begin by going through an overview of the probate process. The second part of the chapter will detail the steps of probate in much greater detail.

Opening the Estate

The first step is for the decedent's last will to be offered and its execution proven. This simply means that it is shown that the will was signed and properly witnessed. If there is no will, the deceased's intestate heirs (spouse, children, grandchildren, parents, etc.) are set out by the court.

At this same meeting, the decedent's personal representative (executor or administrator) is formally appointed (approved) by the court, and letters testamentary (if there was a valid will) or letters of administration (if there was no will) are issued. These "letters" are proof to the rest of the world as to the authority and legitimacy of the personal representative. Only this representative can legally act on behalf of the estate. As a side note, *trust assets* are controlled by the trustee, a person appointed by you.

In every state there is an order of succession in the event that an executor was not named in the will, refuses to serve, or is unable to serve. Generally, the order of priority is: (1) the person named in the will as executor, (2) the surviving spouse if he or she is provided for in the will, (3) any other beneficiary named in the will, (4) the surviving spouse (if not provided for), (5) any other next of kin, and (6) any creditor (if 45 days have lapsed since the decedent died).

In most states, whoever the personal representative ends up being, he or she must be bonded unless waived by the will. If a bond is required, the dollar amount of the bond is for double the value of all personal property in the estate. The personal representative is entitled to compensation for his or her services. The majority of states have a statutory rate of compensation that is based on the size of the estate.

A personal representative's powers and responsibilities are terminated for any one of the following reasons: (1) death or disability, (2) resignation, or (3) the court's finding that there has been misconduct.

A majority of states allow an interested party up to 6 months to contest the will once it is presented to the probate court. If the will is contested at this first meeting, the person(s) who claim that the will *is valid* have the burden of proof to show validity. A claim made by a contestant *after* the probate proceedings automatically shifts the burden of proof to the person or persons contesting the will.

Watching Over the Decedent's Property

The second step is for the personal representative to collect and conserve the estate's assets. Although title to a decedent's property goes immediately to his or her heirs and beneficiaries, the representative has the right to possess the property in order to pay claims and taxes. Once ownership is determined, the new owner (the heir) gains legal title. Assets are owned by the decedent until the moment of death; right after death, without any lapse in time, they are owned by the beneficiaries. If a will is contested or the identity of the beneficiaries is difficult to determine, then title (ownership) reverts back to these persons as of the moment of death as soon as matters are cleared up.

If the settlement of the estate is expected to take a long time, it is common for the representative to have all securities and accounts re-registered in the name of the personal representative so that he or she may collect any income, dividends, or interest and sell off assets as needed in order to pay taxes and other claims. In the case of tangible personal property (jewelry, artwork, furniture, clothing, automobiles, mobile homes, etc.), it is usual for the representative to leave these assets with surviving family members.

Allowances

As a spouse or adult child of the decedent it may sound ridiculous, and perhaps humiliating, but it is the personal representative, who may or may not be a family member, who pays out any needed family allowance (money used to pay ongoing bills, mortgages, food, clothing, utilities, etc.). A family member must first petition the court, requesting that an allowance be granted.

Creditors' Claims

The representative's next responsibility is to give notice by publication in a local newspaper to prospective creditors. If the creditor is known, referred to as a "secured creditor," then this person or company is given a personal notice. At this step, the representative either pays, disallows, or settles creditor claims.

Taxes

The representative is responsible for filing all tax returns—state, federal, income, and estate—on behalf of the decedent and the decedent's estate. The personal representative can be liable if all taxes are not paid. Taxes are paid from the estate's assets.

A final *income-tax* return must be filed for the calendar year in which the decedent died. This return, Form 1040, is filed just like any other income tax return. It includes all of the income earned during the year by the deceased until the day of death; the same credits, deductions, and exemptions are used.

If the *estate* has assets that throw off income (interest, dividends, rents, royalties, capital gains), this money will be received by the representative while the estate is being probated. If the estate has more than $600 of income in any year, the personal representative must file a fiduciary tax return (Form 1041). Depending on the size of the estate, the representative may also be responsible for filing a state and federal estate (inheritance)-tax return.

Distribution

After funeral, administration, taxes, and claims have been paid, the representative's final step is to distribute the remaining assets according to the terms of the will or intestate succession. At this point, most states require that before final distributions are made, there is a hearing during which the probate court enters a "decree of distribution" and discharges the personal representative from any further duties and liabilities.

Supervision

The majority of states subject the representative to court supervision and control at every step. A minority of states allow what is known as "independent administration," which means the estate is handled and settled without court supervision. In some community-property states such as California, only the decedent's half interest in any community property is subject to probate and then only if it passes to someone other than the surviving spouse. Furthermore, in these few states, during this process, the surviving spouse can continue to manage and control all community property (even if the decedent's share has been given to someone else).

Each state has its own definition of a "modest" or "small" estate. In these cases, a number of states have greatly simplified the required administrative procedures.

Informal Administration

A major purpose of probate is to clear title to assets so that the beneficiaries or heirs can receive them (and later sell these assets if they so desire). Often, an estate contains only *personal* property of a modest size. In such a situation, a formal administration may not be needed. The clearing of title is needed only for assets that come with a document of title (real estate, automobiles, mobile homes, and securities). Recognizing this fact, every state provides for what is known as an "informal administration." An informal proceeding is not usually allowed if the decedent owned any real estate, including the family home.

If an informal administration is appropriate, the process is quite simple. A family member files a petition that claims the value of the decedent's estate is less than the amount stated by statute. The size of an estate that qualifies for this quick procedure varies from state to state; in Florida it is $25,000, in Texas

it is $50,000, and in New York it is $10,000.

The probate judge or court clerk then issues an affidavit that serves the same function as letters testamentary or letters of administration. Acting under the authority of the affidavit, the family member then gathers up all of the accounts and securities that were in the name of the decedent (as either sole or co-owner). The family member then re-registers these accounts and securities and takes whatever action is necessary to wind up the decedent's affairs (settle claims, pay funeral expenses, file tax returns, etc.).

How a Large Estate Might Qualify for the Streamlined Procedure

Just because your state might have a $10,000 or $25,000 limit does not necessarily mean that your family cannot still take advantage of an informal administration, even if you are a millionaire. First, your probatable estate does not include those assets titled in the name of your living trust, assets held in joint tenancy, or accounts and policies with designated beneficiaries (life insurance, Totten trusts, IRAs, pension plans, etc.). Second, several states do not include estate money used as a family allowance, the personal-property exemption, and any filed homestead.

If your estate is probated it will probably not qualify for the informal process unless a great deal of planning takes place before your death. Even then the streamlined procedure is not available if you own real estate unless it is titled in the name of a trust or held in joint tenancy. Shown below is the form used in California for an informal administration.

Afffidavit to Exclude Small Estate From Probate

The undersigned declares:

1. I make this affidavit to induce _____ to transfer to me the property described below under California Probate Code sections 13100-13115.

2. _____ (decedent) died at _____ while a resident of the City of _____ County of _____ State of California, on or about _____ , leaving _____ will.

3. At least 40 days have elapsed since the death of the decedent, as shown in a certified copy of the decedent's death certificate attached to this affidavit.

4. No proceeding is now being conducted or has been conducted in California for the administration of the decedent's estate.

5. The gross value of the decedent's real and personal property in California, excluding the property described in California Probate Code Section 13050, does not exceed $60,000 and includes the following

_____ .

9. The affiant requests that the described property be paid, delivered or transferred to the affiant.

10. I agree to hold _____ free and harmless and indemnify _____ against all

liability, claims, demands, losses, damages, costs and expenses whatsoever that _____ may incur because of said transfer, payment, or delivery.

Dated: _____ , 19 _____

Signature: _____

County of _____

State of _____

Subscribed and sworn to before me this _____ day _____ of, 19_____ .

_____

Notary Public

My commission expires on _____

Totten Trusts and Pay-on-Death Accounts

States permit certain financial institutions to let their customers establish accounts in the form of "X, Trustee for Y." These accounts, referred to as Totten trusts, permit the trustor (X in this example) to have *exclusive* control over the account while alive; at death, the account is payable to the named beneficiary (Y in this example).

Monies held in these Totten trusts can usually be paid to the named beneficiary immediately after the death of the trustor, without waiting for probate. This type of account can play an important role in estate planning for small sums of money; owing to their lack of flexibility, they should not be used if a large dollar amount is involved.

Disadvantages of Joint Tenancy

Joint tenancy is sometimes considered an alternative to a living trust. Although joint tenancy avoids probate, it does not have the flexibility or protection of a living trust. Consider the following disadvantages of joint tenancy:

1. You cannot manage property before and after your death.
2. You cannot use discretion in the distribution of income and/or principal.
3. You cannot postpone a beneficiary from receiving property outright.

4. Does not permit flexibility to aid in the reduction of estate taxes.
5. Might create gift tax liability.
6. Only one-half of the property gets a stepped-up basis when one owner dies.

The 19 Steps of Probate

What is wrong with probate is that it is expensive, time-consuming, and often inflexible. Consider the list of things that must be done if a decedent's estate is probated:

Once the process begins, your family loses control and the court takes over. As you can see, this is not something most people want to go through. If probate is required and this process is not completed, property title cannot be transferred. This means that assets cannot be sold in the future.

All of these steps can be avoided by having a living trust. Unfortunately, some of you will either not set up a trust, fail to fully fund your trust, or improperly title assets. For you, I have given a summary description of each of these 19 steps below.

These capsule descriptions have also been included because you may end up probating someone else's estate and this knowledge will be helpful.

Step 1: File Petition for Probate and Get a Hearing Date

This is what initiates the probate process. If a will exists then you file a Petition for Probate; if there is no will, then a Petition for Letters is filed. If the estate contains real estate, the court may require that a bond be posted for the value of the property.

Part of this filing includes the estate's representative listing the name, relationship, age, and residence of everyone mentioned in the decedent's will, whether living or deceased. The surviving spouse and any living children, as well as deceased children, are included. If there are no surviving children, grandchildren, or spouse, then the decedent's living parents are shown. If such parents are dead, then any brothers or sisters of the deceased are listed.

Probate Checklist
1. File a Petition for Probate and obtain a hearing date.
2. File the original will and any codicils with the court.
3. Publish and mail the Notice of Petition to Administer Estate.
4. File proof of publication and proof of mailing (step 3).
5. If required, file Proof of Will.
6. File Order for Probate (and probate bond if necessary).
7. Check calendar notes.
8. File Letters and Duties and Liabilities of Personal Representative.
9. Fill out Application for Appointment of Probate Referee.
10. Prepare Inventory and Appraisement.
11. Mail Notice of Proposed Action to creditors and beneficiaries.
12. Pay all debts that do not require formal notice.
13. File Approval or Rejection of Creditor's Claims.
14. Prepare and file decedent's final state and federal income-tax return.
15. Prepare and file state and federal estate-tax return (if needed).
16. File Petition for Final Distribution.
17. Mail Notice of Hearing to Heirs and Beneficiaries and file proof of the mailing.
18. Transfer assets and obtain receipts.
19. File Receipts and Affidavit for Final Discharge.

Step 2: File Original Will and Any Codicils

At the same time the petition in Step 1 is filed, the will, if there is one, should also be filed. If the deceased had a written will, what is known as a holographic will, then a transcript of it must be typed. Any codicils (changes to the will) are also filed.

Step 3: Publish and Mail Notice of Petition to Administer Estate

Part of the purpose of Step 1 is to have the court clerk give the estate's representative a hearing date. When the clerk gives the representative this information, it must be given to certain persons. This notice must be mailed by first class to all heirs, beneficiaries, and others described in Step 1 above. The person doing the mailing cannot be the representative or any other interested party.

In addition to these mailed notices, the representative must publish the Notice of Petition to Administer Estate in a newspaper of general circulation in the city where the decedent resided. This gives notice to creditors and others who may be interested in the estate. The notification must be published three times before the date of the court hearing.

Step 4: File Proof of Publication and Mailing

This step requires several copies of different documents. First, the representative will need to photocopy two sets of the Petition for Probate. Both copies should then be stamped "filed" by the clerk and sent back to the representative. One of these copies is then given to the newspaper used in the previous step. Second, everyone listed in Step 1 must be sent a copy of the Notice of Petition to Administer Estate. The representative should keep an extra copy for his or her files.

Step 5: File Proof of Will (If Needed)

Three copies of the will and all codicils, if any, are needed so that the court clerk can stamp the case number and filing date on each copy (wills and codicils are described in a later chapter). These copies will be used in the future by the representative.

The next thing that needs to be done is the filing of the original will along with the Petition for Probate. At this point a one-time filing fee is paid. The check, which will be for about $125, should be made payable to "County Clerk." Both of these documents can be filed either in person or by mail with the clerk.

Step 6: File Order for Probate

The purpose of the Order for Probate is to admit the will, if any, to probate and to formally appoint an estate representative. If a bond is required, it will need to be paid at this time.

Step 7: Check Calendar Notes

This is a review step. Before going on, the representative needs to make sure whether the petition has been approved or if there are any problems. The court should be contacted before the hearing to see if everything is all right.

Step 8: File Letters and Duties and Liabilities of Personal Representative

Two copies of Letters Testamentary are certified by the county clerk. These copies are then used to transfer bank and brokerage accounts from the name of the decedent to that of the estate.

The Duties and Liabilities of Personal Representative form provides a summary of the representative's duties. This signed form is filed along with the Letters Testamentary.

Step 9: Fill Out Application for Appointment of Probate Referee

Everything owned by the decedent, whether individually or jointly, must be appraised by a referee appointed by the court. The only exception to this is cash and bank accounts. Before the referee makes these appraisals, the representative has to submit a form showing all of the assets and estimated values, what the rep feels each item is worth. Once this form is sent to the clerk, the representative will then receive a conforming copy with information about how the referee can be contacted for the formal appraisal.

Step 10: Prepare Inventory and Appraisement

Before the court hearing, an inventory of the estate must be made. When filling out the Inventory and Appraisement form, make sure that (a) all partial interests (e.g., joint tenancy) are shown, (b) only those assets subject to probate are included (real and personal property not subject to probate are described in another chapter), (c) the full legal description of all real estate is given, and (d) any mortgages or deeds of trust include the recording reference or legal description. If any real estate is involved, a Change in Ownership Statement will need to be filed by the county assessor's office where the property is located.

Step 11: Mail Notice of Proposed Action

After the testamentary letters are issued, the representative must wait several months before the estate can be closed. This period allows creditors to file their claims against the estate. During this time, the representative may find it necessary to sell assets that are depreciating or causing expenses to the estate. If this is the case, then a Notice of Proposed Action should be filed with the court and copies sent to "interested parties" (creditors and those people who would have normally inherited part or all of the asset that is about to be sold). Anyone who has filed a Request for Special Notice with the court should also be given notice.

Step 12: Handle Decedent's Debts

The representative of the estate has the power to pay, reject, compromise, or contest any claim against the estate without court supervision. All known creditors are first sent a written notice. The creditors have only a few months to come forward and make a claim. Generally, once this period lapses, all other claims are barred.

Step 13: File Approval or Rejection of Creditor's Claims

If claims are filed, the representative needs to fill out a form called Allowance or Rejection of Creditor's Claim to let the creditor and court know what action has been taken. The original is filed with the court and a copy is sent by a disinterested third party to the creditor.

Step 14: Prepare and File Final Income-Tax Returns

The executor of the estate (called an administrator if there is no valid will) is responsible for filing the decedent's final income tax returns. It is important that returns are filed and taxes paid before any substantial distributions; otherwise the executor could find himself personally liable to the IRS or the Franchise Tax Board.

Step 15: Prepare and File State and Federal Estate-Tax Return (If Needed)

Depending upon the size of the decedent's estate, state inheritance and federal estate-tax returns may need to be filed. Again, this liability should be taken care of before the distribution of assets. Under most circumstances, these estate-tax returns must be filed within 9 months of the decedent's death.

Step 16: File Petition for Final Distribution

After the creditor's claim period has expired, the time limit for rejected creditors to file suit has lapsed, all administrative expenses have been paid, and a state income-tax clearance certificate has been obtained, the representative can petition the court requesting an Order Distributing the Assets to the Beneficiaries.

Step 17: Prepare and Mail Notice of Hearing; File Proof of Notice

The notice for final distribution is mailed a couple of weeks before the hearing date to all the beneficiaries or heirs, to anyone who filed a Special Notice, and to any trustee. Proof of these mailings is then filed with the clerk. Along with this, an Order for Final Distribution is also filed. This form details the property to be distributed to each person, including its appraised value.

Step 18: Transfer Assets and Obtain Receipts

Each person who receives property should sign a receipt. If real estate is being distributed, the representative needs to file a statement identifying the date and place of the recording.

Step 19: File Receipts and Affidavit for Final Discharge

Once all property has been transferred and receipts have been filed with the court, the representative can request to be discharged from his or her duties. This Affidavit for Final Discharge is signed by the judge and concludes the court proceeding. If an earlier bond was posted, a copy of the Order of Final Discharge should be sent to the bonding company.

The Costs of Probate

Probate fees are based on the *gross* value of your estate (e.g., market value of your real estate *including* any mortgage), not its net value. Your state's probate- and administrative-fee schedule may be higher or lower than what is shown below.

Gross Estate Value	California	New York
$100,000	$6,300	$10,000
$200,000	$10,300	$18,000
$500,000	$22,300	$38,000
$1,000,000	$42,300	$68,000
$2,000,000	$62,300	$118,000
$5,000,000	$122,300	$268,000

These are *statutory* fees. The attorney handling your estate can always petition the court for "extraordinary" expenses. Such requests are usually granted and further reduce the size of the estate. *According to the Estate Research Institute, 10–70% of a deceased's assets will be siphoned off by probate fees, estate taxes, accounting, and other costs.*

When reviewing the chart above, do not forget to factor in the effects of appreciation either due to prudent management and/or inflation. As an example, if inflation were to average 7%, a $300,000 estate today (a $14,300 probate) would double in value in 10 years (resulting in a $30,300 probate).

Other Problems Associated with Probate

Not only is probate time-consuming and expensive, there are several other unfavorable side effects to the process. In order to protect the estate, assets are usually frozen during probate. This means that your loved ones cannot receive their inheritance; assets may not be sold or money distributed without the court's permission. All of the court filings, appearances, and publications are a matter of public record. "Unintended heirs" are put on notice, and business competitors now have access to the decedent's assets and liabilities.

When Probate Can Affect You

The probate court can step in when (1) you die, (2) you become incompetent, or (3) your minor children inherit property. If you are married, the chances of probate double. If your spouse dies, becomes incompetent, or has minor children from a previous marriage, and these children inherit property, you may be subjected to probate.

How People Attempt to Avoid Probate

There are four ways people think probate can be avoided: (1) a will, (2) a will that has a trust in it, (3) not having a will, or (4) owning property jointly.

First, a will has no effect *until* it is probated. The will must be declared valid by the court before assets are transferred. Second, a will with a trust built into it still means that a will exists. These types of trusts are known as "testamentary trusts" and, unlike a living trust, cannot become effective until the will has been probated. Third, even if you do not have a will, the state you reside in has one for you. Every state wants to make sure that debts are paid and all of your assets are distributed. The state's will must also be probated.

Finally, joint ownership does avoid probate, but usually only temporarily. Married couples often hold title in joint tenancy in part to avoid probate. The same is true with single people who own an asset with a family member or friend. This form of ownership merely postpones probate. Upon the death of either joint owner, the surviving owner will receive the property without having to go through probate. However, when the survivor dies, assets may be probated. Most important, joint ownership can cause a great deal of legal and financial problems. Since this is the solution used by most people, you might wish to review the last chapter and reacquaint yourself with all of the problems associated with such form of ownership.

The Trust Process
Although not mandatory, if you have a living trust it is advisable for your trustee to place a newspaper notice. If you do not publish, creditor claims are bound by the statutes of limitations for contracts, which is one year in most states but up to 7 years in a few states.

Under probate, the time within which creditors are entitled to file claims is severely limited, usually to no more than 4 months. Under a living trust, the rights of creditors are determined by the statutes of limitations that apply within contract law. But in a time-based contract, such as an installment agreement, the statute of limitations may exist for the entire life of the contract.

Summary

As you can see, probate is not something you would wish upon your worst enemy. The proceedings can be expensive, there are numerous steps that must be fulfilled, and you do not have control over how long each step will take.

You might be thinking that this is no concern to you; after all, you will not be around to see the estate probated. Well, think again. You may be subjected to the process if your spouse or child predeceases you. Even if you are certain that this is not a possibility, think how long it took you to save, on an after-tax basis, the ten or twenty thousand dollars that will be drained from your estate to pay the probate bill. Or perhaps an appeal should be made to your ego. After you have passed away, do you want people near you wondering how financially savvy you really were if you were so ignorant as to not properly plan your affairs? The only way to make sure that this does not happen is by having a living trust.

The purpose of probate is to change the legal title of property from your name to that of your heirs. These heirs may be the ones you intended, meaning you had a valid will *or* family members that you would have preferred not receive anything, meaning that you died intestate (without a valid will). In addition to making title changes, probate allows the state or other interested parties to come forward and contest the validity of a will or some of its provisions.

If you have real estate located in more than one state, your estate will be subjected to multiple, known as ancillary, probates. Legal counsel will have to be consulted (and paid) in each of these states. The only way to ensure that probate is avoided in every state is by having a living trust. Joint tenancy is not the answer.

Once the court agrees that the will is in order (or intestate succession is determined), the estate's representative goes about winding up your affairs. Claims are settled, taxes are paid, and assets are distributed to the heirs. The probate process can be done in less than a year but often takes 2 or more years. During this entire process, beneficiaries in need of money, including your spouse and children, are required to petition the court for an allowance.

The person chosen to administer your estate was either named in your will or appointed by the court. This person or entity is under the control of the court at all times. The level of supervision depends upon the resources of the court and state statutes. For certain estates, a lengthy and expensive probate process can be avoided if an informal administration is allowed. The next chapter talks about estate taxes. This expense is on top of whatever your estate was charged for probate. When people talk about the costs of probate, they very often fail to consider how an estate is further diminished by estate taxes. Fortunately, with proper estate planning and the use of a living trust, both estate taxes and probate fees can be completely eliminated.

Checklist of Things to Do

1. Make sure that all of your titled property, with the exception of your car and checking accounts that total less than $30,000, are titled in the name of a revocable living trust.
2. Talk to your spouse, making sure that he or she understands that investments in the future should be done in the name of the trust.
3. Verify with your attorney that you also have a will to take care of assets left outside of the trust. If you get a "living-trust package," then look for what is known as a "pour-over will" (described in another chapter).
4. Have a talk with one or two beneficiaries of your estate; inform them that if there is a probate, the lawyer is to be instructed to first pursue an informal administration.

CHAPTER 3

ESTATE TAXES

ALL U.S. CITIZENS and everyone owning property in the United States is subject to estate taxes at death. Several states also impose an inheritance tax. The tax rate and the amount due is determined by the size of the *taxable* estate. When reading this chapter keep in mind that estate taxes and probate fees are completely different. Whether or not part or all of your estate is subjected to probate or completely avoids the probate process has nothing to do with tax liability.

Certain exemptions and tax-planning devices allow you to transfer part or all of your estate without paying any death taxes to the state or the feds. Your estate will not be subject to any of these taxes to the extent it is (1) worth less than $600,000, (2) given to a surviving spouse *who is a U.S. citizen*, or (3) left to a tax-exempt charity. This chapter will show why you may not want to use any of these strategies.

To approximate your federal estate-tax liability follow these steps: (a) estimate the value of your taxable estate, (b) deduct any estate tax exemptions, and (c) look at the estate-tax table to determine the amount of tax that will be due, if any.

Estimating the value of your estate is a two-part process. First, you will need to determine your net worth. This is simply all of your assets minus all of your debts, including any mortgage(s) you might have. The next several pages contain a worksheet that will help you determine your net worth.

Net Worth Worksheet

I. Assets

Description of Your Property	Type of Shared Ownership	Percentage You Own	Net Value of Your Ownership
COLUMN 1	COLUMN 2	COLUMN 3	COLUMN 4

A. Liquid Assets

1. cash

_____   _____ _____ _____
_____   _____ _____ _____
_____   _____ _____ _____
_____   _____ _____ _____

2. savings accounts

_____   _____ _____ _____
_____   _____ _____ _____
_____   _____ _____ _____
_____   _____ _____ _____

3. checking accounts

_____   _____ _____ _____
_____   _____ _____ _____
_____   _____ _____ _____
_____   _____ _____ _____

4. money-market accounts

_____   _____ _____ _____
_____   _____ _____ _____
_____   _____ _____ _____
_____   _____ _____ _____

5. certificates of deposit

_____   _____ _____ _____
_____   _____ _____ _____
_____   _____ _____ _____
_____   _____ _____ _____

6. mutual funds

_____   _____ _____ _____
_____   _____ _____ _____
_____   _____ _____ _____
_____   _____ _____ _____

	COLUMN 1	COLUMN 2	COLUMN 3	COLUMN 4
	Description of Your Property	*Type of Shared Ownership*	*Percentage You Own*	*Net Value of Your Ownership*

B. Other Personal Property
   (all your property except liquid assets, business interests, and real estate)

1. stocks

2. bonds

3. bank accounts (CDs, checking, etc.)

4. automobiles and other vehicles, including planes, boats, and recreational vehicles

5. precious metals

6. household goods

_____   _____   _____   _____
_____   _____   _____   _____
_____   _____   _____   _____
_____   _____   _____   _____

7. clothing

_____   _____   _____   _____
_____   _____   _____   _____
_____   _____   _____   _____
_____   _____   _____   _____

8. jewelry and furs

_____   _____   _____   _____
_____   _____   _____   _____
_____   _____   _____   _____
_____   _____   _____   _____

9. art works, collectibles, and antiques

_____   _____   _____   _____
_____   _____   _____   _____
_____   _____   _____   _____
_____   _____   _____   _____

10. tools and equipment

_____   _____   _____   _____
_____   _____   _____   _____
_____   _____   _____   _____
_____   _____   _____   _____

11. valuable livestock/animals

_____   _____   _____   _____
_____   _____   _____   _____
_____   _____   _____   _____
_____   _____   _____   _____

12. money owed you (personal loans, etc.)

_____   _____   _____   _____
_____   _____   _____   _____
_____   _____   _____   _____
_____   _____   _____   _____

13. vested interest in profit-sharing plan, stock options, etc.

_____   _____   _____   _____
_____   _____   _____   _____
_____   _____   _____   _____
_____   _____   _____   _____

14. limited partnerships

_____   _____   _____   _____
_____   _____   _____   _____
_____   _____   _____   _____
_____   _____   _____   _____

15. vested interest in retirement plans, IRAs, death benefits, annuities

_____   _____   _____   _____
_____   _____   _____   _____
_____   _____   _____   _____
_____   _____   _____   _____

16. life insurance

_____   _____   _____   _____
_____   _____   _____   _____
_____   _____   _____   _____
_____   _____   _____   _____

17. miscellaneous (any personal property not listed above)

_____   _____   _____   _____
_____   _____   _____   _____
_____   _____   _____   _____
_____   _____   _____   _____

C. Business Personal Property

1. patents, copyrights, trademarks, and royalties

_____   _____   _____   _____
_____   _____   _____   _____
_____   _____   _____   _____
_____   _____   _____   _____

2. business ownerships (partnerships, sole proprietorships, corporations, etc.)

name and type of business

_____   _____ _____ _____
_____   _____ _____ _____
_____   _____ _____ _____
_____   _____ _____ _____

name and type of business

_____   _____ _____ _____
_____   _____ _____ _____
_____   _____ _____ _____
_____   _____ _____ _____

3. miscellaneous receivables (mortgage, deeds of trust, or promissory notes held by you; any rent due from income property owned by you; and payments due for professional or personal services or properties sold by you that are not fully paid for by the purchaser)

_____   _____ _____ _____
_____   _____ _____ _____
_____   _____ _____ _____
_____   _____ _____ _____

D. Real Estate

address

_____   _____ _____ _____
_____   _____ _____ _____
_____   _____ _____ _____
_____   _____ _____ _____

address

_____   _____ _____ _____
_____   _____ _____ _____
_____   _____ _____ _____
_____   _____ _____ _____

address

_____   _____ _____ _____
_____   _____ _____ _____
_____   _____ _____ _____
_____   _____ _____ _____

E. Total Net Value of All Your Assets

II. Liabilities (What You Owe)

Many of your liabilities will already have been accounted for because you listed the net value of your property in Part I of this worksheet. For example, to determine the net value of your interest in real estate, you deducted the amount of all mortgages and encumbrances on that real estate. Similarly, the value of a small business is the value after business debts and other obligations are subtracted. For this reason, the only liabilities you need list here are those not previously covered. Do not bother with the small stuff (such as the phone bill, or what you owe on your credit card this month), which changes frequently. Just list all major liabilities not previously accounted for, so you can get a clearer picture of your net worth.

COLUMN 1	COLUMN 2
To Whom Debt Is Owed	*Net Amount of Debt You Owe*

A. Personal Property Debts

1. personal loans (banks, major credit cards, etc.)

_____   _____

_____   _____

_____   _____

_____   _____

_____   _____

2. other personal debts

_____   _____

_____   _____

_____   _____

_____   _____

_____   _____

B. Taxes (include only taxes past and currently due. Do not include taxes due in the future or estimated estate taxes)

_____   _____

_____   _____

_____   _____

COLUMN 1	COLUMN 2
To Whom Debt Is Owed	*Net Amount of Debt You Owe*
_____	_____
_____	_____
_____	_____

C. Any other liabilities
   (legal judgments, accrued child support, etc.)   _____

D. TOTAL LIABILITIES
   [excluding those liabilities already deducted in Section 1]   _____

III. NET WORTH
   [Total Net Value of All Your Assets (Section I.E.)
   minus Total Liabilities (Section II. D.)]   _____

The second step is to project the value of your estate at death. This is done by taking your net worth and adjusting it for the future effects of inflation and prudent investing. Once you have determined your life expectancy (see Appendix F), an assumed rate of future growth and inflation needs to be chosen.

Over the past half century, inflation has averaged 4% (if you believe the government's figures). According to internal bank memos and studies, the true rate of inflation has been about twice what the government has reported. Perhaps you feel that the banking industry's figures are too high or that inflation will dramatically escalate during the later part of the 1990s. Whatever your beliefs, choose a figure. I suggest that the figure you use be somewhere between 3 and 10%.

Now that you have an inflation figure in mind and you have looked at Appendix F to determine your life expectancy (add a couple of years if you do not smoke), we can now calculate the growth rate of your portfolio by using "the Rule of 72."

The Rule of 72

The calculation involved in the Rule of 72 is simple and will show how long it takes money (or a portfolio) to double in value. Take the number 72 and divide it by your assumed rate of inflation or growth. The resulting number is how long it takes an estate to double in value. As an example, let us suppose that your estate will grow, owing either to inflation or effective investing and/or savings, at a rate of 8%. Seventy-two divided by 8 is 9. This means that a $175,000 estate will be worth $350,000 in 9 years. At the end of the second 9-year period, it will double again and be worth $700,000. Let us go through one more example to make sure that you understand the math.

As a second example, let us assume that you have a net worth of $825,000. Your holdings are evenly divided among real estate (your home), a broad mixture of stocks, and tax-free bonds. You spend the interest from the municipal bonds and the dividends from the stocks; it is not expected that you will need to sell any of the securities. The house is owned free and clear. Let us assume that the $225,000 tied up in tax-free bonds does not appreciate, the stocks increase in value at roughly 12% per year, but the value of your home just keeps pace with inflation. You have a positive outlook about inflation and feel that it will, overall, average approximately 4% during your remaining years. According to the life-expectancy table, being a 65-year-old single female who does not expect to remarry, your life expectancy is 18 more years.

Based on the facts given in the paragraph above, here is the illustration broken down by its component parts:

Asset	Current Value	Value at Death
personal residence	$300,000	$600,000
common stocks	$300,000	$2,400,000
tax-free bonds	$225,000	$225,000
total values	$825,000	$3,225,000

The house will "grow" to $600,000 because, based on a 4% inflation rate, the value of an asset that keeps pace with inflation will double every 18 years (72/4 = 18).

Over the past 50 years, stocks have appreciated between 10 and 16%, depending on whether or not you are looking at blue chips or aggressive-growth companies. If it is assumed that your blue-chip stocks will appreciate at 12%, then "money" doubles every six years (72/12 = 6). If the stocks double in value every 6 years and we are looking at a time frame of 18 years, this means that there are three doubling periods (18/6 = three). During the first doubling period, $300,000 grows to $600,000; during the second doubling, $600,000 grows to $1,200,000, and $2,400,000 after the third doubling.

It is hard to imagine that an existing portfolio valued at $825,000 will eventually be worth $3,225,000 with little effort on the part of its owner. Nevertheless, this is what happens when natural growth and/or inflation take over.

As you can see, making these projections is very important. As previously mentioned, estate taxes are based on the net value of your estate *at death*, not its value today. You may think that you do not have much now, but think about the future and what the effects of inflation and/or savings can do to your "modest" estate.

Federal Estate-Tax Exemptions

The person appointed to supervise the distribution of your estate has the responsibility of getting your estate appraised. If an executor was named in your will, then it is his or her responsibility. If an executor was not appointed, then the court will name an administrator to take charge. If you have a living trust, then it is usually the responsibility of the successor trustee (co-trustee if you have a surviving spouse). If all your property is in joint tenancy, then the co-owner has the duty to make sure all assets are appraised and an estate-tax return filed.

The $600,000 Lifetime Exemption: We All Get It

Everyone has what is known as a $600,000 federal exclusion. You get this lifetime exclusion whether you are married, single, an adult or a child. This means that you can gift, will, or transfer up to $600,000 without having to pay any federal estate or gift taxes. This does *not* mean that you can bequeath up to $600,000 *per* child, friend, or relative. The exclusion belongs to you and is singular in nature. If you have an estate that has a net value of $1,000,000 at death, taxes may be due on up to $400,000 ($1,000,000 − $600,000).

The $10,000 Annual Exclusion

In addition to the $600,000 exclusion, the feds allow you an annual exclusion of $10,000 per donee. This is different from the $600,000 lifetime exclusion for two reasons. First, the exclusion applies to *each person* you make a gift to. This means that if you have three children and six grandchildren, you can gift up to $90,000 each year ($10,000 per donee times 9 donees) without filing a gift tax return or incurring any taxes, assuming that no single donee's gift totals more than $10,000 for the year. Second, unlike the *lifetime exclusion of $600,000*, this $10,000 exclusion is annual. This means that you can make gifts each and every year without paying any gift taxes (again assuming that no one donee ends up with cash or property that exceeds more than the $10,000 limit per calendar year).

If you are married and your spouse joins in on the gifting, the effective annual exemption doubles to $20,000. Thus, a married couple with three kids could gift each child a total of $20,000 any year they wanted, without having to file a gift-tax return ($20,000 × 3 children). Once the calendar year is over, you are out of luck for that particular year. If you miss one year you cannot double up the next year.

There is no annual limit to the exemption if the gifted money is used for educational or medical purposes. If your son, daughter, relative, or friend needs $53,000 for an operation or $21,000 for school tuition and room and board, there are no gift taxes due. To get this unlimited annual exclusion, make sure that the check (gift) is made payable to the educational or medical institution, not directly to the child, friend, etc.

Using Both Exemptions: $10,000 ($20,000) Annual Plus $600,000 Lifetime
If you exceed the $10,000 annual limit per donee, then you must file a gift-tax return. If you are married and your spouse joins in on the gift, then no filing is necessary unless the gifts to a person exceed $20,000 for the calendar year. When you file this form, you have a choice. You can either pay taxes on the excess above $10,000 ($20,000 if married) or eat into your $600,000 lifetime exclusion. Taxes on any excess begin at 37% and go up to 55%.

As an example, let us suppose that you are married and have two children. Gifts to one of the children total $19,000 for the year. Since you and your spouse joined in on these gifts, no gift tax is due and no return needs to be filed. During the same year, you and your

spouse made a $6,000 gift to the second child in March, an $8,000 gift in July, and a $10,000 gift in October, all to the second child. Since these gifts to the other child total $24,000 and none of this money was used for educational or medical purposes, a gift-tax return has to be filed. Since the gifts for the year exceeded the allowable annual exemption by $4,000, Mom and Dad can pay taxes on this excess amount (which would total 37% of $4,000) or skip paying any such taxes and reduce *each* of their lifetime exclusions by $2,000.

If the reduction was opted for, this would mean each parent would now have a lifetime exclusion of $598,000 ($600,000 minus $2,000). The remaining exclusion of $598,000 could be reduced even further in future years before death. Assuming this did *not* happen, each parent would then be able to pass on up to $598,000 without the estate incurring any estate or inheritance tax.

The Unlimited Marital Deduction
In addition to the exemptions described above, *if you are married*, anything you leave your surviving spouse is also exempt from state and federal estate taxes. This is true if you leave your spouse one dollar or ten billion. This is commonly referred to as the "marital deduction." There is no distinction between inheritances or gifts of cash, real estate, or personal property. Anything you leave to your wife or husband is free from estate taxes. Likewise, it makes no difference as to how the asset was titled before or after death. You can gift or will property that is owned individually, jointly, as community property, or in a trust.

A Potential Problem
There is a potential problem when the marital deduction is used. Married couples who have estates worth over $600,000 mistakenly believe that the best solution is to leave everything to the surviving spouse, thereby avoiding estate taxes. This may merely be a postponement *and compounding* of estate

taxes that ultimately need to be paid on the death of the second spouse. Worse, leaving everything to your wife or husband may actually create a future tax liability where none would have existed.

All of the problems in the paragraph above arise when the *second* spouse dies. The survivor's estate now comprises what you left, any interim growth, and the assets of the survivor. The second spouse can still pass up to $600,000, but any excess amount will be taxed, beginning at 37%. By leaving everything to your surviving spouse, you will be throwing away a $600,000 exemption that your estate could have had. Fortunately, there is a way for each spouse to take advantage of the $600,000, thereby eventually passing on $1,200,000 to children, relatives, and/or friends. This estate planning strategy is known as an A-B Trust and is detailed in a later chapter.

If you have a will or trust that was written before September 13, 1981, make sure an attorney reviews it. There is a strong likelihood that your will contains provisions that deal with old tax laws. Specifically, this means that you can pass only a certain amount to your spouse without incurring an estate tax.

The unlimited marital deduction is available only to married couples. The estate-tax laws do not favor couples who are simply living together. If you are a couple who has a *common-law marriage* in Alabama, Colorado, the District of Columbia, Georgia, Idaho, Iowa, Kansas, Montana, Ohio, Oklahoma, Pennsylvania, Rhode Island, South Carolina, or Texas, then the marital deduction is recognized.

Deciding If You Should Take Full Advantage of the Marital Deduction

It is probably a good idea to consult with your financial advisor before you decide whether or not you should take full advantage of the 100% marital deduction. As you may recall, a spouse may gift or leave the other spouse an unlimited amount of money, real estate, per-

sonal property, etc., without incurring any estate or gift tax, either on the federal or state level. As tempting as this may sound, there are some things you should first consider.

First, review the size of your estate and that of your spouse's. Second, decide how important it is for both of you to have a single-minded estate plan. Third, think about how important it is to benefit your children, or other heirs, before you and your spouse die. Fourth, consider the potential income-tax savings of a B and/or C Trust. A-B and A-B-C trusts are described in later chapters. Fifth, you may want to protect assets from subsequent spouses. Sixth, a great deal in estate taxes may be saved by using an A-B or A-B-C Trust in which the appreciation of property in the B and/or C Trust escapes any future estate taxes after the death of the first spouse (these assets can be taxed when the first spouse dies, but there will not be a second estate tax due). Seventh, how important, psychological or otherwise, is it for your spouse to have complete and absolute control over all assets.

Spouses Who Are Not U.S. Citizens

If your spouse is not a U.S. citizen, then estate taxes may be due if the survivor inherits more than $600,000. There is one exception to this form of discrimination. By setting up a Qualified Domestic Trust, the unlimited marital deduction is restored. In order for the decedent's estate to be able to pass on an unlimited amount to a spouse who is not a U.S. citizen, the Qualified Domestic Trust must meet all of the following requirements: (1) at least one of the trustees must be a U.S. citizen, (2) the surviving spouse who is not a U.S. citizen must be entitled to receive all income from the trust, and (3) it must comply with other IRS regulations governing these trusts.

As you can see from the description of these domestic trusts, the spouse who is not a U.S. citizen cannot receive *principal* that totals more than $600,000. There is no dollar limit to the amount of income that can be received, but there is a cap on principal. The cap of $600,000 is arrived at by looking at everything the survivor has inherited, not just distributions of principal from the trust. If the cumulative total of principal distributions does exceed $600,000, there will be an estate-tax liability that begins at 37%, no matter what kind of trust there is.

If your spouse is not a U.S. citizen, there is one more bit of good news. You can gift this spouse up to $100,000 a year in cash or property, free from federal estate taxes. This annual exclusion is on top of any benefits that might be reaped from a Qualified Domestic Trust.

Disclaiming (Refusing) Your Inheritance

No one can force you to accept a gift or inheritance. If a beneficiary makes a valid disclaimer, the disclaimed interest passes as though the disclaimant (you) predeceased the person who made the gift (or left the inheritance).

Believe it or not, there are special situations where it may not make sense to inherit part or all of someone's estate. The reason for refusing such gifts or bequests is motivated solely by estate taxes. If you are extremely secure financially and already have a large estate, then you may not want to increase the later taxation of your estate. Instead, you may wish to have the inheritance pass directly to your children.

As an example, suppose your brother Murray had a will or living trust that stated "All of my estate is to go to my brother Bob. If he does not survive me, my estate shall be divided equally among Bob's three children." If Bob already has a large estate, has very good disability, medical, major medical hospital insurance and makes a lot of money from a secure job, then maybe Bob does not want or need Murray's inheritance. By disclaiming the inheritance, Murray's estate would go to Bob's three kids.

To do otherwise may mean that Bob's estate would be huge (once Murray's estate was added to it) and the resulting estate taxes when Bob died would be in the 50% range. In short, Bob's decision to say "pass" means that Murray's property is not added to Bob's estate when Bob dies. By having a smaller estate, more of Bob's estate will pass intact to his kids (or whomever he likes).

By accepting assets from a trust or will, you may needlessly be subjected to additional taxes. When you receive the property, it becomes part of your estate; taxes on an estate, once deductions and credits have been applied, begin at 37% and go to as high as 55%. By accepting property that you do not need and had planned on leaving to your children anyway, your estate could end up paying taxes that would have been avoidable. A disclaimer means that what you would have received from a trust, will, or intestate succession goes to the contingent beneficiary. If the "original" inheritance was from your mother or father, this means that the next in line is probably your children.

For a disclaimer to be legal, the following must be strictly complied with: (1) the disclaimer must be written, irrevocable, and unconditional refusal to accept a full or partial interest in the asset, (2) the trustee or executor must receive the notice within 9 months of the grantor's death, (3) you cannot have received any benefit from the asset (i.e., no interest, dividend, or rent checks), (4) the disclaiming heir cannot designate the recipient of the rejected property, and (5) the asset cannot go into a trust that benefits you unless you are the decedent's spouse. A few states require that the disclaimer also be notarized.

Charitable Gifts

Any gifts made to to a charitable group that has received a tax-exempt status from the IRS is exempt from federal estate taxes. Before you make a gift to any charity, particularly one that is politically active, make sure that it has qualified under Internal Revenue Code Section 501(c)(3).

Making gifts to charities can offer you some income-tax benefits while you are alive and lower or eliminate any estate taxes at death.

Planned giving is described in Chapter 22, "The Charitable Remainder Trust."

Miscellaneous Exemptions

Generally, the costs incurred for treating the last illness of the now deceased are fully deductible. Burial expenses, probate fees, and legal bills are also fully deductible. The person filling out the estate-tax return will also receive credit for state inheritance taxes or any foreign taxes imposed on properties owned by the decedent outside of the United States.

Deferring Estate Taxes

In most cases, if estate taxes are due, the IRS wants payment within 9 months. Going beyond this period of time can result in penalties and interest. Under certain circumstances, a district or service center director of the IRS, according to IRC (Internal Revenue Code) Section 6161, may extend the time for payment of estate taxes for up to 12 months after the 9-month period (for a total of 21 months). The director must be convinced that there is "reasonable cause" to grant such an extension.

Reasonable cause includes: (1) there are no liquid assets in the estate or trust, (2) the estate or trust has a claim to other assets that cannot be collected, and/or (3) the fiduciary (trustee, personal representative, administrator, or executor) is unable to borrow money to pay the taxes due. If an extension is granted, the interest on the deferred payment will not be waived and is not deductible on an income-tax return; it is deductible on the estate-tax return.

Closely Held Businesses

If the decedent's interest in a closely held business represented more than 35% of the adjusted *gross* estate, the estate's representative may elect to pay estate taxes in 10 installments or less. If you think that this is a situation that might later apply to you, consult with your attorney and financial advisor for further guidance. Among other things: (a) passive assets held in your business are not considered

business assets for purposes of meeting the 35% test; (b) the first installment can be postponed for up to 5 years—in such a case, taxes could then be pro-rated over the next 10 years (a delay which effectively totals 15 years); (c) an election for any delay must be made at the time the estate-tax return is due (this includes any extensions that may have been obtained); the estate will be charged 4% interest on the first $345,000 of federal estate taxes due, reduced by the decedent's unified credit (which may be as high as $192,800)—any balance due will incur normal deficiency interest charges (a rate much higher than 4%), and (d) the actual amount of taxes that can be deferred is determined by a formula (divide the value of the estate's or trust's interest in the closely held business by the adjusted gross estate. The resulting figure is the percentage that can be deferred).

Taxing Estates and Trusts (Income Taxes Only)

Estates and *irrevocable* trusts are subject to the following *income tax* rates (to be adjusted for inflation in 1992 and beyond):

Taxable Income	Tax Liability
not over $3,450	15% of taxable income
$3,450–$10,350	$517 plus 28% of excess over $3,450
over $10,350	$2,450 plus 31% of excess over $10,350

Estates and *irrevocable* trusts (which would be created upon the death of the first spouse *if* there was an A-B or A-B-C) are required to make quarterly estimated tax payments for any taxable year ending 2 or more years after the date of death. The estate and/or irrevocable trust will not be subjected to a penalty for underpayment of estimated taxes if the payments equal 90% of what turns out to be the current year's tax liability or if the executor pays 100% of the prior year's tax bill.

Generally, distributions from B and C Trusts are deductible by the trust and reportable as income by the beneficiary. Keep in mind that the A Trust or traditional revocable living trust are not considered taxpaying entities; no special tax returns are filed for these trusts since they do not pay any income tax (because they are revocable). Income from these trusts flows directly to the trustor and is taxed on the individual's return.

A passive loss is a loss that results from a trade, business, or certain investments (such as limited partnerships) in which the taxpayer does not materially participate. Generally, passive losses may offset income from passive activities (i.e., a limited partnership that shows a gain) but not income from other activities (i.e., stocks or bonds sold at a profit, income from a business, etc.). Passive losses, like other losses, can be carried forward on your tax return for offsetting purposes in future years.

If you have any passive losses that have not been used up by the time you die, they are lost forever. The one exception is that passive losses, if they are in excess of the step-up in basis the property receives at death, may be used to offset nonpassive income (salary, interest, dividends, etc.) on the decedent's final income tax return.

Capital losses, charitable deductions, and net operating losses of the decedent cannot be used later by the trust. Once you die, these types of losses, which could normally be used to offset gains or ordinary income, are lost forever. Furthermore, capital losses that accrued prior to death cannot be carried forward on the surviving spouse's return.

The IRS allows the estate's executor to file a joint return with the surviving spouse, but only for the year of the death. The surviving spouse may file a joint return for 2 additional years if he or she meets all of these conditions: (1) maintains a household that is the principal residence of a dependent who is a son, stepson, daughter, or stepdaughter, (2) the surviving spouse is entitled to a tax deduction for the dependent, (3) does not remarry during the calendar year and (4) would have been eligible to file a joint return in the year of death if the decedent had lived.

State Inheritance Taxes

Although Nevada is technically the only state that has no death taxes, your estate, for practical purposes, will not be penalized if you live in one of the following states: Alabama, Alaska, Arizona, Arkansas, California, Colorado, the District of Columbia, Florida, Georgia, Hawaii, Illinois, Maine, Minnesota, Missouri, New Mexico, North Dakota, Oregon, Texas, Utah, Vermont, Virginia, West Virginia, Washington, and Wyoming. All of these states impose a tax on estates that have a net worth over $600,000, but whatever this tax ends up being, the federal estate-tax liability is reduced by this amount, dollar for dollar.

For example, you might find that your federal estate-tax liability was $26,000. Just before your executor was about to write the IRS a check for the $26,000, it was discovered that there was a state inheritance tax of $3,000. Instead of writing one check, the executor would now write two checks, one to the IRS for $23,000 and one to the state for $3,000. As you can see from this example, the federal government will credit you for any state inheritance taxes paid.

For those 26 remaining states, death taxes are based on the fair market value of all real estate owned in the state, no matter where the decedent lived, and all personal property, no matter where it is located, for residents of the state. To be considered a resident of a state, you must be domiciled there; meaning the place you intended to be your home. Usually, it is easy to determine the state of domicile. The court looks at where a person voted, worked, lived most of the time, and owned a home.

Reducing Estate Taxes

There are four ways to reduce estate taxes: (1) make sure that the value of your estate is less than $600,000 at death, (2) leave your estate to your spouse, (3) set up an A-B Trust, or (4) start a gifting program. As already discussed, you can gift up to $10,000 ($20,000 if you are married) annually to as many people as you like. The A-B Trust is detailed in chapter 18. Leaving everything to your wife or husband means that your $600,000 lifetime exclusion is being wasted. The IRS estimates that fewer than 2% of all estates are subjected to estate taxes.

If Estate Taxes Are Due

A federal estate-tax return, Form 706, is due within 9 months from the date of death if the decedent's *gross* estate exceeds $600,000. A return must be filed even if the net value of the estate turns out to be well under $600,000. As previously mentioned, all assets transferred to the surviving spouse are excluded when computing the net estate. You may find that filing a return is required, even though no taxes will be due because of the size of the *net* estate.

The "net estate" for federal estate-tax purposes may not be the same as the estate that goes through probate. Form 706 requires that all property in which the decedent had any interest be listed. This includes property that passes outside of probate; property such as retirement accounts, life-insurance proceeds, pay-on-death bank accounts, and assets held

as joint tenancy with rights of survivorship (jtwros). The "probate estate" is defined in more narrow terms (see probate chapter).

If estate taxes are due, then the Federal Estate-Tax Chart should be consulted.

Computing Estate Taxes

The IRS publishes a 20-page set of instructions for completing the federal estate-tax return called "Instructions for Form 706." You will find another IRS publication, number 448, "Federal Estate and Gift Taxes," helpful.

To help you determine any potential estate-tax liability, let us go through an example so you can see how the computations are made. Assume the following portfolio:

- $250,000 home with a $150,000 mortgage
- $100,000 worth of tax-free bonds
- $100,000 in bank CDs
- $200,000 of life insurance

The gross value of this estate is $650,000; the *net* value is $500,000. As you can see, the difference is that whereas the "gross estate" ignores any outstanding mortgages or liens, the "net estate" makes allowances for such encumbrances. Since the gross estate is over $600,000, Form 706 must be filed. However, no estate taxes will be due since the net value is under $600,000.

FEDERAL ESTATE TAX CHART

Taxable Estate	Tax	Taxable Estate	Tax
$600,000	$ 0	$1,250,000	$255,000
$750,000	$ 55,000	$1,500,000	$363,000
$850,000	$153,000	$2,000,000	$588,000

55% on the excess over $3,000,000

Summary

This chapter has covered estate-tax ramifications and things you can do to stop your estate from being taxed when you die. You learned about the annual exclusion and how its effectiveness can be doubled if your spouse joins in on the gift. You also learned that the exclusion is per *donee*, not *donor*. In addition to the annual exclusion, everyone is entitled to a lifetime exemption. Only married couples are afforded the third benefit: the unlimited marital deduction.

Chapter 4 covers gifts in greater detail. An effective gifting program, described briefly in this chapter, can be very beneficial to the family. Chapter 4 will thoroughly discuss the pros and cons of making gifts during your lifetime.

Checklist of Things to Do

1. Calculate a rough projection as to the value of your estate at death.
2. Determine if there is a potential for estate-tax liability.
3. Find out if you live in a state that imposes an inheritance tax.
4. If you have a projected worth greater than $1,200,000, talk to your spouse about a gifting program.
5. If you are single and will end up with an estate greater than $600,000, consider gifts.
6. If your spouse is not a U.S. citizen, look into a Qualified Domestic Trust.

CHAPTER 4

GIFTS

THERE ARE TWO parties whenever a gift is made: the donor and the donee. The donor is the person making the gift, and the donee is the recipient. The federal government attempts to tax gifts that exceed $10,000 per calendar year per donee. The tax is imposed on the donor, not the donee. There is no limit to the number of donees that can receive up to $10,000 per year from you. The $10,000 limit is doubled if your spouse joins in on making the gift with you. This $10,000 or $20,000 limit applies to donees whether or not they are related to you or are an entity, institution, club, or group.

Only a few states have state gift taxes. They are: Delaware, Louisiana, New York, North Carolina, South Carolina, Tennessee, and Wisconsin. Generally, if your state imposes a gift tax, it will be at the same rate or level as the state's death tax. Only a small percentage of people even need to think about state gift and death taxes. If your net estate is projected to be worth many millions of dollars at death, you could consider changing your domicile to a state that imposes no such taxes, or concentrate on a gifting program.

For tax purposes, a gift is defined as a voluntary transfer of property or forgiveness of debt without receiving anything in exchange.

In order to be effective, the donee must acknowledge and accept the gift. Equally important, the donee must have a present right to the property, whether the asset is personal property or real estate.

To be perfectly legal, the property should be delivered to and accepted by the recipient (the donee); the donor must release all control over the property. When personal property or cash is given, it is easy to determine if a gift has occurred. In the event of an audit, the IRS would look to see where the gift was deposited and under whose name. In the case of real estate, the IRS is concerned with who has physical possession of the property, which party is paying taxes, any outstanding mortgage and maintenance, as well as how the property is titled at the county recorder's office.

There are no gift-tax concerns for property placed in a living trust. This is because the trust can always be revoked, and the beneficiaries, usually the children, have no present interest or right to the trust property. Furthermore, the person who made the trust can always revoke or amend the trust, canceling the entire document, omit previously included property, or change heirs. In short, if someone sets up a trust and retains the power to change who will benefit from it, even if the trustor himself is specifically excluded as a possible beneficiary, there is still no gift.

Computing Gift-Tax Liability

There may be a gift tax due if (1) the gifts to a specific donee total more than $10,000 for the year ($20,000 if the donor is married), (2) the gift is not used for medical or educational purposes (as previously mentioned in another chapter, there is no dollar limit for this exclusion), or (3) the gift is not to a recognized charitable group. Assuming that none of these points apply, the excess amount over $10,000 is deducted from your lifetime exclusion of $600,000. Gift taxes are still not due unless any single donee receives over $10,000 for the year and the entire $600,000 lifetime exclusion has been used up.

The gift-tax rate increases with the size of the cumulative gifts. The reason for this is to prevent large amounts being sporadically transferred at a lower tax rate. The gift-tax rate is determining by adding up all of the taxable gifts (the excesses over $10,000 or $20,000) for each year from 1971 through the present.

If you change the ownership of your life-insurance policy to someone else, you have made a gift. The value of this gift needs to be determined to see if a gift-tax return must be filed. You are still the insured, and perhaps the designated beneficiary has not changed, but ownership has. A gift of a life-insurance policy within 3 years of death is disallowed for estate-tax purposes. The disallowance means that the IRS will include the value of this gift as part of the decedent's property for estate-tax purposes. The worth of a life-insurance policy at this point would be its death benefit minus any outstanding loans against the policy.

The Gift-Tax Return

A gift-tax return must be filed by April 15 of the year following the year in which the gift was made. Thus, if you made a large gift in February of 1992, you would have to file a 1992 gift-tax form, but it would not have to be filed until April 15, 1993. You must file such a return if you made gifts to any one person or entity that exceed $10,000 during the calendar year. The IRS does not require a gift-tax return to be filed for gifts between spouses or to pay for education or medical help, no matter how large the amount(s). Surprisingly, a return must still be filed if the gift exceeds $10,000 and is made to a qualified charity, even though no taxes will be due.

Gifting Strategies

For estate-planning purposes, whenever possible gift property that is likely to appreciate in the future. You do not want the future appreciated property as part of your estate when you die. Keep in mind that once a gift is made, you cannot later change your mind and take back the gift. A gift to a minor cannot be given back by the minor since the child lacks legal capacity. Similarly, you cannot force an adult, even a relative, adult child, or spouse, to give you back an asset you had previously gifted them. Gifts cannot be "reversed" even if you are in severe financial trouble.

On the other hand, it is usually unwise to give away property while you are still alive that has substantially appreciated in value since you first acquired it. There is a significant tax benefit to the heir if the property is transferred after your death and not before it. To appreciate this distinction, you must first understand what is meant by "basis." An example of how the basis or cost of an asset can be changed was given in the first chapter. However, you may find a review of this concept useful.

Defining Basis

When you acquire anything, either by purchase, exchange, gift, or inheritance, you take on a certain cost basis. Basis is the value placed on the property when it is acquired by you. It is used by the IRS and your state franchise tax board to determine any taxable profit or loss when the property is later sold. Normally, basis is the price you paid for the property. Basis can be reduced if the asset can be depreciated according to IRS guidelines. Basis can also be increased if the property is fixed up or altered. A couple of examples may be helpful.

Assume you bought a house for $200,000 and spent $50,000 fixing it up. Since your personal residence cannot be depreciated, when you sell the house it will have an adjusted basis of $250,000. If the sale of the house nets you anything more than $250,000, you will either have to pay taxes or buy another home within two years in order to satisfy the rules the IRS has concerning tax-free exchanges. The only exception to this is if either or both spouses are age 55 or older and take advantage of the one-time $125,000 exclusion. If you sell the house for less than $250,000 there will be a loss. Unfortunately, your personal residence is one of the few things you cannot take a loss on. Let us look at another example.

Let us suppose that you bought some rental apartment units, and the total purchase price, which would include any closing costs, commissions, or fees, was $800,000. Once you owned these apartments you began to depreciate them, as allowed by the IRS. For sake of illustration, let us assume that a total of $250,000 in depreciation was taken. *At this point*, the apartments have an adjusted basis of $550,000. Let us now suppose that you are ready to sell these apartments, but before you do, you want to spruce them up a little bit by putting on some new roofs, adding new landscaping, and fixing the fences. All of these fix-up costs total $60,000. You cost basis is now $610,000. Suppose the property is sold for $1,000,000 but you net only $930,000 after real estate commissions and the advertising for selling the property are deducted. The gain for income-tax purposes would be $320,000 (the *net* amount received from the sale minus the *most current adjusted* cost basis).

Let us now move on to a slightly more complex issue: determining basis for estate- and gift-tax purposes. We will begin with how basis is determined when gifts are involved.

Determining Basis for Gifts: the Worst of Both Worlds

The value of a gift is its fair market value on the date the gift is made, as far as the donor is concerned. If I gave you some stock that was worth $9,000 on the day the gift was made, my concern as the donor is its value on that day. For gift-tax liability purposes, I and the IRS are not concerned with what the stock was worth earlier in the year or how much I originally paid for it. However, if you decide to later sell this stock, *your* profit or loss for tax purposes is determined by taking the net sales proceeds and subtracting from it: (a) the value of the stock on the day you received it or (b) the price I originally paid for it, *whichever is less*. In this example, if you later received $14,000 from the stock, one might automatically assume that there was a $5,000 gain (the net sales proceeds minus the value of the stock, $9,000, on the day you received it). This would be wrong. If I had originally paid $8,000 for the stock, then there would be a taxable gain of $6,000 ($14,000 minus $8,000).

The best way to remember how basis for gift-tax purposes works is that the IRS uses the figure that shows the lowest possible "cost basis." Let us now see what happens if you receive property from an inheritance instead of as a gift while the donor is still alive.

Basis and Inheritances: the Only Good Thing About Death

There is only one good thing about death and this is it. Inherited property gets a step-up in basis based on the fair market value of the property on the date of the decedent's death. If I leave you some stocks, bonds, or real estate in my will or living trust that I paid $100,000 for, and they are worth $700,000 when I die, you have inherited property worth $700,000. Your cost basis is also $700,000. Eventually when you sell the property, whether that time is one day after I have died or 50 years later, your profit or loss for tax purposes is based on a basis of $700,000.

If those stocks are sold by you for $500,000, you can take a tax loss of $200,000

($500,000 minus your "cost," or basis, of $700,000)! As hard as it might be to believe, that is how it works, even though the IRS may know that I had paid only $100,000 for that stock a week, year, or half century ago. If, instead, you sold this inherited stock for $740,000, you would owe taxes on the $40,000 gain ($740,000 – $700,000); the gain, of course, would be reduced by any fees or commission paid to the brokerage firm. Before you begin feeling sorry for the IRS, read the next paragraph.

When you die, your property is valued, for estate-tax purposes, based on its fair market value on the date of death. You do not get to choose an alternate date. The fact that the property, whether it is real estate, stocks, or a rare coin collection, happens to have peaked in value on exactly the same day that you died is tough luck.

50% Step-up in Basis for Joint Tenancy

The example described above assumes a single person or married person who does not hold *joint* title to any property. If you own a brokerage account, stock, bond, or piece of real estate with someone as joint tenancy, then *your share* of the property will get a step-up in basis upon your death; the co-owner's share retains its original cost basis (adjusted for any depreciation or fix-up costs). Both halves of the property do not get a step-up in basis when just one of the owners dies.

As an example, let us suppose that you and a friend opened up a joint account at a brokerage firm and purchased $70,000 worth of stocks. The value of the stock is now $170,000. If this asset were sold while both of you were alive, there would be a $100,000 taxable gain. If one of you died, then *that share* would get a step-up in basis. For tax purposes, the property now has a value of $85,000 (one-half of the value on the date of death) plus $35,000 (the original cost basis of the surviving tenant). This means that if a sale were to occur after one of the owners died, the *adjusted* basis would be $120,000 ($85,000 plus $35,000). If the stocks were sold the day after

death for $170,000, there would be a gain of $50,000. This is certainly better than the taxable gain of $100,000 if the property had been sold while both you and your friend were alive. Unfortunately, this income-tax savings comes at a price: someone must die.

Can the step-up in basis be even greater? Yes; read the next section on community property.

100% Step-up in Basis for Community Property

There are 8 community-property states: Arizona, California, Idaho, Nevada, New Mexico, Texas, Washington, and Wisconsin (Wisconsin is technically not a community-property state, but it has adopted laws that are very similar to those found in community-property states). This distinction is not only important if you become divorced, it is also important for tax-basis purposes. To take advantage of community-property laws, you must be married and reside in one of these states.

For income- and estate-tax purposes, it is not enough that you live in a community-property state. The title to the asset must be shown as community property. Instead of that grant deed or brokerage account titled as "John and Mary Smith" or "Betty and Frank Jones, joint tenancy," it must be listed as "John and Mary Smith, community property" or "Betty and Frank Jones, c/p."

If you live in one of these community-property states and personal property or real estate is titled as "community property," or abbreviated as "c/p," then there will be a 100% step-up in basis upon the death of either spouse. This is in contrast to the 50% step-up in basis received if property is titled as "joint tenancy" or "jtwros."

As an example, let us suppose that you and your spouse lived in California, a community-property state, and the two of you bought some raw land for $160,000 in New York (the state where the property is located is not important and will not affect the outcome of this example). Title to the property was taken *or later changed to* "community property." The land is now worth $500,000 and the two of you decide to sell it. The taxable gain would be in the neighborhood of $340,000 (the $500,000 selling price minus your basis of $160,000). If one of you died just before the property was sold, there would be an adjustment to the basis. In the eyes of the IRS, the basis of the property is now $500,000. The resulting sale for $500,000 would mean that there would be zero capital gains and therefore no taxes due on the "gain."

Like joint tenancy, there must be a death before a stepped-up basis is received. And, just like joint tenancy, it does not make a difference when the property was acquired or subsequently sold, as long as both parties were alive when the purchase was made, the account was titled as community property, and there was a death before the property was sold. For estate- and income-tax purposes, there are three differences between joint tenancy and community property: (1) the co-owners do not have to be married in joint tenancy in order for there to be a step-up in basis but they do in the case of community property, (2) joint tenancy can occur in any state where the property is located or where the owners reside, community property requires that husband and wife be residents of one of the 8 community-property states, and (3) upon death of an owner, joint tenancy receives a step-up in basis only on that part that represented the decedent's share; community property gets a step-up in basis for each half.

Only One Negative Thing About Community Property

Most people who are residents of a community-property state should immediately change the title of jointly owned property from "jtwros" to "c/p." This change can be done without hiring an attorney. Any necessary forms can be sent by your stockbroker, mutual-fund representative, or county recorder's office. *Property held in a living trust can just as easily be changed from joint tenancy to*

community property. The cost for making the change is either nominal or zero. There is no need to hire legal counsel. However, before you make the change, make sure that you have complete faith and trust in your mate.

Community-property laws dictate that either spouse can bequeath his or her one-half share in the property without the other spouse's permission or knowledge. Your wife or husband may have a secret will that you do not know about. If your spouse predeceases you, you may be thinking about the 100% step-up in basis only to find out that the decedent has left his or her share to someone else. So you now have a new partner, perhaps someone you have not even met. As co-owners, you and your new "buddy" cannot sell or transfer the property without the other's consent.

Before moving back to gifting strategies, one final point should be made about basis. Property owned individually gets a 100% step-up in basis for estate-tax as well as capital-gains purposes when the property owner dies. Basis is not changed if the sole owner happens to have a spouse or lover that dies first. Many married people own some property separately and some property jointly. A married couple can also own property separately within a living trust, even if each spouse is a co-trustee.

Using Gifts to Reduce Estate Taxes

Using gifts to reduce or eliminate any eventual estate taxes on a state and federal basis can make sense if (a) your estate will exceed $600,000 at death, (b) the anticipated gift has not appreciated greatly in value since you acquired it, and most important (c) you are certain that you will not need the gift to live on later. This final point should not be of concern if you strongly believe that the *adult* donee will "re-gift" the asset back to you if an emergency does arise. After all, there is no law saying that just because someone makes a gift to you, you cannot make a gift back to them, even if that gift is exactly what they originally gave you.

One of the advantages of a lifetime gifting

program is that you can see the benefits and the joys of the gift while you are still alive. Another advantage is that you may use the gifts as a kind of "test program"; seeing how the gift is ultimately squandered or prudently managed. Making a gift will also reduce the size of your portfolio for estate-tax purposes. When properly done, gifts can also make you qualify for government assistance faster if you are struck with a financially devastating disease or illness, such as Alzheimer's.

If you want to make gifts to your children but feel that there may be a time in the future when you will need that money or property back, think long and hard before you make the transfer. You may trust that child completely, but what would happen if the child changed because of drugs or alcohol? Would that asset be protected for your future use if the child incurred expensive medical or legal bills? Finally, if the child is married, what is the mate like? Is your daughter-in-law or brother-in-law likely to use the money to buy a new car or go to Las Vegas? These are all questions that you should be asking yourself before the gift is made.

One last point about gifts to children. If a gift is made to a minor child, a custodial account will have to be set up. This is true for most titled property such as real estate and brokerage-firm accounts. There is no cost or fee for setting up one of these accounts; no special forms or attorneys are needed. Instead of being titled "Johnny Jones" (the name of the child), the account will read "Mary Jones, custodian for the benefit of (often abbreviated as FBO Johnny Jones."

Custodial accounts include the child's date of birth and social security number. Until the child reaches adulthood, only the custodian can trade in, sell, or transfer the account. The custodian has a strict fiduciary duty to act on behalf of the child. This means that gifts cannot be made back to the donor. The custodian can be any adult. This means that the custodian could be the donor, the child's parent, grandparent, or friend. Only one person can be the custodian on the account; this makes it easier for decisions to be made and also makes the court's job simpler in determining fault if something goes wrong in the account. The account must be turned over to the child as soon as he or she reaches 18 (age 21 in some states).

Gifting Life Insurance

When an insured dies, life-insurance proceeds are included as part of the decedent's estate unless the owner and deceased were different people. Usually when life insurance is purchased, the owner and the insured are the same person; a husband or wife takes out a policy and pays for the premiums. But it does not have to be this way.

If someone *other than the insured owns the policy*, then the death benefit is not included as part of the decedent's estate when computing potential death taxes. By the way, it does not matter who the owner is when it comes to income taxes. Beneficiary(s) do not pay any income taxes on the death benefit. Life-insurance proceeds are always received free from state and federal income taxes. Let us get back to *estate* taxes.

In order to remove the policy from the "future deceased's estate," ownership must be transferred by written documentation. The necessary form is freely supplied by the insurance company. The important thing is that the gift must have been made at least 3 years before the death of the insured. This "three-year" rule applies only to gifts of life insurance. Since a gift is being made, there needs to be some concern as to the value of the gift.

According to the IRS, the value of a life-insurance policy is its "cost." In the case of a brand-new policy, this would be the first year's premium. In the case of a seasoned policy, value is based on what it would cost to replace the policy at the time of the gift. The cost to buy a similar policy may or may not equal any cash value in the policy. In the case of a policy that has accumulated a cash value, the value of the gift, according to the IRS, is the "interpolated terminated reserve as of the date of the gift, plus any prepaid premiums." You may not know what this is, but your insurance agent can get this information for you.

Do not be intimidated by any terminology or the process of changing ownership. You may find that the value assigned to the policy is less than $10,000. In such a case, no gift-tax return needs to be filed. If the value is greater than $10,000, you will need to file a gift-tax return along with Treasury Department Form 938. Whatever the value turns out to be, it will be much less than the death benefit. It might be time-consuming to go through this process, but think how much money will be saved if the decedent has an estate valued at over $600,000 and the insurance proceeds are not included for estate-tax purposes.

Trying to Use Gifts to Reduce Income Taxes

Some people are under the mistaken belief that they can lower their income taxes by making gifts of their salary or other earnings to the children. Unfortunately, this does not work. For income-tax purposes, the IRS always taxes the earner, not the eventual recipient. In short, you cannot assign part of your wages to someone else and avoid or minimize your own income taxes.

Gifts to children or relatives make sense if you are providing support to that person(s).

One of the goals of making a gift is to make sure that once the gift is made, earnings from that gift are taxed to the donee and not to you (the donor). From an income-tax point of view, it does not make sense to make a gift to someone if that security, trust deed, or piece of real estate will now be taxed in a higher bracket. This is not usually a point of concern, since most parents are in a higher tax bracket than their child. But there is a catch.

Income earned by the child is always taxed under the child's bracket, which is a zero bracket unless the child earns several thousand dollars each year. What is not always taxed under the child's bracket is what is known as "unearned income." *Unearned* income is money generated by stock dividends, proceeds from the sale of something, interest from government or corporate bonds, and interest from savings accounts and bank CDs.

Until the child reaches age 14, unearned income in excess of $1,000 each year is taxed under the bracket of the parent or parents. It does not make any difference that part or all of the unearned income was generated from an asset purchased by the child or from a gift by a relative, such as Grandpa or Grandma. Once the child reaches age 14, all income, earned and unearned, is taxed to the child, based on his or her bracket, even if it is still zero and Mom and/or Dad are multimillionaires.

Summary

Only gifts made to a qualified charity result in a tax deduction. Some people mistakenly believe that a gift to a child should result in a write-off. The purpose of making gifts to children or other relatives is to ensure that the income from the asset will now be taxed under that person's tax bracket and not yours. If your child is under age 14, only the first $1,000 of unearned income each year is taxed to the child; any excess is taxed to Mom and Dad, even though they may not have made the gift. A second reason to make a gift is to reduce the eventual size of your estate. A smaller estate means a reduction or elimination of estate taxes.

A gift, unlike an inheritance, does not receive a step-up in basis. The donee takes on the donor's cost basis or fair market value on the date of the gift, whichever is less. This negative may be small in comparison to a gifting program that is well thought out.

Checklist of Things to Do

1. Sit down with your wife or husband and review your net worth.
2. Consider making gifts to your children if your net worth is such that you can easily live without the gifted property.
3. Try to gift assets that have appreciated little since you purchased them.
4. If you completely trust your spouse, retitle all growth assets into community property so that one of you can take advantage of the 100% step-up in basis.

PART II

CHAPTER 5

YOUR LIVING TRUST

A LIVING TRUST is a document that allows you to transfer property ownership from your individual name(s) to the name of the trust. You control the trust. The property that can be placed in your living trust includes (1) personal residence, (2) all other types of real estate, (2) checking accounts, (3) brokerage accounts, (4) mutual funds, (5) any securities in which you have physical possession of the certificate, (6) second-trust deeds, (7) automobiles, (8) boats, (9) motor homes, (10) family heirlooms, (11) art, (12) jewelry, and (13) furniture. In short, everything you partially or fully own.

Keep in mind, nothing changes except the names on the titles. You continue to buy, sell, transfer, gift, and make decisions just as you did before. *Although it is simply a legal technicality, this is what keeps you and your family out of probate.* Since you no longer own anything in your own name, there is nothing to probate when you die or become incompetent.

Trusts were invented by the English about 400 years ago. They probably grew out of a thirteenth-century practice of giving overlords title to lands for the use of the Franciscan friars, who by the laws of their order were not allowed individually or as a community to own property.

The trust grew out a unique concept: a double form of ownership. The trustee has the legal title to the trust property, and the beneficiary has the equitable interest in it. The development of the trust idea was a gradual one, involving decisions handed down by the English courts throughout the reigns of numerous kings.

Advantages of a Living Trust
A revocable living trust offers the following benefits and features:

- complete flexibility: can be changed or canceled at any time
- lets you keep control even during incompetency and after death
- prevents conservatorship and court-imposed guardianships
- allows quick distribution of assets to beneficiaries
- avoids the problems of joint ownership
- very difficult to contest
- eliminates unintentional disinheriting
- completely confidential
- no court or attorney involvement needed
- can protect loved ones who have special needs
- valid in all 50 states

· never needs to be updated
· avoids the costs, delays, and emotional stress of probate

Several of these features were briefly discussed in the introduction. The descriptions that follow are more thorough and raise issues not previously mentioned.

Complete Flexibility: Can Be Changed or Canceled at Any Time

Since you and your attorney are setting up a *revocable* living trust, changes can be made at any time while you are still alive and competent. If you and your spouse set up a trust together, then both of you must agree if any changes are to be made.

Alterations to your trust may be desirable owing to personal, family, or economic changes. There may come a time when you decide that you no longer want to manage the trust's assets. This change of heart may be owing to age, a physical impairment, or lack of interest or time. If this ever happens, you can resign as the trustee and select someone else to oversee the trust and its assets.

At some later date you might decide that the eventual distribution of your estate should be changed. This may be owing to a divorce or marriage or to the fortune or misfortune of a child or grandchild. As an example, you could decide to send a grandchild to a private high school and want to ensure that the necessary funds are available in the event that you are not. Or you might conclude that one child will need more financial help than another owing to an accident or because the child wants to establish her own business or buy a house. These types of things can be accommodated easily by making a simple change to your living trust.

Finally, economic conditions or forecasts may change such that you now want the trustee to be able to invest in gold or invest only in mutual funds that concentrate on growth stocks from the largest corporations in the country. The fact that you dictate how the trust is to be invested gives you the ability to select investments that can be held and those that must always be avoided. It is these powers that can ensure the safety and financial well-being of the family long after your death. The investment parameters set forth by you will be part of your legacy; such direction must be adhered to *until all assets are distributed out of the trust*, even though that may be decades after your death.

Since you created this document, only you can destroy it. A trust is very easy to amend or revoke. Your attorney should charge you a nominal fee to amend a trust. Revocation is even easier: Transfer all assets that were previously titled under the trust to another name (single, joint, etc.) and then tear up all copies of the trust.

Lets You Keep Control at All Times

The trust you create concerns itself with your assets. While alive, you are the trustee, managing the trust's (your) property. What a successor can or cannot do with these assets is spelled out in a section of the trust called the "powers of the trustee." These powers can be as liberal or restrictive as you wish. As an example, you can limit the trustee's investment options to certificates of deposit and government bonds. You can also make sure that a certain asset is not sold (e.g., "*Income from the apartment buildings owned by the trust is to be distributed evenly to my three children. Only after the death of all my children may these apartments be sold*"). As you can see, these types of provisions mean that you are controlling your estate from beyond the grave. And you thought you couldn't take it with you!

This control is maintained even if you become incompetent or simply decide to step down as trustee. The successor or co-trustee(s) must follow the directions set down in the trust document. If a successor trustee does something that is not allowed by the trust, this person can be hauled into court.

The control you have over your living trust lasts until you say otherwise. If you can no longer legally speak for yourself, the trust cannot be changed unless you had previously given someone a *durable* power of attorney. A durable power of attorney is valid if you become incompetent but is automatically terminated upon the death of either you or the person you gave the power to.

Prevents Conservatorships and Court-Imposed Guardianships

If you have minor children or grandchildren who are not all adults, then you should be concerned about a court-imposed guardianship. These guardianships can occur whether or not the child's parents are alive or dead. Since minors cannot legally transfer titled property (stocks, bonds, mutual funds, real estate, etc.), the court may intercede to protect the child's interests even if both parents are still alive. If a minor child inherits titled property, a retirement account, the death benefit from a life-insurance policy, or becomes the joint owner of property, the court will have to sign for the child if any of these assets are sold or refinanced.

If you are divorced, then a provision naming a guardian for a minor child is imperative. If you were to die while your child was still a minor, or was an incompetent adult, the court must name someone to take your place. If you do not have a will that contains guardianship provisions, the court has no choice.

Unless your ex-spouse can be shown to have severe problems with alcohol or drugs, there is a strong likelihood that he or she will be named to raise the child. This is what happens even though the now deceased mother or father felt that their former spouse would make a terrible parent.

A conservatorship is used to oversee the personal and financial affairs of an adult, usually an elderly person such as your father or grandmother. Again, unless you had the proper document drafted before your death or incapacity, the court will step in and choose the person they think will act in that person's best interests. Unfortunately, the court will not be able to make as informed a decision as you would have. You know the

family secrets, desires, dislikes, and hopes; the court, on the other hand, is forced to rely on limited information.

Quick Distribution of Assets to Beneficiaries

You may want some of your beneficiaries to receive their inheritance immediately and others over a number of years; the choice is yours. A quick distribution may be important for an heir to continue running a family business, to take advantage of timely investment opportunities, or simply to continue on with his or her life. An estate that is subject to probate does not provide such needed timeliness. Heirs must hire an attorney and petition the court for an allowance to pay household bills, buy groceries, and make new purchases. During the period of probate, which may last anywhere from several months to over a dozen years, a beneficiary could end up being in financial limbo, unable to move forward or make business and investment decisions until assets are finally distributed.

A living trust avoids all of these problems by allowing for assets to be distributed immediately after the decedent's demise. In order to make speedy transfers, the trustee needs only a certified copy of the death certificate and the trust. These two items alone are all that is required. There are no special formalities. Assets in the trust that are supposed to be distributed outright to specific persons can be turned over to their new owners a few days after death. Other assets that are to remain in the trust for the benefit of future generations or until the beneficiary reaches a certain age are left intact and stay under the trustee's supervision.

Avoids Joint-Tenancy Problems

As mentioned elsewhere, individuals and couples try to avoid probate by titling accounts in joint tenancy with rights of survivorship (jtwros), commonly referred to as simply "joint tenancy." There are numerous problems with joint tenancy. First, nontitled property such as jewelry, art, furniture, coin collections, and cash cannot pass outside of probate without proper documentation or unless the cumulative value of all property, titled and untitled, is less than a statutory amount (which is as high as $60,000 in some states). Second, when you title anything in joint tenancy you are making a gift. This may require the filing of a gift-tax return and possibly the payment of a gift tax. Third, since you have made a gift, you cannot take the asset back; part of it now belongs to someone else. Since there are now co-owners, the property cannot be sold, transferred, or given away without the permission of every owner. Fourth, if the new joint owner is sued, the asset can be used to help satisfy the claim or judgment.

If you think that the new co-owner could *never* ever be sued, then you must be talking about someone who does not drive a car, own a business, who is not married, has no children or pets, will never need medical attention (or have children that need help), or owns no real estate. In short, you are not talking about anyone I have ever met.

A joint tenancy may also mean that you are helping the IRS and hurting the beneficiary. A gifted interest, which is what happens when you make someone else a partial owner, does not receive a 100% step-up in basis when you die. However, property owned by a trust can receive a 100% step-up in basis when the grantor (trust maker) dies. Another monetary harm that can be caused is qualification for financial assistance. A college, graduate school, or government-assistance program will not make grants or lend money to a student, medical patient, or handicapped individual who owns half of some real estate and maybe part of a securities account.

Difficult to Contest

We have all heard the expression "If she could see what was going on, she would turn over in her grave." Well, this is how the deceased would probably feel if an unwanted heir came forward and successfully contested the wishes of the decedent. Wills are not easy to contest, but it does happen; particularly if someone was very close to death or taken care of by someone who ends up inheriting what is felt to be a disproportionate share.

A living trust is a different matter. It is a document that was used by the decedent before death, perhaps for several years or decades. The trust is something that the now deceased had probably reviewed at leisure before signing instead of a will which could have been made while in a hospital or after learning of a terminal condition. A living trust is something under which the trustor managed his or her affairs. It is also quite likely that additional input was provided from an unbiased attorney.

There is a more practical reality which makes the living trust more difficult to contest: finding out about the death before assets are distributed. Since most trusts provide for the immediate distribution of assets upon the death of the trust maker (trustor), it is very likely that the decedent's estate will no longer exist by the time a hopeful heir comes forward. Once partial or full distribution has occurred, it is less likely for someone to go through the added expense of bringing multiple claims against different individuals and/or institutions.

Eliminates Unintentional Disinheriting

As previously mentioned, most individuals and couples have their trust drafted, signed, and funded long before there is an incapacity or death. The person making the bequests is more likely to have all of his or her senses when these decisions are being made.

If you die without a will or living trust, your intended beneficiaries may end up with nothing. This is because the state has its own ideas as to how your estate should be distributed if you did not make such plans while alive. The laws of intestate succession, dying without a valid will (or trust), vary from state to state. Your spouse may end up with everything when, in fact, you only wanted him or her to receive half or a third. Conversely, your children may end up with one-half or two-thirds of your separate property when, instead, you wanted everything to go to your spouse.

A living trust can avoid intestate succession and thereby make sure that your estate goes to those people and/or institutions that you intended. Your lifetime of work and saving can be wasted if your property is given away to a family member who ends up wasting away the fruits of your work.

Ensures Privacy

If you die without a will, chances are that your financial history will now become public record. Intentionally disinherited parties, the press, creditors, and even your business competitors can now find out what you owned at death and whom you owed money to. The only reason we know about John Wayne's holdings was because he died without a trust. A great deal of Bing Crosby's financial affairs were made public when his first wife died. Learning a valuable lesson, Bing later had a living trust drawn up for himself and his second wife. It is for this reason, and this reason alone, that we know nothing of who Bing's heirs were or the size of his estate. There is, however, a more serious concern about this issue of privacy.

Certain salespeople and organizations thrive on court records. These same people will mercilessly solicit immediate family members in the hopes of selling them services, products, or investments; items that may not only be unneeded, but harmful. No one would like to see their carefully laid out financial plan ruined by a convincing stockbroker who talks an heir into liquidating everything and buying high-commission and/or risky investments. There are also businesses that charge fees to "prospective heirs" by notifying them of your death and telling them that they may be entitled to some of your estate. And, for a percentage of the take, they will help pursue the bounty. Solicitors and salespeople learn about grieving widows, widowers, and children by combing court records. By law, these records are made available to everyone; that is why they are referred to as public records.

If you do not care that parts of your life become an open book once you are gone, think about your family. The burden of settling an estate, providing comfort to others, and dealing with one's own grief are great enough. Do not prolong or compound this emotional strain by giving public notice to a bunch of hyenas.

No Court or Attorney Involvement Needed

Whether justified or not, the public feels that the fees charged by lawyers and doctors are too high. If someone's sole possession is a house worth $125,000 that has a $124,000 outstanding mortgage, it is not difficult to figure out that the net worth of this individual is $1,000. What may surprise you is that the probate fees on such an estate can easily top $7,000. In many states, these fees are statutory; not something that can be negotiated. These costs may be just the beginning. Hopefully this $1,000 estate will not incur "extraordinary fees" (something that can be petitioned for by the attorney or the estate's representative). These extras may be several thousand dollars more. But wait, there may be more. On top of legal fees and court costs there are usually charges for appraisals, accounting, and administration.

By having just a will (or dying without one), you may *think* that the fruits of your labor are going to your loved ones. Instead, your family may learn that a large percentage, perhaps the entire estate, ends up going to accountants, administrators, appraisers, and attorneys.

There is, of course, more to this involvement than fees and expenses. Court intervention may mean a judge second-guessing what she thought you were trying to do with your estate. Or worse, a judge who has to follow the strict schedule of intestate succession. Not only may bad decisions be made, there are also delays (see "quick distribution of assets to beneficiaries" above). Again, *all* of this can be avoided by having a living trust.

Protect Loved Ones with Special Needs

One of the great things about a living trust is your ability to have it tailored to fit special situations that exist now or may come into being long after your death or disability. Imagine the following tragedy: You have a will that divides up your estate evenly among 4 children; at the time of your death, all 4 children are healthy and financially secure. A few months or years after your death, one child is permanently disabled in an auto accident. The child is no longer able to work; the inheritance is eaten up during the next couple of years. Now the child needs help from his other brothers and sisters. Your other kids would like to help, but (a) their spouses will not let them, (b) they have their own problems, or (c) they are selfish and maybe even blame the disabled child for driving carelessly or not having sufficient insurance. It is too late for you to do anything; you (and your wife) are dead.

If there was a living trust instead of a will, this situation could have been avoided. Given the right powers, your successor trustee can decide who gets the income from your estate, when, and how much. The power to "sprinkle" income among beneficiaries is a commonly used technique. It ensures that accidents and unforeseen circumstances (e.g., bad investments, marriages that do not work out, grandchildren who need special assistance, etc.) are taken care of, even though you may no longer be around.

Valid in All 50 States

Sometimes when we enter into an agreement it does not work the way we expected if we later move to another state or country. The living trust you have drafted in one state is valid in Texas, Florida, Idaho, etc. The conditions of the trust will be honored in all 50 states. There are also several countries that recognize revocable living trusts that are drafted in the United States. Your wishes continue to be carried out no matter what state you end up residing or dying in.

Never Has to Be Updated

Certain parts of a living trust *package* need to be periodically updated, but this is not true with the living trust, even if these ancillary documents are not updated and become invalid. Thus, even though a durable power of attorney for health care is not renewed every 7 years or your living will is not revalidated every 5 years (these numbers vary depending upon your state of residency), it does not mean that the living trust is not good.

A living trust is something that stands on its own. It is not required that you include one or more ancillary documents. Additional provisions and powers will probably be helpful to you and your family, but their legality will not void your entire estate plan.

Your living trust should be reviewed whenever there are major estate-law changes (very infrequent) or if there is a major event in your family. These events would include such things as a death, marriage, divorce, birth, or permanent disability of a loved one. Only after such a review may you find it necessary to have your trust changed.

Minimizes Emotional Stress

Nobody likes to be told what to do. Yet, this is precisely what can happen without adequate estate planning. As mentioned throughout this book, if you do not make certain decisions before your death or incapacity, someone else will do it for you. This person may be someone chosen by the court. If you do not care about yourself, think about your family.

Do you want an outsider intruding on your spouse or children, asking them questions, making them almost beg for an allowance while the estate is being settled and periodically sending them bills for "services rendered"? The answer is probably not. Yet this is what happens all the time to survivors who cannot rely on the protection afforded by a living trust. There is also the issue of emotions.

A living trust can settle an estate within a few days. On the other hand, an estate that is probated may be tied up for several years. Every court appearance, every letter from solicitors, every call from an executor, administrator, or lawyer means that your loved ones' wounds will heal that much slower. Survivors go through a natural period of mourning; the length of that mourning is something private and personal. Do not let your family be subjected to a grieving period that is not only unnatural but unfair.

Avoids Probate

This is the first thing brought up by just about every book, seminar, and article dealing with living trusts. True, probate can be easily avoided if you have a living trust, but there are many other benefits afforded by the trust. Many of these benefits have been covered in previous pages; others will surface as you read on. These are things that can make your life easier and more secure while you are alive. There are also provisions and additional documents that can help family members immediately after your death and possibly for decades that follow.

Under certain circumstances it is a good idea to subject a small part of an estate to probate. An inexpensive probate proceeding means that, once completed, no more creditors can come forward, and unintended heirs cannot challenge your wishes or bequests. Do not get me wrong; several of the "advantages" of probate can also be accomplished with other estate-planning techniques and, for most people, probate should be avoided completely. Your estate-planning specialist can help guide you in this area. Counsel can review your particular situation and advise you accordingly.

The Parties to a Living Trust

There are three parties to every trust: (1) the grantor, (2) the trustee, and (3) the beneficiary. The person creating the trust, you, is referred to as the *grantor* or "trust maker." If you are married and set up a trust with your spouse, you are both grantors of the trust. The person you name to manage the assets in your trust is called the *trustee*. If you are married, you and your spouse can be co-trustees. You should also name someone as the successor, or backup, trustee. This is the person or entity that will manage your affairs if you and/or your spouse are unable due to death or incapacity. The people who will receive your property when you die are called your *beneficiaries*. You can determine who will inherit your assets and when such distributions are to be made (e.g., when an heir reaches a certain age or accomplishes a certain task). All of these parties will be described in greater detail in the next chapter.

Setting Up a Living Trust

An estate-planning attorney will prepare the trust based on what you would want to happen upon death or disability. You decide who will inherit your property and when. You decide who will be responsible for the estate's management. You can also decide who will take care of you if you become physically or mentally incapacitated.

A great deal of what goes into a trust is standardized. As long as you use a lawyer who is experienced with the preparation of living trusts and wills, the process can be simple, quick, and inexpensive.

After the trust has been prepared, most of which can be done on a word processor, and you have read the document, it must be signed and notarized. All of the property that you want to be in your trust then needs to be transferred into the name of the trust. Beneficiary designations to your retirement accounts (in certain cases) and life insurance proceeds should also be changed.

Changing the title to your property is easy. As an example, instead of owning your home as "John and Mary Smith," the deed will now read, "John and Mary Smith, trustees of The Smith Family Trust, dated May 15, 1992" (the date of the trust is included to help identify it). In the case of real estate, the county recorder's office is notified; the recorder charges a fee of less than $50 to make the change. Banks, brokerage firms, and other institutions where you own assets should also be contacted. These institutions will not charge you any fee but will require you to provide them with a generic form or request that you use a form they have prepared. When an asset is sold or transferred, the owner or owners still sign their name, but include the word "trustee" after it.

Personal property does not include a formal title. Standard provisions found in most living-trust documents will automatically include all of your untitled and personal belongings into the trust. Unlike the probate process, you do not need to list or inventory your possessions or other assets.

Certain assets are not subject to probate or are not allowed to be owned by the trust. You cannot obtain life insurance on a trust but you can name the trust as the beneficiary. The same is true with retirement accounts such as IRAs, Keoghs, pension plans, profit-sharing programs, 401(k)s and 403(b) plans, although there may be income-tax reasons why the change should not be made. Everything that has a designated beneficiary will escape probate. You may find it helpful later to name the trust as the beneficiary of these accounts and policies for three reasons.

First, if the beneficiary is incompetent when you die, the court will set up a conservatorship (described in chapter 10) in order to control and protect the proceeds. This happens even if there is a living trust. However, if the trust is listed as the beneficiary, the proceeds will be paid to the trust, the "actual" owner, who is not incompetent. The successor trustee(s) will then be able to use the money received to care for your heir without court supervision.

Second, if you and the named beneficiary both die at the same time, the court may have difficulty deciding who will receive the proceeds. A trust can avoid this uncertainty by naming successor beneficiary(s).

Third, by having everything go through a single document, your living trust, it is easy to make changes. This can be particularly important if there are ex-spouses or children you wish to later add or delete as beneficiaries.

A Special Word About Retirement Accounts and Life Insurance

One of the decisions you need to make is whether or not your retirement accounts should have their beneficiary designations changed. The advantages of making such a change have already been described. But a retirement account that names a trust as beneficiary may not be rolled over if the beneficiary is a trust and not a person or persons. This means that taxes on such a distribution could not be postponed for more than 5 years.

In the case of life insurance, it may be wise to not only change the beneficiary designation but also the ownership. This is because only the owner can borrow money from the policy. If you become incompetent, the *successor trustee* could borrow out the cash value of the policy and use it to help pay for your care. Life insurance is considered one of your assets for estate-tax purposes.

When the Trust Becomes Effective

The trust becomes valid as soon as it is signed, notarized, and "funded." This simply means that the title of at least one asset is now in the name of the trust. At this point, your lawyer's responsibilities for the establishment of your trust ends.

One of the biggest mistakes people make is thinking that everything is fine simply because trust documents have been signed. This is incorrect. Any assets not titled in the name of the trust may be subject to probate. Make sure that everything you own, with the exception of those items described in a later chapter, is titled in the name of the trust. Assets acquired after the revocable living trust have been set up are simply titled in the name of the trust.

When you die, the successor trustee, or co-trustee if you are married, will act as your representative without having to report to the court. Assets are distributed or managed based upon the trust instructions you left. Nothing is frozen; the process can be quick, inexpensive, and no lawyers are necessary. And, since there are no mailed or published notices, uninvited "heirs" will not be able to easily make claims against the estate.

Successor Trustees

Make sure that the person(s) you name as successor trustee(s) is trustworthy *and* willing to take on this responsibility if it ever becomes necessary. The co-trustee or successor trustee has a great deal of power if you die or become incompetent. But this power is limited by the trust instructions you set down while you were alive and competent. A trust is a legally binding contract. As fiduciaries, trustees have a duty to follow your trust instructions and act in a prudent manner at all times. The trustees must act in a manner that will help the beneficiaries. A successor or co-trustee who abuses this fiduciary responsibility can be held liable and taken to court.

If you become incompetent, the successor, or co-trustee, steps in and handles all financial affairs. This "new" trustee can write checks, make deposits, sell assets if necessary, and even apply for disability benefits on your behalf. Again, no courts, attorneys, conservatorships, or special people need to be notified. Everything is confidential and tasks can easily be performed. If you regain competency, no special paperwork or legal intervention is necessary for you to take back control. The acting trustee simply steps aside and once again takes on the position of successor or co-trustee. A competent adult who sets up a trust can always hire, fire, or change trustees at any time without reason or permission.

Minor Children and Grandchildren

If you leave property directly to your minor children or grandchildren, make a child a joint owner, or list a child as beneficiary of your life insurance or retirement plan, you could be setting up a probate guardianship for the child. The court must make sure that the child's interests are "protected," even if one or both parents are still alive. This protection is not free; the child or parent(s) will have to pay the costs of a lawyer and any court expenses. The court-appointed guardian will raise the child and/or control the inheritance until he or she reaches legal age.

The way to avoid a court-appointed guardian is to set up a children's trust within your family trust. This way, the trust "inherits" on behalf of the children. At death, assets are immediately transferred to a trust that is administered by the person(s) you designated; the custodian must manage all such property for the benefit of the children.

Having a court-appointed guardian for a minor is similar to what happens under a conservatorship—the procedure is expensive and can take a great deal of time. Every expense must be documented, audited, and approved by the court.

Courts prefer to see a natural parent as guardian. Even if you specify someone else, your "ex" will probably become the guardian. A disinterested or irresponsible parent may suddenly become very interested once they learn that guardians are entitled to be paid for their services. Furthermore, courts often do not have the resources to carefully monitor all guardianships; your spouse or "ex" may end up with unsupervised access to the child's inheritance.

Summary

Trusts have been around for hundreds of years. Many members of Congress have living trusts because they understand the benefits of this estate-planning device. Perhaps the greatest feature of a trust is that you can change it whenever you like. Depending upon how the trust is worded, you can also ensure that no changes can be made after your death.

A revocable living trust is not a substitute for a will but it does things that a will cannot. First, it can be effective if either you or your spouse become incapacitated. Second, it avoids the problems created by joint tenancy. Third, the estate can be distributed quickly. Fourth, assets can remain within the trust and managed for the benefit of your spouse, parents, children, etc. Fifth, there is no need for an attorney or the courts to get involved. Sixth, it can be structured to protect family members who may later become disabled. Finally, it avoids the costs, delays, and emotional stress created by probate.

Checklist of Things to Do

1. Talk to your spouse about all of the benefits of a revocable living trust.
2. Determine who will make decisions after your death: (a) your spouse, (b) someone other than your spouse, or (c) your spouse and someone else.
3. Think about who your heirs will be and decide if their share of the estate is to be given outright or at some later date.
4. If trust assets are to remain in the trust after your death, consider a "sprinkling" provision that will allow your spouse and/or successor trustee the power to make special distributions to children who may later have special educational or medical needs.

CHAPTER 6

YOUR TRUST TEAM

THERE ARE THREE parties to every trust: the trustor, the trustee, and the beneficiary. More than one person call fill each of these roles. There can be two trustors, co-trustees, and multiple beneficiaries. Thus, the trustor can, and usually is, the trustee; a trustee may also be a beneficiary, etc. In addition to these team members, it is strongly recommended that you have "alternate players": successor trustee(s) and successor beneficiary(s). By having these backup players, your trust will have people who can step in immediately if a trustee resigns, becomes incapacitated, or dies; contingent beneficiaries allow you to leave your estate to those who are your "second choices."

This chapter will detail what each of your team members is supposed to do and what they can expect in return. The focus on the chapter will be suggestions and a sense of direction as to who should be chosen for each position.

Trustor (the Person Who Creates the Trust)

The person who creates the trust is called the trustor. If two or more people set up a trust, then each would be called a co-trustor. The trustor(s) is the only person who can change,

alter, amend, or revoke the trust. Once the trust has been created and signed by the trustor(s), his and/or her duties have ended. The only time the trustor would get involved again with the trust would be to change or revoke it.

Whoever transfers assets into the trust is called the settlor. There can be one or more of them. The settlor is usually the trustor. The same person or persons usually sets up and funds the trust. In this book, the term "trustor" and "settlor" can be used interchangeably. You may also come across the terms "grantor" and "grantor trust." The IRS and some legal writers refer to the settlor as the grantor; living trusts are occasionally called grantor trusts.

Trustee (the Person Who Manages the Trust Property)

This is the person who manages and administers the trust. If there are two or more such people, each is referred to as a co-trustee. If you and your spouse are going to set up a trust together, it will most likely show each of you as co-trustors and each of you as co-trustees. In the case of a married couple, assets in the trust can be bought, sold, mortgaged, used as collateral for a loan, transferred, or gifted away without the permission or knowledge of the other spouse. It does not have to be this way, but this is how most living trusts with married couples are structured.

Once the trust has been created and partially or fully funded (assets have been retitled in the name of the trust), the trustee steps in and can immediately buy, sell, mortgage, transfer, etc., any of the trust assets, provided the powers of the trustee include such latitude. Even though you were the person who created the trust, as the trustee you must stay within the guidelines imposed by the trust document. If you, as the trustor, want to be more aggressive or conservative with the trust's investments, you can simply amend the powers of the trustee section.

From a practical point of view, the *trustors* can pretty much do what they want. After all, they are the ones who created this thing; it was also their money, property, and other assets that went into the trust. If they happen to intentionally or negligently stray outside of what the trustee is supposed to be able to do, who is going to know? A court would not be very amused to learn that you were bringing a lawsuit against yourself. On the other hand, and on a more serious note, in the case of co-trustees, it is very possible that one spouse (co-trustee) might stop the other spouse (co-trustee) from doing something contrary to what they had both previously agreed to.

As an example, if you set up a living trust with your husband and the trust states that only blue-chip stocks and government bonds can be bought or traded in the trust, you would have recourse against your husband if he went out and started trading in commodities or purchasing apartment buildings with trust assets. And this would only be fair. After all, this is something that both of you agreed to, terms, powers, and all; acts outside of the wording of the trust could be contrary to what you had agreed to.

If all of this sounds a little too heavy, do not despair. The wording of most trusts allows the trustee or co-trustee quite a range in the investment and management of the trust's property. It is very rare to hear about one co-trustee suing another.

The Successor Trustee (a Backup for the Trustee)

When one or both trustees are unable to act because of death or disability, or because they have given written resignation, a successor trustee steps in. You always have the right to replace your successor with anyone you wish (including reinstating yourself) at any time—the only requirement is that you must be competent when the change(s) takes place. The reason you have this power is that you are the *trustor*. A trustee does not have the right to name a replacement.

If you are not married, it is pretty likely that you are the sole trustee. If something were to happen to you, the person you named as successor trustee would now assume the duties of the trustee. If you are married, most trusts are set up so that if one spouse no longer acts as a co-trustee, the other spouse will then act alone. Some trusts are set up so that if one spouse is removed, a substitute trustee takes this spouse's place, thus ensuring that there are two trustees at all times, at least while one of the spouses is alive.

If you and your spouse set up a trust, the survivor usually has the right to change successor trustees. This gives the estate maximum flexibility, since unforeseen events may occur after the death, resignation, or incapacity of the first spouse.

When talking about what the surviving spouse can and cannot do, keep in mind the following: (1) *you* may end up being the surviving spouse—just because you are older than your spouse does not necessarily mean that you will be the first to die or become incapacitated; (2) the powers of the trustee are something that cannot be changed without your permission—once you die, resign, or become incapacitated, your spouse must act within the framework of the trust, and (3) if you resign or become incapacitated, you can always reclaim your position (title) as co-trustee whenever you like, as long as you are mentally capable at the time the demand is made.

A successor trustee assumes management of the trust (co-manager if another trustee exists) immediately. As soon as you die, resign, or become incapacitated, your successor steps in. No court proceeding, legal action, or special notice is needed. One of the features of a living trust is privacy; the substitution of a successor trustee without any fanfare goes along with this theme.

Whether there are one or more persons who eventually take your place as trustee is not the critical issue. What is important is that you understand what that person(s) can and cannot do. The successor trustee will perform one or both of these duties: (1) manage the trust's assets and/or (2) distribute the trust's assets. Management and distribution must be done in accordance with the instructions you laid out when the trust was first formed. The only way these instructions or powers can change is if you make an amendment to the trust before your resignation, death, or incapacity.

Management must be carried on in a "prudent manner." Assuming the trust is fairly broad in latitude, this does not necessarily mean that only conservative investments such as CDs, government bonds, and money-market accounts are the only choices. "Prudence" can mean maintaining purchasing power; in other words, seeking investments that historically have been hedges against inflation: common stocks, certain categories of mutual funds, and real estate.

A frequently asked question is whether or not trust property can be mortgaged or encumbered. The answer is a qualified "yes" in most cases. This means that the successor trustee could take out a first or second mortgage in order to improve the property, use the proceeds for another piece of real estate, or for another investment. What the trustee could *not* do would be to use the money as a loan or an "advance" to a beneficiary. In short, trust management and investment decisions are for the benefit of the trust, not the trustee(s), successor trustee(s), or beneficiary(s).

Successor Co-trustees (a Backup Team for the Trustee)

About a third of the trusts I have seen provide for successor co-trustees. This means that when both spouses "step down," two or more other people step in; these people are usually two or more of the parents' adult children. The successor co-trustees must act in a way that you and your spouse did not: these successors must agree on every action. In contrast, while you and your wife or husband were acting as co-trustees, either one of you was free to make decisions without approval by the other.

Trusts *can* be worded so that either successor co-trustee can make a decision without the consent of the other successor co-trustee(s). Much of this discussion talks about two people acting together. You and your spouse may have three, four, or more children. In such a case, you are free to name one or more as your successor trustee(s). The only requirement is that your child, or whomever you choose (friend, banker, broker, etc.), is an adult and competent at the time the person is acting as a trustee.

Some trusts that name multiple successor co-trustees require unanimous agreement; others allow majority rule. If an agreement cannot be reached owing to a split or non-unanimous vote, some trusts are worded so that a neutral source, usually a professional arbitrator, casts the deciding vote. The names, addresses, and telephone numbers of several arbitration panels can be found in the phone book. Arbitration will cost the estate a fee, and a decision will take more time. Fortunately, experience has shown us that it is exceedingly rare for an arbitrator to be used. Once the successor co-trustees are aware that an arbitrator can easily be brought in to resolve the matter, probably at a cost to the trustee (since he or she is likely to be a beneficiary), stalemates seem to disappear.

A person who does not want to hurt the feelings of his or her children will sometimes name a financial institution, such as a bank's trust department, as a successor trustee. If you and/or your spouse are seriously considering an outside entity for the management of your trust, do some checking around. By contacting a few of these institutions you can get an idea as to the fees involved, the type of statements you will be receiving, and the trust department's investment style.

Beneficiary (Who Gets the Final Distributions)

The person who creates the trust, the trustor, is also the beneficiary. If you and your spouse set up a living trust, each of you is a co-trustor *and* a beneficiary. If you and your wife or husband set up a trust, the surviving spouse is the sole beneficiary of the trust. There are other beneficiaries at the death of the first spouse if there was also an A-B or A-B-C Trust; separate chapters are devoted to each of these types of trusts. In the case of a married couple, the primary purpose of a living trust is to provide for the surviving spouse, whether that ends up being you or your wife or husband. In certain cases, this may mean that most or all of the estate (trust property) is used for that spouse's later benefit.

Most trusts are worded so that before a beneficiary can inherit his or her share, three conditions must be met. First, the trustor (or co-trustors) must be dead. Second, the beneficiary must be living after your death. Third, assets must be remaining. *If all of these conditions are not met, the beneficiary gets nothing.*

Something most beneficiaries want to know is who gets what and when. As the trustor, you, perhaps along with some guidance from your attorney, will make these decisions. There are several ways you can have your estate distributed, but any way you think of will come under one or more of these three headings: outright, at a specific age(s), and deferred.

Immediate Distribution

Outright distribution is used when the beneficiaries are adults. Your decision should not be based on age alone. Presumably, you have a good sense of which child or children are more responsible than others. You are probably also familiar with special needs: college education, graduate work, help in buying a first home, starting a business, therapy needs, supplemental income, etc. One of the beauties of a living trust is that you can decide that one child is to get an immediate distribution (his or her share) and the other (or others) is not.

Distributions at Specified Ages

A second alternative is to make the distribution at a specific age. Some estate-planning specialists recommend that you postpone distribution of principal until the child (or other heir) is at least 25 years old. Such a delay will have given the beneficiary time to finish college and perhaps graduate school and experience the "real world" for a couple of years (learning to appreciate how difficult it is to *save* $1,000). By this time, the beneficiary may have even developed a stable relationship. As my father has always told me, "It is easier to spend money than it is to save it." There is no substitute for life experiences and maturity. At age 25, a down payment on a house might not seem as important as that new Porsche.

Deferred Distributions

Deferred distribution is the third way to pass on your assets. Under a deferred approach, it is quite possible that nothing is immediately distributed upon your death. Instead, the beneficiaries must reach certain ages, complete specific tasks, or wait until a set number of years have passed since the trustor has died (or death of the surviving spouse in the case of a married couple). Three of the most commonly used benchmarks are: graduation from college, purchasing a home, and getting married. There are two common methods of deferred distribution based on age: (a) the heir receives one-third of his or her share at age 25, one-third at age 30, and one-third at age 35, or

(b) the adult heir receives one-third of his or her share outright, one-third 5 years later, and one-third in 10 years.

There *may* be an unfairness to deferred distribution. It makes little sense to unintentionally defer part or all of a beneficiary's share until he or she reaches age 45 or 50. And this is precisely what can happen if part or all of the distribution is predicated on certain events (e.g., getting married, having a child). The same thing can happen when the beneficiary must wait a certain number of years after your death(s) to receive the final one-third or two-thirds of his or her share. It is doubtful that most parents really want a child to get the balance due in 5 or 10 years after the parents' death if the surviving child is already 45 years old.

Besides outright distributions of *principal*, immediate or deferred, you might also want to consider distribution of *income*. Income from a trust would include such things as rents collected, interest payments, dividends received, and royalties paid. Deferred or permanent delays of principal are appropriate under the following situations: (1) the child is already financially secure and you want to provide for your grandchildren, (2) the child is too immature, (3) the child is married to someone who is "controlling," (4) the child's marriage is troubled, (5) the child is prone to lawsuits, or (6) the child appears to be a gambler when it comes to investments. Keep in mind two things. First, reference to "the child" includes other heirs such as parents, brothers, sisters, friends, etc. Second, once a distribution is made, it cannot be taken back and is no longer within the control of you or the trust.

Income distributions may be appropriate for some of your beneficiaries but not others. The level of income will largely depend upon the investment powers afforded to the trustee and how that trustee acts. Trust powers that allow for investments in stocks, bonds, and limited partnerships (all of which are categorized as "securities") can produce significantly different results. As an example, if the trustee invests largely in foreign stocks, particularly securities from Pacific Basin countries, the dividend (income) may be only in the zero to one percent range. Conversely, an investment in high-yield bonds or a leasing program can provide a yield or distribution (income) in the 10–15% range. This is certainly a case in which the income beneficiary will want to stay on very friendly terms with the trustee(s).

For whatever reason, you may decide to disinherit one or more of your children. Technically, this can be done by simply leaving their name out of the trust. No special disclaimer needs to be made. If disinheritance is what you want, it is best to be safe: include the names of all children in your pour-over will (described in a later chapter; this shows the court that you did not forget any of your children—their existence was acknowledged but it was decided they were to receive nothing).

A common concern of parents is being "unfair." Our law firm comes across people who think that they are the only parents in the world who are considering uneven distributions among their children. Do not despair. A fair number of single parents and couples give more to one child or beneficiary than to another; usually for some very sound and noble reasons.

Handicapped Children

Before moving on, you should know about how the government could treat your estate if you have mentally or physically handicapped children. First, you do not have to provide for their welfare. If it is your goal to have public assistance for that child, do not make this person a beneficiary of income or principal. Second, if an inheritance is received by the handicapped child, government benefits may cease at this point or a state or federal agency can step in and take part or all of the inheritance.

In the case of handicapped children, there is another alternative. Your trust can be worded such that the successor trustee can provide for the child's "welfare." This means that things like room, board, education, medical care, transportation, and entertainment can be *directly* paid for (i.e., not actually paid to the child). By using this tactic, government payments *may* not be in jeopardy.

Executor (the Manager of Your Will, Not the Trust)

Executors, guardians, and conservators are not members of your *trust* team, but they are integral players. It is a necessity that you have an executor; a guardian is strongly recommended if you have minor or incapacitated adult children. A conservator is needed only if you are judged to be incompetent.

Like a trustee, an executor is a manager. The trustee oversees assets in the trust; the executor administers everything outside of the trust. You name an executor in the pour-over will. A pour-over will is included as part of a living-trust package and covers property not titled in the name of the trust. The executor is also needed in case there is a probate. Probate will not take place with proper estate planning, which often includes the use of a living trust. However, if by accident there was a probate (too many assets not titled in the name of the trust), the executor, not the trustee, would then represent your estate. As soon as any probate ends, the executor would then "pour" any remaining assets outside of the trust into the trust. Once "poured in," the trustee would then have the additional responsibility of managing and/or distributing these "new" assets. This is why you have a pour-over will.

Normally, people name the same person to act as executor *and* successor trustee. In the case of a married couple, each spouse names the other as executor.

Guardian (Watching Over Minor or Incapacitated Children)

As mentioned above, a guardian should be named if you have minor children or adult children who are handicapped. This should be done even if you are married and have a younger spouse. There is no certainty that something might not happen to both of you before the child or children become adults or recover from the handicap.

Naming a guardian is tricky. You may have to look to the future needs of the child and hopefully not offend your parents, in-laws, brothers, sisters, or best friends. You can name only one guardian per child; however, the same person could be the sole guardian of several children. If you have more than one child, then a different person could be named for each. When listing a guardian, consider the following: (1) where would the child live—would school, friendships, or family ties be damaged?, (2) does the prospective guardian share your views about education, discipline, religion, etc.?, (3) how much of a financial strain will the guardian be under?, and (4) is the person you are thinking about naming willing to raise the child or children if something happens to you and your spouse?

Conservator (Taking Care of You at a Later Age)

None of us like to think about growing old or becoming unable to manage our personal affairs because of physical or mental limitations. However, the reality is that something could happen: a stroke, an auto accident, disease, advanced cancer, or Alzheimer's. If something like this does happen, you have a choice: you can select someone to care for you before the disablement or you can let the court do it. The person the court selects will probably be your spouse, but what would happen if your spouse were no longer alive or was unable to take care of you? The answer, as usual, is to make sure that a backup is named, a contingent conservator.

There is nothing pleasant about a conservatorship, but at least with proper estate planning you will have some control over the process if it becomes necessary. This is because your conservator is named by you when the trust is established. The named conservator can be changed only by you. Equally important, your trust can also name the facility you are to go to and a minimum amount that should be spent each month on your care.

As an example, your trust could state that if hospitalization or a nursing home were ever needed, and you were unable to speak for yourself, you would go to the La Jolla Rest Home, a private room with an ocean view would be provided if available, and that you would receive three gourmet meals a day. The fact that your beneficiaries or successor trustees might not think this is a good idea is not important. True, this could exhaust most or all of your estate, but after all it is *your* money.

Summary

Once broken down into parts or parties, a revocable living trust is easy to understand. There are three parties to every trust. The same person could be the trustor (the person who created the trust), the trustee (the person who manages the trust), and/or the beneficiary (the person who inherits part or all of the property titled in the name of the trust). Usually, when someone sets up a trust, he names himself as the trustee and someone else as a beneficiary. Remember, the beneficiary is entitled to something only after your death.

Alternates should be listed in the event that you are no longer able to serve as your own trustee or in case a beneficiary dies before you do. One of the great advantages of a living trust, unlike a will, is that distributions can be made as soon as you die, or they can be delayed. A distribution that is delayed may be a wise course of action for beneficiaries who are still too immature, have trouble completing school, are in a troubled marriage, or should use the inheritance to purchase a home or income-producing asset.

How the trustee manages assets in the trust depends on the flexibility given to this person or institution as worded in your trust document. The "powers of the trustee" section of the trust can be worded so that only conservative investments can be bought and sold, or the wording can be very liberal, allowing the trustee (and any successor trustees) to seek out aggressive and other high-risk assets.

Finally, by including other documents as part of your estate plan, you will have done everything possible to ensure the orderly disposition and management of your estate after you have gone. You will have also helped to protect the interests of your spouse and any children.

Checklist of Things to Do

1. Show your spouse how nothing changes with a trust while you are alive.
2. Decide if you want your trust worded so that either co-trustee (spouse) can act without the permission or knowledge of the other. In the case of spouses, most trusts are structured this way.
3. Choose successor trustees who are honest and are good money managers.
4. Determine who your heirs are and when their shares are to be received.
5. Consult with your spouse and agree upon whether a child is to receive only income from their inheritance or income and principal.
6. The executor (the person who manages any property left outside of the trust) should probably be your spouse. If you are single, the executor should probably be the same person or institution you named as successor trustee.

CHAPTER 7

THE POWERS OF YOUR TRUSTEE

YOUR SUCCESSOR TRUSTEE'S powers depend on the wording of your trust, powers granted by statute, and those *implied* by law. Your trust document will list those powers that may be exercised by the trustee. If they conflict with those granted by statute, those powers listed in your trust will control. The Probate Code grants an extensive list of powers to the trustee for any trust created after July 1, 1987. Thus, unless you make limitations in the trust document, a trustee can:

- collect and hold property
- receive additions to the trust
- operate or participate in a business, subject to limitations
- invest in stocks and bonds
- invest in U.S. government and municipal obligations (T-notes, T-bonds, Series EE and Series HH bonds)
- deposit funds in certain types of accounts
- acquire and dispose of property
- manage property
- encumber property
- make alterations and repairs to trust property
- develop land
- enter into leases
- enter into mineral leases

- grant or take options
- vote shares or give proxies
- pay assessments
- sell or exercise stock subscriptions and conversions
- consent to corporate reorganizations and other changes
- hold securities in the name of a nominee
- deposit securities in a securities depository
- insure trust property
- borrow
- settle and pay claims
- pay taxes and reasonable compensation for the trustee and agents, as well as other expenses
- make loans to beneficiaries on fair and reasonable terms or pledge property to guarantee loans
- distribute property to a beneficiary who has a legal disability
- employ agents
- execute and deliver instruments
- prosecute or defend legal actions

While reviewing the above 29 powers, keep in mind the following: (a) you can eliminate one or more of these powers in your trust document, (b) all of these powers refer only to those assets titled in the name of the trust, and (c) there are restrictions on some of these powers. For example, if the business consists of something other than fewer than 5 rental property units, the trust must expressly authorize such action (see power #3) or a court order is required.

The Probate Code also includes "implied powers." These are powers that the trustee may use to accomplish the purposes of the trust, so long as such powers fall under the general standard of care required of all trustees.

Finally, the Probate Code gives a trustee the right to petition the court for additional powers. If granted, the trustee is then assured that his or her actions will not later be successfully challenged by a beneficiary. In the alternative, the trustee can always obtain releases from the beneficiary(s), rather than petition the court. If you opt for written releases, make sure that the beneficiary fully knows the ramifications of your intentions. Consent by the beneficiary does not bind those beneficiaries who did not give their consent, nor does it have any effect upon a minor beneficiary or unborn beneficiary. Conversely, a court order is binding on all beneficiaries, current and future.

Duties of the Trustee

The "prudent-person" standard of care applies to all trust property, investments, and actions of the trustee. Additionally, the Probate Code requires that the trustee (a) take control of and preserve trust property, (b) make trust property productive, (c) dispose of improper trust investments, (d) keep trust property separate and identified, (e) enforce the claims of the trust, (f) defend actions that may result in loss of trust property or assets, and (g) not delegate those duties that he or she is expected to perform personally.

While you are alive and competent, if you name someone other than yourself as trustee, the trustee is required to follow all of your written instructions and follow your directions, even if they have an adverse effect on the beneficiaries. In short, while you are alive, you owe no duty to the beneficiaries and they have no right to your estate. After your death (and the death of your spouse if you are married), the trustee must be loyal to the beneficiaries, administering the trust as set forth in the "powers of the trustee" section.

Conflicts of Interest

As part of his or her duty, the successor trustee must avoid even the appearance of a conflict of interest or self-dealing. To do otherwise would be a violation of one's fiduciary duties. Courts are not very lenient when it comes to self-dealings and conflicts of interests. Successor trustees have been successfully prosecuted even when they did not even know that there was a conflict, when there was no profit involved, and when they did not act in bad faith. Potential problems arise in any one of the following situations: (1) the trustee is also a beneficiary, and part of the trust property includes a family business, (2) the trustee leases or purchases trust assets for himself, (3) the trustee sells or leases her assets to the trust, (4) the trustee competes in business with the trust, (5) the trustee loans or borrows from the trust, or (6) the trustee receives extra pay from the trust for additional work.

The potential conflicts of interest described above can be avoided if the trustee gets the informed consent of all beneficiaries *before* entering into one of these transactions. A letter of release from the beneficiaries after the fact is the next-best thing.

Being Fair to the Beneficiaries

Your successor trustee must also be impartial when it comes to the beneficiaries; again, within the context of the trust's powers. As an example, if you want two-thirds of your estate distributed to Johnny when he reaches age 30 and the remaining one-third to go to Mary when she becomes 40, the trustee is not being impartial just because he or she is carrying out your wishes.

The question of impartiality arises most

often when the trustee has the ability to make discretionary distributions and investments. One problem area is whether or not the trustee should consider the resources of a beneficiary when deciding if a discretionary distribution should be made. The trust may offer guidance or it may be necessary to seek help from the court. These problems can be solved by omitting discretionary clauses or setting down distribution guidelines in the trust.

What Happens If You Use Co-trustees

Unless your trust states otherwise, if there are two or more co-trustees, then agreements must be unanimous. The only times when a co-trustee could be excluded from the decision would be if he or she were absent, ill, or temporarily incapacitated and action needed to be taken in order to avoid "irreparable injury to trust property." Most married couples have their trust set up so that either spouse can act without the permission of the other. Your trust can certainly be worded to the contrary. If there are three or more co-trustees, another way around the problem of unanimous consent is to have your trust worded so that only a majority is needed. In any case, each trustee is supposed to participate in the administration of the trust and take "reasonable steps" in order to prevent another trustee from committing a wrong.

You can have your trust worded such that duties are divided up among trustees. Thus, you might state that one co-trustee (or successor co-trustee) is responsible for investments and that another is to make income distributions to the beneficiaries.

Standards for Trust Investments

Generally, what a trustee can or cannot invest in depends on the type of asset and whether the particular investment was proper under the circumstances. Some states have rules or guidelines that should be followed when choosing the *type* of investment (i.e., common stocks, preferred stocks, government bonds).

The particulars of the specific investment chosen are reviewed in light of the trust's objectives, distribution requirements, circumstances of its beneficiaries, and the need for diversification in the trust.

If a trust is so worded as to authorize the trustee to make a certain type of investment, to make a specific investment, or to follow a described pattern of investing, the trustee is in the clear, despite a state's "statutory list" or "prudent-investor" rules. *The tricky part, and indeed the purpose of this entire section, is to find out what is allowed if the trustee is given discretion.* Here we must divide up those states that follow statutory lists and those that adhere to the prudent-investor rule.

A small number of states follow a statutory or legal-list approach to determine whether an investment is acceptable or not. In these states, government bonds, certain types of first mortgages, corporate bonds, and a limited number of common stocks are allowed.

Fortunately, the great majority of states are guided by the prudent-investor rule. Under this approach, the trustee is held "only to a standard of good faith and prudence, requiring the exercise of care, skill, and caution, as well as impartiality, in making trust investments." Thus, the trustee should look at the *probable* income and *probable* safety of principal. Despite the broad interpretation that is found under the prudent-investor, referred to in the past as the "prudent-man" standard, there are some considerations that must always be kept in mind.

First, the trustee needs to look at the interests of any remainder beneficiaries. A remainderman, or in this case "remainder beneficiary," is a person or entity that may be entitled to some or all of the trust's assets at a later date. An example of this type of interest would be trust instructions that said, "Income paid to my spouse during his lifetime, upon his death, all assets are to go to my son." In this example, the son is the remainderman. The duty owed by the trustee to this "future" beneficiary should be to protect against loss of purchasing power. This would mean some type of growth to offset the effects of inflation.

Second, the notion of "prudence" is looked at when the investment is made; how it actually turns out should not be the responsibility of the trustee if he or she is acting with care. Things that the trustee would consider include how easily the investment can later be sold (marketability), security, and tax ramifications. Even though the trustee is not expected to be able to look into the future, bad choices should be sold. The prudent-investor rule requires the trustee to continually review all investments. If the trustee holds on to assets that have become improper for the trust, he or she could be personally liable for losses that resulted from holding such investments too long. Deciding how long "too long" is may not always be an easy task.

The foundation of the prudent-investor rule is diversification. A proper investment may become "improper" if there is too much of it in the trust's portfolio. Let us now take a more detailed look at what is acceptable in all states (jurisdictions).

What Trusts Can Invest In

While reading this section, remember that a trust can allow more or less than what is described below. This is one of the attractive features of your living trust. You can allow the trustee to invest in options, commodities, and risky penny stocks, or you can restrict the powers such that the trustee can purchase only bank CDs and money-market accounts; while you are alive and competent, the choice is always yours—after all, it is your money.

Government, municipal, and high-grade corporate bonds are almost always acceptable for trust purposes. First mortgages and first deeds of trust, if well secured, are also allowed. Second mortgages or second deeds of trust are not generally allowed.

A few states that use statutory lists may exclude common and preferred stocks. Most states, which follow the prudent-investor rule, permit these securities. If a dispute arises, the court will be looking at the *particular* stock involved. Specifically, it will want to look at the corporation's value, record of paying dividends, how long the company has been around, and its management. Mutual funds that invest in common and preferred stocks are likewise allowed in these jurisdictions.

Raw land as a speculative investment is not allowed. However, such an investment will probably be allowed if the land is to be improved with an income-producing building (apartments, shopping center, etc.).

Trustee Selection

Often it makes sense to give removal power to your beneficiary. However, the IRS might try to impose extra income- and/or estate-taxes if the heir can change trustees at will, especially if the trustee has the power to invade principal. The theory is that by shopping for trustees, the heir can get whatever he or she wants. And then, the IRS reasoning goes, the money is not really in a trust at all; it is in the heir's hands, with the full taxes due as if it had been bequeathed outright.

A Corporate Trustee

Trustees manage two things for you. They manage assets, and they decide when and how much to disburse to your heirs. How much should these services cost? Pure money management is offered by mutual funds. The Vanguard Group, one of the most cost-efficient of the large mutual-fund groups, charges under ½% of the assets annually to manage a typical fund. That includes both portfolio management and such overhead as accounting and coupon-clipping.

As for hand-holding, which a mutual-fund group across the country cannot properly do, there is no obvious low-cost comparison. But a ball-park number is, again, ½% a year. Thus, if a bank trust department will do both money management and hand-holding for an all-inclusive 1% of assets annually, you are not faring badly. New York's U.S. Trust charges a $2,000 base fee plus 1% annually on accounts of $3 million or less for everything from asset management to disbursements to the trust's tax return.

Teach your heirs to look over their trustee's shoulder. There are about 100 heirs who are campaigning for better treatment by their trustees (write to Mrs. Joan Smith, P.O. Box 292, Villanova, Pa. 19085).

Summary

The powers of your trustee are defined in three ways: those granted by statute, those implied by law, and those granted by the trustor (you) in the trust document. With few exceptions, these powers can be as creative or restrictive as you like. The fact that there are laws allowing a trustee to perform certain acts does not mean that they have to be permitted in your trust.

Besides being restricted by statute and provisions within the trust, the trustee must always follow the guidelines set forth by the prudent-person standard of care. Even *appearances* of a conflict of interest must be avoided. A completely neutral trustee, one who is not trying to benefit himself or herself in any way, is generally protected from disgruntled beneficiaries. If the trustee's actions even remotely seem to be at odds with the interests of the trust, beneficiary letters of permission can be sought.

If you are married and have a living trust with your spouse, many estate-planning attorneys recommend that you allow either you or your spouse the ability to make trust decisions without the other's permission. It is further recommended that after the death of the first spouse, the survivor be allowed to make decisions alone. Upon the death of the second spouse, successor trustees can be used. In many situations it is best to have only one successor trustee (as opposed to successor *co*-trustees) in order to avoid conflict and delays.

Checklist of Things to Do

1. If you are married, explain to your spouse how the trust's "chain of command" works.
2. Get input from your lawyer about using co-trustees and/or successor co-trustees.
3. When choosing successor trustees, consider the geographic location of the person being chosen, his or her management and investment skills, and willingness to serve.
4. Consider leaving a letter to your children *that will be read only after the death of both you and your spouse.* The letter can explain why one son or daughter was picked over another to act as trustee. This explanation can point out that the decision had nothing to do with love or favoritism.
5. Try not to discuss the issue of successor trustees with anyone other than your spouse and attorney. There is no need to cause any family resentment at this point. As your children mature even more, they will be more understanding of your decision. There is also the possibility that the successor trustee will be substituted by either you or your mate one or more times.

CHAPTER 8

How to Transfer Assets into Your Trust

In most states, your trust is not valid unless it is "funded." This means that at least one asset must show the trust as "owner." The fact that a trust is valid in no way means that all of your other property will avoid probate. It would be a big mistake to think this. Only those assets titled in the name of the trust will completely escape probate. Sometimes a trust will contain a Schedule A (assets other than life insurance) and Schedule B (life-insurance policies). It is mistakenly believed that the mere listing of your assets on one of these schedules is all that is needed. This, too, is incorrect. Such schedules are useful for *non-titled* property (furniture, jewelry, paintings, etc.) but nothing else.

To help you prevent these common mistakes, this chapter will show you how different types of assets are transferred to a trust. As you will see, some of these retitlings can be done by you, some by your financial advisor, and some by the county recorder's office. Once you have finished this chapter, you will see how easy the process is.

Institutions will usually require you to furnish them a copy of the trust. This is not necessary; you can supply them with a "certified copy of the trust." The certified copy may consist only of a few pages of the trust: (1) the page showing that you are the trustee, (2) the section indicating the powers of the trustee, and (3) the signature page. The banks, savings and loan associations, brokerage firms, and other entities that you deal with have certain legal responsibilities and also a fiduciary duty to their customers. Having said this, it is not their right or duty to know who your beneficiaries are, the size of your estate, what you own, or who your successor trustees are. This is none of their business and has nothing to do with them or the validity of the trust. The shortened form of your trust, what is referred to as a certified copy, is more private, less costly to make photocopies of, and cheaper to send through the mail.

Even though your name is, say, Margaret Kopechne, and the name of the trust is "The Margaret Kopechne Trust, dated 4/6/92," it does not mean that Margaret Kopechne is the trustee. Sometimes a trust is set up by someone who names someone else as the trustee. It is for this reason that you must show the institution that you are the actual trustee.

A trustee cannot act outside of the scope of the living trust. If the trust says that trust assets can be invested only in blue-chip stocks and raw land, then that is the only thing the trustee can do. The fact that you are the sole trustee, trustor (person who created the trust), and beneficiary means nothing. If you want the trust to be able to open up a checking account, then your trust needs to be amended to include such powers. Institutions you do business with want to protect themselves by making sure that what you want to do is "legal" within the contexts of the trust. This is why the "Powers of the Trustee" section of the trust document is so important.

Finally, whoever you deal with, again in order to protect themselves, will want to make sure that the trust is valid. The easiest way to do this is to look at the final page of the trust: the signature page, which will have your signature(s) notarized. The company you are dealing with will rest easier knowing that you are also the person who created the trust and that you are really acting on "your own behalf."

As you read through the trust-transfer instructions below and come across the phrase "seeing the trust," or words to that effect, it is an abbreviated way of saying that only those key pages described above are necessary.

Real Estate
This is one of the few assets (see also "trust deeds" and "time shares" below) that you should not attempt to retitle unless you specialize in real estate or get help from your attorney. The law firm you deal with will probably charge you a fee in the $50 range for each deed of trust that needs to be retitled. This fee includes the nominal charge levied by the county recorder's office.

Since real estate is the most important and valuable asset owned by most people, this is not something you want left to amateurs (you). Informal surveys have shown that a great number of people who try to do this themselves for the first time make mistakes. By trying to save 50 or 100 bucks, you may make the transfer ineffective and later force the property into probate. Probating property that is worth $150,000 will cost your estate close to $10,000. You have to ask yourself if it is really worth it.

In order to transfer your property, the attorney will need a copy of your grant deed. In some states title to property is taken under a land grant or land lease. Whatever the name is, this document gives you title to the property. Some people mistakenly believe that there is no grant deed until the house is paid off; this is incorrect. If you cannot find your grant deed (land grant or land lease), call the county recorder's office for information. The request for the document must be in writing and a nominal fee will also be charged.

From an earlier chapter you learned that transferring a piece of property from your name to the name of the trust will not affect its tax base or increase your property taxes. In fact, several states have enacted legislation that even allows parents to transfer property to children or vice versa without affecting the tax base of the asset. Similar legislation in these states also "ignores" transfers from a surviving spouse to his or her new spouse, meaning that there will not be a reappraisal.

The Homestead Act, a federal law, protects homes from creditors for up to $45,000 in equity, provided the protection of the bankruptcy court is also sought. This is something you should consider doing. Placing your home in a living trust will not affect the protection afforded by bankruptcy or the Homestead Act.

Automobiles
The motor-vehicle code in most states exempts automobiles from probate. However, if you own a car or a mobile home that is worth more than a certain amount, $30,000 in some states, including California, these vehicles should be registered in the name of the trust. Retitling cars and motor homes is easy, but requirements vary. Contact your department of motor vehicles and request the proper form.

Bank Accounts
Bank accounts can be changed by filling out new account-registration forms, signed by you, as the trustee. Most banks will want a

copy of your trust, showing that you are the trustee, that the powers of the trustee include dealing in bank accounts, and that the trust is valid (the notarized signature page).

Certificates of Deposit

Bank CDs can be retitled in the name of the trust by simple written correspondence and a certified copy of the trust. The same process is used for credit-union accounts.

Mutual Funds (Including Money-Market Accounts)

Write the different mutual-fund families you are involved with and send along a certified copy of the trust. The fund's transfer agent will put the fund(s) into the trust without a charge. The process should take less than three weeks. You will know that the retitlement has taken place because your next account statement(s) will show that the new owner is the trust.

Securities (Stocks, Bonds, and Limited Partnerships)

Publicly traded stocks and bonds can be put into your trust by contacting the issuer's transfer agent. The corporation's transfer agent will require a written request, an Irrevocable Stock or Bond Power and a certified copy of the trust that includes a handwritten verification by you that the trust is still valid. All three of these documents should have your signature guaranteed. It takes anywhere from four to eight weeks for new certificates to be issued and sent out. There is no cost for the new security certificates.

A signature guarantee is different from a notarized signature. Notaries can be found in banks, savings-and-loan associations, financial-planning firms, and real-estate offices. A signature guarantee can be done only by a brokerage firm that is a member of one of the stock exchanges or a commercial bank (not a savings and loan). There is no charge for a signature guarantee. Notaries often charge five dollars. Brokerage firms, mutual-fund groups, and transfer agents that require a sig-

nature guarantee will not honor a notarized signature under any circumstances. Brokerage firms and mutual-fund groups, like transfer agents, will also require a signature guaranteed stock or bond power.

A partnership interest is also considered a security. To transfer a partnership interest, whether you are a limited or general partner, have your attorney draw up a Bill of Sale/Letter of Assignment. This document describes the business and transfers it to your trust. Sole proprietorships are retitled in the same manner. In the case of limited partnerships, one of the general partners will usually make the transfer for you, making an attorney unnecessary.

Security certificates should be sent by certified mail, return receipt requested. Unsigned certificates are not negotiable; it is the stock or bond powers that make them marketable. The brokerage firm, mutual-fund company, or transfer agent simply opens each envelope and attaches a power to each certificate. There is no problem using certified mail. In the alternative, you can insure the securities and use registered mail. Over 90% of all diamonds are sent registered mail. In either case, make sure the stock or bond power or the back of the certificate is signed exactly as the front of the certificate is made out. As an example, if you have a 100-share certificate of IBM stock made out to "John James Jones, Jr.," you will need to sign the power or certificate as "John James Jones, Jr.", not "John Jones" or some other variation.

The easiest way to transfer stocks, bonds, money-market accounts, limited-partnership interests, and mutual funds is to take statements and/or certificates to your stockbroker. The brokerage firm you deal with will do all the necessary work, usually for free. If you do not have an account with the firm, this may be a good time to open one up.

Life Insurance

Like retirement accounts (see next section), life-insurance policies have a designated beneficiary. The person(s) listed as beneficiary(s) will receive your life-insurance proceeds even if you do not want them to (i.e., a former spouse), unless you change the beneficiary by writing to the insurance company.

A beneficiary letter of transfer is all that is needed. This letter states that you want to change the beneficiary from —— to —— (your living trust). The letter should reference the policy number and it needs to be signed by you *twice* (as the policy owner and as the trustee).

IRAs, Pensions, Keoghs, Profit-Sharing Plans, ESOPs, and 403(b) Plans

All of these assets include a provision for a designated beneficiary. Sometimes when these types of accounts are opened, the place to name the beneficiary is left blank. If a beneficiary has been listed, then this will take precedence over any will or trust. *For tax purposes*, make sure that *individuals* are listed as beneficiaries (see below). The contingent beneficiary(s) should be the trust.

To include your living trust as beneficiary of your retirement account(s) write to the account custodian and use language to the effect that "The contingent beneficiary should be ——." Make sure you include the name of the trust and its social security number (which is your number if you were the person who created the trust).

The letter you send to these custodians should reference the account number(s). As ridiculous as it sounds, these letters will need to be signed twice: once by you as the owner and once by you, in the name of the trust, as the transferee. Many law firms will provide you with several transfer forms to make the process easier. These forms can be used for non-retirement accounts as well.

Review future confirmations or statements to make sure that the *ownership* of your retirement account was not changed. Occasionally, the custodian will make a mistake.

One of the reasons that your retirement accounts should not list your trust as the beneficiary is that the survivor's ability to opt for a joint life payout (a means of stretching out

distributions and thereby possibly decreasing income taxes) may be lost if the trust is named as the beneficiary. A joint life payout can also be helpful to a non-spouse beneficiary.

Another reason is that if your spouse does not directly inherit this account—meaning it is inherited by the trust or someone else—a rollover for more than 5 years is not allowed. A spouse who inherits a retirement account can decide to roll part or all of the account into his or her name, continuing to postpone taxes indefinitely or receive outright distribution, paying income taxes in the year in which the money is received. A non-spousal beneficiary (a living trust, brother, parent, child, etc.) can have the account liquidated immediately and be subject to income taxes (but not a penalty) or roll it over for up to 5 years. At the end of 5 years, such an account must be fully depleted.

Trust Deeds

If you sold property and took back a second or lent someone money using a house as collateral, you have a trust deed. The other person's obligation to pay you is an asset. Since this is a titled asset, it should be in the trust. To transfer a trust deed you will need an attorney to draw up a new document, which in turn would be recorded with the county recorder's office. The recording protects you in the event that the property owner tries to sell the property without having first repaid you.

Annuities

You may have purchased your annuity through a brokerage firm or financial planner, but all annuities are issued by insurance companies. Even though insurers issue these contracts, all annuities are investments, not life insurance. Nevertheless, the application includes a place where the beneficiary(s) is to be listed. You will want to name your living trust as the *contingent* beneficiary. As mentioned under the retirement account section above (IRAs, pensions, etc.), it is the contingent beneficiary you should change if you are married, not the beneficiary. The tax benefit of such a change is that surviving spouses can inherit or take over annuities and retirement accounts without triggering a tax event within 5 years. The remaining spouse is always free to liquidate part or all of the account, but continued tax deferral would be lost on any amounts distributed.

Business Interests

If you are the sole or part owner of a privately owned corporation, your interest (shares of stock) can be easily transferred by having the existing shares voided and new stock certificates reissued in the name of the trust. The blank stock certificates you will need are normally found in your corporation's minutes book.

Business interests that are not partnerships or corporations can be transferred by one of the transfer form letters provided to you for free by the attorney who drafted your will. Your signature on the form should be notarized. This type of ownership is also referred to as a sole proprietorship.

Safe-Deposit Box

It is a good idea to include safe-deposit boxes as part of your trust since it may be necessary for a co-trustee or successor trustee to get into the box in order to retrieve important documents or articles (e.g., the original trust, cash, security certificates). To change title, go to the bank with a copy of your trust and have a bank officer rewrite your file card.

Time Shares

A time share is considered to be ownership of real estate. As such, title transfer is done through the county recorder's office.

Summary

A trust can protect only those assets that are titled in the name of the trust. A common mistake is to set up a trust and not fund it properly. When changing the title on accounts and property, the entities that you deal with need only to see a certified copy of your trust. This abbreviated version is only a couple of pages long. Your privacy is maintained since a bank or brokerage firm will not find out the size of your estate or its intended beneficiaries.

With the exceptions of real estate and trust deeds, all other assets can be easily retitled by you or your financial advisor. There is no cost or fee involved in transferring these items. A nominal fee is charged for real estate, time shares, and trust deeds. For later income-tax purposes, retirement accounts should list your spouse as primary beneficiary and the living trust as the contingent beneficiary. Retitling your assets so that the trust is now shown as "owner" will take a little time but the process is easy. More important, it is critical to effective estate planning.

Checklist of Things To Do

1. Make a list of all of your titled property (real estate, securities, bank accounts, etc.).
2. Find out what your attorney will charge, if anything, to retitle these assets.
3. Discuss the retitling with your stockbroker, financial planner, and/or insurance agent.
4. Note when the requested name changes were made; with the exception of interests in real estate, a statement showing the trust as the new owner should be sent to you within a month.
5. Find out the procedure for protecting your home under the Homestead Act.
6. Inform your spouse that all future purchases of titled property, with the exception of most automobiles, should be in the name of the trust.

CHAPTER 9

WILLS

A WILL IS an instrument executed in accordance with certain formalities that directs the disposition of a person's property at his or her death. A will, therefore, is an instrument that operates to transfer title to real or personal property at death.

The principal difference between a will and any other type of conveyance is that a will takes effect only upon the death of the maker. It has no operative effect during the testator's lifetime. It is fully revocable or amendable at any time and does not establish any property rights until the testator's death. The beneficiaries named in a living person's will have no rights or benefits thereunder until the testator dies. Until that time they have nothing but an expectancy. A codicil is a supplement to a will. It may add to, take from, or alter the will's provisions.

Written wills have been known for thousands of years. There is evidence of them in the Old Testament. Another indication is the Code of Hammurabi, enacted around 2270 B.C., during the reign of the ancient Babylonian king; this contains certain rights of disposition by will. The oldest known written will was made in Egypt about 1805 B.C. In it Uah gives his property to his wife, Sheftu, including his house and his slaves, and asks that he be buried in his tomb with only his wife.

What You Can Accomplish with a Will

A will is not a substitute for a living trust and vice versa. With a will you can (1) decide who is going to receive your estate, (2) choose beneficiaries, (3) revoke all previous wills, (4) forgive debts owed to you, (5) nominate a guardian for your minor children or incapacitated adult children, (6) appoint the person who will make sure that the terms of your will are carried out (this person is referred to as the executor), (7) determine what will happen to your estate if you and your spouse were to die simultaneously, (8) disinherit anyone you want (with the possible exception of your spouse), (9) choose what will happen to your body after death, and (10) possibly help you minimize or eliminate estate taxes.

Do You Need More Than a Will?

Living trusts offer almost all of the features of a will but also provide flexibility and features not found with a will. A living trust can benefit and protect you while you are alive; a will is worthless while you are alive or if you become incompetent. There are also several aspects of estate planning that cannot be accomplished with a will.

A will cannot help you (1) avoid probate, (2) safeguard against your own incapacity, (3) transfer property in the most economical way before or after death, (4) handle a personal situation (e.g., former spouses and/or children from a previous marriage), (5) stagger distributions, (6) stop a court-appointed conservatorship, or (7) manage your estate after death.

Requirements for Making a Valid Will

If your will is valid in the state you reside in, it will be recognized in any state where you die. Your "residence" is where your principal home is, where you spend most of your time. To make a will you must be an adult. (A few states allow minors who are married or in the military to make valid wills.) You must also be of "sound mind." This definition, which would also apply to the making of a living trust, includes your knowing: (1) that you are making a will and what a will is, (2) the relationship between you and your immediate family members (e.g., who your father is, whether or not a child is alive, who your spouse is, etc.), and (3) the type of property you own and a rough idea of the extent of these holdings.

It is not very common for a court to rule that someone was not of sound mind when their will was drafted and signed. Proving that you cannot recognize friends or that you are absentminded is, by itself, not enough to prove mental incapacity. A will can be declared invalid if fraud or undue influence can be shown; this usually means that the wrongdoer was manipulative and that the person being manipulated (you) was mentally weak. The best way to sum up this issue is to point out that you do not have to show competence or a "sound mind"; it is *presumed* that you were fine. Except in movies and on television, challenging a will is rarely done.

Capacity to Make a Will

When you execute a will you must have testamentary intent. Similarly, the testator must have testamentary capacity at the time he or she executes a codicil to the will or attempts to revoke a will. The testator's capacity before or after execution is not controlling.

In general, it takes less mental capacity to make a will than to do any other legal act. Perfect sanity is not required. Even someone who has been declared incompetent is not conclusively proven to lack mental capacity for testamentary purposes. In order to establish that the testator had the requisite capacity to make a will, it must be shown that the testator:

- knew the nature of the act she was performing
- knew the natural objects of her bounty
- knew the nature and extent of her property
- understood the disposition she was making

Drunkenness, eccentricities, physical infirmities, or mental illness in and of themselves do not negate mental capacity. Habitual drinking or extreme intoxication do not automatically constitute testamentary incapacity. Conditions such as old age, deficient memory, or even childishness are not sufficient. Psychiatric treatment or attempted suicide do not imply a lack of capacity.

In addition to being an adult "of sound mind," there are a few technical (drafting) requirements. In all states except Louisiana, a will is technically valid if it (1) is typewritten (word-processed paper or printed forms are acceptable substitutes) and the document states that it is your will, (2) contains at least *one* substantive provision (e.g., disposing of some or all of your property or naming a guardian for a minor child), (3) appoints an executor, also known as a "personal representative" (the person responsible for distributing your property after death), (4) is dated, signed, and (5) witnessed and signed by at least 2 people (3 in some some states) who do not inherit under the will. A will does not have to be notarized, recorded, or filed.

What Happens If You Die Without a Will

Dying without a valid will is also referred to as dying intestate. Sadly, most Americans die without a will, including such notables as Abraham Lincoln, Ulysses S. Grant, and Howard Hughes. If you die without a will or living trust, then the following events occur after your death: (1) a court petition is filed so that your property is distributed under intestate laws (i.e., your state will now decide who gets what), (2) a guardian is appointed to raise any minor children and manage their property, including what they receive from your estate, (3) a judge will appoint an administrator to supervise matters, and (4) after the payment of administrative, legal, and court costs, your estate will be distributed according to state laws. It is not likely that the state's plan of distribution is the same as what you *would* have wanted.

Intestate Succession

When someone dies without a valid will, trust, or when the will and/or trust does not make a complete disposition of the estate, there is always the question as to who is entitled to the property and to what extent. This part (or whole) of the estate that is not "spoken for" comes under the heading of "intestate succession." Determining who such heirs shall be is the responsibility of the state. In nearly all states, the rules governing intestate succession are the same for real estate and personal property.

The state you consider your residence is known as your state of domicile. At death, your state of domicile (which may be different from the state you die in) determines who gets your personal property. On the other hand, the state where your real estate is located governs the disposition of such property.

As an example, let us suppose Mary Jones lives in California and owns some real estate in Oregon. While traveling, Mary dies in Arizona. If Mary died without a trust or a will, all of her personal property (automobile, clothes, furniture, investments, jewelry, etc.) would be distributed according to California, her state of domicile. The state of Washington, through its intestate succession laws, would govern only the disposition of the real estate located in Washington.

Except for the 14 states (Alaska, Arizona, Colorado, Idaho, Maine, Michigan, Minnesota, Montana, Nebraska, New Jersey, New Mexico, North Dakota, Pennsylvania, and Utah) that have enacted the Uniform Probate Code, there are no two states whose intestate laws are identical. In fact, some of the states that have enacted the code have not adopted all of its provisions, thereby making even these states a little different from each other. If you are concerned about intestate succession, first determine if the decedent was single, married, and/or had children.

In most states, *if there are no children or grandchildren*, the surviving spouse gets everything; if there are children or grandchildren, the spouse gets one-third or one-half, depending on the number of kids. In some states the survivor gets a stated dollar amount and one-third or one-half of the balance of the estate. If there are children or grandchildren, then the line stops at this point; parents, brothers, sisters, etc., would get nothing.

In order for your grandchild to receive anything, your son or daughter (whichever is the parent of the child) must be deceased. If this is the case, then the grandchild is entitled to what his or her parent would have gotten. If your son or daughter has two or more children, each grandchild would then have to equally share what your son or daughter would have received under intestate laws. This is known as "by right of representation."

As an example, suppose you are a grandparent, not married, and you have 3 children: Sharon, John, and Ben. A couple of years before you die, one of your children, John, dies, leaving 3 children, Alice, Andrea, and Andrew. Your other 2 children are both alive when you die without a valid will or trust. Your estate would be divided as follows:

⅓   to Sharon
⅓   to Ben
⅑   to Alice
⅑   to Andrea
⅑   to Andrew

Even though John's wife is still alive, she would not get any part of your estate in this example. The fact that Sharon and Ben each had children of their own means nothing since both Sharon and Ben are alive.

If you were to die without a spouse or children and left property that was not controlled by a trust, in joint tenancy, or left by will, your grandchildren would inherit everything. Even if there was only one grandchild, he or she would get it all. In most states, if there were also no grandchildren, then your parents would be the sole heirs. In a few states, if only one of your parents was alive, then he or she would get half and the other half would be equally divided by the decedent's brothers and sisters.

Intestate Succession in Community-Property States
If you are a resident of Arizona, California, Idaho, Louisiana, Nevada, New Mexico, Texas, or Washington, then you live in a community-property state. Upon death, "intestate property" division would be determined by whether or not the asset in question was separate or community property. Separate property is inherited, as described in the section above.

Community property, which is everything that is not separate, goes to the surviving spouse if there are no grandchildren or children of the decedent. Keep in mind that in the case of community property, you can only will, gift, or bequeath *your* share (meaning your half of the community). In some states the surviving spouse gets the decedent's share of the community property even if there are children or grandchildren. In other states, the decedent's share of the community (which is always half of the community property) is inherited by his or her children (grandchil-

dren if no children exist). In all cases, the other half of the community always belongs to the surviving spouse.

Types of Wills
There are three kinds of wills: typed (this would include form wills or wills drafted from a software program), handwritten, and oral. The most common type of will is the typed version. A blank-form will has been included in this chapter. If you decide to use a living trust, you may not need this sample will.

Unlike a typed, printed, or form will, a handwritten will does not need to be witnessed. This type of will, also known as a holographic will, must be entirely in the handwriting of the person making the will and must also be signed only by this person. Handwritten wills are not recommended for several reasons: (1) they are recognized by only about half the states, (2) since they are not witnessed, the courts believe them to be less reliable, and (3) if they are not completely handwritten they are often thrown out (i.e., invalid if written on personalized stationery, the date is typed, etc.).

There are also problems with the oral, or nuncupative, will. Only a few states recognize oral wills and only for special situations: (1) the amount in question must be less than a certain dollar amount, (2) the person making the will must be in imminent danger and/or (3) a member of the Armed Services.

What You Cannot Do with a Will
A will cannot dispose of property that you have obligated yourself to transfer by other means: assets owned in joint tenancy, a living trust, life-insurance proceeds, or the designated beneficiary of a retirement account, your spouse's share of any community property and certain bank accounts (Totten trusts). Additionally, you cannot use a will to encourage someone to commit illegal or anti-social acts. Finally, you cannot make a bequest dependent on marriage or divorce.

What Happens After Someone Dies

If there is a will, the first thing that happens is that the executor finds the will, hires an attorney for the probate process, and then waits for the judge to confirm him or her as the personal representative (executor). Once confirmed, the executor now has legal authority to conduct the estate's business. If there are minor children, the court will officially appoint the person named in the will as guardian.

The executor's job includes paying bills and estate and income taxes. After the probate is completed, when creditors can no longer come forward, the executor's final task is to distribute estate assets according to the terms of the will. Assets titled in the name of a trust are turned over to the trustee for management and/or distribution.

How to Choose an Executor or Personal Representative

Most married couples choose the other spouse as executor. If you are single, or for some reason do not trust your spouse, or feel that he or she is physically or mentally not strong enough, use the following criteria: (1) try to choose an executor who lives near you, (2) do not request the executor of your estate to post a bond, (3) name someone who is in good health, (4) attempt to name someone as executor who is also an heir (this makes sure their interest does not wane), and (5) make sure this person is willing to serve as executor when called upon.

Determining If You Are Still Married

Unmarried people usually have no trouble with ownership issues. Surprisingly, many people are not quite sure if they are still technically married or single. If you are in doubt, contact the county clerk where the divorce took place and get a copy of the records; if records cannot be found, start by assuming that you are still married.

There is a great deal of talk about common-law marriage, the idea that you are married just because you live with someone. There are only 14 states that recognize common-law "marriages": Alabama, District of Columbia, Colorado, Georgia, Idaho, Iowa, Kansas, Montana, Ohio, Oklahoma, Pennsylvania, Rhode Island, South Carolina, Texas, New Hampshire, and the District of Columbia. The mere act of living together does not create a common-law marriage in any of these states; the couple *must act* as if they were married.

In most states if you get divorced, then your former spouse will not inherit under your will or by intestate succession. In some states, a divorce automatically revokes the *entire* will.

Property and Marriage

If you are married, state laws determine what you can and cannot leave by will. Your state of residence has the final say for everything but real estate located elsewhere. In the case of real estate, the state laws where the property is located is the determining factor.

If you are a resident of one of these states *when you die*—Arizona, California, Idaho, Nevada, New Mexico, Texas, Washington, or Wisconsin—then you are covered by community-property laws. These laws vary somewhat in each state, but all of these states agree that all income, retirement accounts, property, and assets acquired during marriage is community property. The only exceptions to this definition are assets inherited or received by gift as separate property and gifts of the "community" to one of the spouses. Arizona, California, Nevada, New Mexico, and Washington have all ruled that acquisitions and income derived from separate property retains its separate-property status. Lastly, all community-property states except Washington honor written agreements that treat *earned income* (salary, tips, bonuses, and commissions) as separate property if such monies are kept separate.

If a state is not a community-property state, then it is a common-law state. Thus, the remaining 42 states and the District of Columbia believe that how title is taken determines if the asset is owned by one or both spouses. If there is no title (antiques, paintings, jewelry, etc.), then the person whose income was used to pay for the asset is considered to be the owner. Common-law states do protect the surviving spouse. At death, if you live in a common-law state, your spouse is entitled to a third of the property left in the will (one-half in a few states). The exact amount depends upon the common-law state, if there are minor children, and whether or not the surviving spouse has been provided for by other means.

When Married Couples Move to Another State

A couple that moves from a common-law state to a community-property state will find that most community-property states do not treat property acquired in a common-law state as community property. California and Idaho are the only exceptions; Arizona and Texas go along with California and Idaho in the event of divorce but not when it comes to death.

The reverse is also true. Generally, if you move from a community-property state to a common-law state, that common-law state will recognize the community-property status of all such assets acquired before moving to one of the 42 common-law states.

Simultaneous Death

In the case of property jointly owned with your spouse, when you die your share automatically goes to your spouse; when your spouse dies, his or her share also goes to you, even if both of you die at the same time. Obviously, if such an event were to occur, neither one of you would be around to receive the property. This is why it actually goes to your estate. Your will, trust, or intestate succession would then decide who receives such interest(s) and to what extent.

Property No Longer Owned at Death

When you die, your will may list assets that you no longer own; property that was lost, stolen, sold, or given away. Such references do not make the will invalid; the expected beneficiary is simply out of luck.

Children

In the case of minor or handicapped children, there are two issues: who will raise them and how will their financial needs be protected. As long as one parent is alive, the custody of the child or children is not an issue—the remaining adoptive or natural parent is chosen by the court. This is true even if there was a divorce years before the death of the parent who was awarded custody.

The child's guardian must be named in a will; an alternate document such as a living trust is not sufficient. Whether the guardian or someone you divorced is named in a will, the court must make a formal declaration. The judge always has the authority to supersede your decision. Usually this is done only if the named person has a serious criminal, drug, or alcoholic background.

Uniform Transfer to Minors Act (UTMA)

In your will, you are free to name a minor or handicapped child as a primary or alternate beneficiary. However, since we are dealing with a minor or incompetent, adult supervision is necessary until the child becomes an adult or becomes competent. Most states allow gifts or inheritances of up to $5,000 without such supervision. The two ways to make a gift to a child are by using the Uniform Transfer to Minors Act (UTMA) or a children's trust. California, Florida, 31 other states, and the District of Columbia have adopted the UTMA. If you live in a UTMA state, then the real estate or assets are managed by the adult custodian until the child becomes an adult (age 18 in some states and age 21 in others). Once the child becomes an adult, the custodian must turn everything over to that young adult. *Without a trust*, there is no choice, except if you live in California, which allows you, in your will, to list any age between 18 and 25.

Every state has adopted either the UTMA or the UGMA (Uniform Gifts to Minors Act). The only differences between these two acts is that the UTMA allows gifts to be made by will and the UGMA does not; in some states you cannot make gifts of real estate under the UGMA but you can under the UTMA. Each of these acts is beneficial for estate-planning purposes, since you now have a way of "supervising" gifts to minors without incurring court costs or bringing in an attorney to draft some special agreement.

A Children's Trust

A children's trust is valid in all 50 states and the District of Columbia. A children's trust allows you to specify in the trust at what age the trustee is to relinquish control and turn over the asset(s) to the child. The children's trust may end up lasting until the child becomes 18 years old or 100. It is not generally recommended to have such a trust last past the "child's" 40th birthday.

A children's trust can be created as part of your will if the UTMA has *not* been adopted by your state, or if you do not want the child to have full control over the property(s) as soon as he or she legally becomes an adult. Keep in mind that there are two ways to create a children's trust: by will or as part of a living trust. Children's trusts created by will must go through probate and are not valid in most states. *Children's trusts created within a living trust are valid in most states* and avoid the problems of probate.

The children's trust, the UTMA, and the UGMA all have to do with making gifts or providing for the inheritance of your kids. However, you may decide that one or more of your children are not to receive anything. You do not need a reason. If you want to disinherit a child, state this in your will; this way, the court knows that you did not mistakenly leave someone out. As an alternative, you could also name a child and leave him or her a nominal amount, such as one dollar.

Effect of No-Contest Clause

A no-contest clause in a will means that any person who contests the will shall forfeit all interests he or she otherwise would have received under the will. Obviously, if the con-

test is successful, the no-contest clause fails along with the rest of the will. The contestant would then be concerned with his or her rights under intestate succession or a prior will. However, there are differences of opinion as to what happens if the beneficiary loses the contest. In most states, a beneficiary who unsuccessfully challenges a will does not forfeit anything if the court finds that the challenge was made in good faith and on the basis of probable cause. The forfeiture provision is given effect if the beneficiary had no reasonable basis for contesting the will. Some states, including California, give full effect to no-contest clauses even if there was probable cause. Florida law states that no-contest clauses are unenforceable in all cases. The following do not constitute a contest (meaning the no-contest law is not applicable):

1. An action brought to construe the will (i.e., "What did the decedent mean by ——?").

2. Challenging the court's jurisdiction (i.e., the will should be probated in a different state).

3. Challenging the appointment of the executor or an accounting made by that person.

Determining the Value of Your Probate Estate

As mentioned elsewhere in the book, property left by will, with certain exceptions, must be probated. Intestate succession—dying without a will—is subject to the same probate proceedings. The purpose of probate is to transfer clear title of property to the new owners; probate is also intended to satisfy creditors' claims and to help ensure that the estate is properly distributed. As you can see, by not having a will, probate is not necessarily avoided. Assets in a living trust avoid probate.

If your estate is probated, the fees and costs of probate are largely determined by where you live, what kind of deal you can work out with the attorney, and the size of the probatable estate. Your estate, for probate purposes, is calculated by taking inventory of everything you own, including retirement accounts, jointly owned bank accounts, life insurance, the value of your furniture, jewelry, etc., and first subtracting all property that will be transferred by means other than by will or intestate succession laws. This means that you would subtract all property owned in joint tenancy, "pay-on-death" bank accounts, *property titled in the name of a living trust*, life-insurance proceeds (unless your estate was named as the beneficiary), and retirement accounts (unless there was no designated beneficiary or your estate was named as the beneficiary). The fair market value, on date of death, of all remaining assets is the probatable estate.

There are several states that allow a certain amount of property to either escape probate or be subjected to an informal probate that is quick and fairly easy. This amount ranges anywhere from $5,000 to $60,000 cumulatively, depending on your state of domicile at death.

Why Wills Are Necessary

After reading some articles and books on living trusts, you might be left with the impression that wills are not necessary, especially since they might subject an estate to probate. This is just not true. There are several advantages to having a will, particularly when it is combined with a living trust. With a complete estate plan that has been thoroughly thought out, you will discover that a will is a good thing. And, speaking of an estate plan that has been carefully arranged, you will learn all about that by the time you finish reading this book.

The advantages of having a will are: (1) it is an easy way to make a quick estate plan, when there are time or money constraints, (2) it is the only way for you to name a guardian for your children, (3) upon your death it may be discovered that some assets were left outside of a living trust; the will can aid in the disposition of such property, (4) in the event of the simultaneous death of you and your spouse, a will may be the best way to dispose of jointly owned property, and (5) if your estate is worth $5,000 or less (this figure is as high as $60,000 in some states), there will be no probate in some states.

When You Should Consider Changing Your Will

There are several things that may make it a good idea to either review or change your will. The events include: (1) wanting to add or subtract a beneficiary, (2) a desire to increase or decrease the amount of someone's inheritance, (3) moving from a common-law state to a community-property state or vice versa, (4) marriage, (5) death of your spouse, (6) divorce, (7) adoption or birth of a child, (8) the death of the person named as guardian for your child, (9) the death of a beneficiary, including a child, (10) death of the person who was going to be your executor, or (11) substantial increase or decrease in the value of your estate.

Changing Your Will

In the case of major changes, your existing will should be revoked and replaced by a new one. An attempt to make extensive changes could be confusing to the court and/or the executor. Simple changes can be made by an amendment to the will, formally known as a codicil. "Simple changes" include adding or subtracting bequests, changing beneficiaries, or altering who your executor or guardian for the children will be. The codicil can revoke a clause in the will or add a new provision.

A codicil is executed in the same way that a will is; in the case of a typed (printed or word processed) amendment, this means dated, signed, and witnessed by two people (three in some states) who do not have an interest in the will or codicil. The codicil should also refer to the will. Once completed, it is a good idea to give everyone who has a copy of your will a copy of the codicil; this helps to avoid confusion after your death. A sample codicil form is provided for you at the end of this chapter.

Revoking Your Will

There are two ways to revoke a will: (1) a deliberate act by the person who created the will (you) and (2) by law. You can revoke your will (and/or any codicil) by tearing up or burning the original and all copies. The safest way is by a written statement; this makes your intentions clear. The law will step in and revoke your will when a left-out spouse or unmentioned child is concerned, but not in the case of any other provision.

Contesting a Will or Revocable Living Trust

The grounds for contesting a trust are similar to those for a will contest: fraud, duress, or incompetence of the creator. As a practical matter, a trust that has been in active operation for a period of time before the settlor's death or incapacity is more difficult to upset because it is harder to prove the necessary grounds. The trustor's contacts with the trust are a continuous validation. The contestant, however, has more time to contest a trust: 4 years from the date of death as opposed to 120 days after a will has been admitted to probate.

Sample Will

Shown below is a form will you may wish to copy or reproduce. This sample will is designed for a married person who does not have any minor children or adult children who are handicapped (there is no provision for a guardian).

LAST WILL AND TESTAMENT OF _____
(your name)

I, _____ , a resident of _____ , _____ ,
(your name)   (city)   (county)

_____ , declare that this is my will and revoke all previously made will(s) and codicil(s).
(state)

I am married to _____ ; all references in this will and any subsequent codicil(s)
(your spouse's name)

to my spouse are to him/her.

I used to be married to _____ ; the marriage ended by _____ .
(name of previous spouse)   (death, divorce, etc.)

I am the parent of the following children whose names and dates of birth are:

_____   _____
(name)   (date of birth)

_____   _____
(name)   (date of birth)

_____   _____
(name)   (date of birth)

_____   _____
(name)   (date of birth)

The following is a list of my beneficiaries and what each is to receive:

_____   _____
(name of beneficiary)   (description of property; e.g., cash, % of estate, etc.)

_____   _____
(name of beneficiary)   (description of property)

_____   _____
(name of beneficiary)   (description of property)

_____   _____
(name of beneficiary)   (description of property)

_____ (name of beneficiary)

_____ (description of property)

_____ (name of beneficiary)

_____ (description of property)

_____ (name of beneficiary)

_____ (description of property)

If _____ does not survive me by 30 days,
  (name of beneficiary)

_____
  (description of property)

shall go to _____ .
  (name of alternative beneficiary)

If _____ does not survive me by 30 days,
  (name of beneficiary)

_____
  (description of property)

shall go to _____ .
  (name of alternative beneficiary)

I give the rest of my estate to _____ ; if he/she fails to survive me by 30 days,
  (name of residuary beneficiary)

then the residue of my estate shall go to _____ .
  (alternate residuary beneficiary)

If a named beneficiary or alternate beneficiary fails to survive me by 30 days, his/her share shall be equally divided by the then remaining beneficiary(s).

If any beneficiary under this will, either directly or indirectly, contests or attacks this will or any of its parts, his/her share is revoked and such share shall then be evenly divided among all of the remaining beneficiaries.

I nominate_____ as the executor of my estate, to serve without bond.
  (executor)

If he/she dies, resigns or for any other reason is unable to act as executor, I nominate

_____ to act as executor, also without bond.
  (alternate executor)

My executor is to have the following powers: (1) to retain property that may or may not depreciate or lose value; (2) to sell, exchange, or lease, by private or public means, real or personal property of my estate and to administer any such monies received; (3) to exercise all rights of a person who owns securities; (4) to settle or defend all claims in favor of my estate, including any estate and income tax liability; (5) to operate, sell, encumber, maintain, or dispose of any business or business interest which is part of my estate; (6) to distribute property to the custodian or guardian for the benefit of any minor or incapacitated adult that receives any part of my estate and (7) perform all other acts which he or she feels are necessary and appropriate for the management, investment, and distribution of my estate. These aforementioned powers are in addition to any powers and discretion vested in an executor by operation of law.

If my spouse and I should die simultaneously, for purposes of this will it shall be conclusively presumed that I survived such spouse.

I subscribe my name to this will on _____ at _____ _____ ,
                                          (date)   (city)   (county)

_____ , and declare that: (a) I am a competent adult and (b) I did not enter into or sign
      (state)

this instrument under any type of influence.

_____
(your signature)

On_____ , _____ declared to us, the undersigned, that this
      (date)   (your name)

document was his/her will and asked us to act as witness. He/she then, in our presence, verbally
acknowledged that this was his/her will and also signed it in our presence. We then signed in
his/her presence, and in the presence of each other, our names as witnesses. We further declare
that to the best of our knowledge, he/she is a competent adult and was not influenced in the
making or signing of this will. Under penalty of perjury, we declare all of these things to be true.

_____ residing at _____
(first witness signature)   (his or her complete address)

_____ residing at _____
(second witness signature)   (his or her complete address)

_____ residing at _____
(third witness signature)   (his or her complete address)

How to Complete This Sample Will

There are only five things you should know about before you use this sample will: (1) the will should be typed or word processed on non-eraseable paper, (2) all of the blanks should be filled in by ink, (3) you must sign the will in front of three witnesses (make sure they are all in the room when you make your declaration and when all four of you sign your names), (4) all of the witnesses must be competent adults and none of them should be a beneficiary of your will, and (5) the will should be stapled when completed.

After you have completed the above, store it in a safe place and tell your executor and alternate executor where the will is located. If you use a safe-deposit box, check with your bank to make sure your executor and alternate executor will be able to access the document after your death.

You may decide that it is a good idea to make copies of your original will and distribute these copies to your spouse, children, executor and/or alternate executor. This is your decision; there is no legal requirement that you do this. However, if this idea appeals to you, do not sign any of the copies. Unsigned copies are not legal but can provide important information after your death. By having only one signed original, revocation or changes become much easier.

Sample Codicil

Shown below is a sample codicil; something you would use if you were to change a beneficiary or an asset. The three witnesses you will need do not have to be the same ones you used when your will was witnessed.

FIRST CODICIL TO THE WILL OF _____
                                              (your name as it appears on your will)

I,_____ , a resident of _____ ,
   (your name as it appears on your will)   (your city and state of residence)

declare that this is the first codicil to my will dated _____ .
                                                           (date of your will)

First, I revoke that part of my will that provided:

(include the exact wording of the sentences and/or paragraphs)

Second, I add the following provision(s):

(include whatever you like)

In all other respects, I confirm and republish my will dated _____ .
(date of your will)

This codicil is dated _____ .
(date)

I subscribe my name to this first codicil on _____ , at _____ , _____ ,
(date)   (city)   (county)

_____ and state that I have signed and executed it without any undue influence.
(state)

On _____ , _____ declared to us, the undersigned, that this was his/her first
(date)   (your name)

codicil to his/her will and asked us to act as witnesses, signing our name accordingly. At the

request of _____ and in the presence of him/her and of each other, sign our names as
(your name)

witnesses. We further declare that we understand this to be _____ first codicil and that
(your name)

to the best of our knowledge, he/she is a competent adult and was under no influence at the

time of this signing. We declare under penalty of perjury that the foregoing is true and correct.

_____ residing at _____
(first witness's signature)   (his or her complete address)

_____ residing at _____
(second witness's signature)   (his or her complete address)

_____ residing at _____
(final witness's signature)   (his or her complete address)

Summary

A will is something that should be used in conjunction with a living trust. A will is not a substitute for a trust and vice versa. A will disposes of property not titled in joint tenancy, the name of a trust, retirement accounts with designated beneficiaries, and insurance policies. A will is also the proper way to name a guardian for your minor children or an adult child who is incapacitated. A *pour-over will,* usually found as part of a living-trust package, takes care of property that you forgot to title in the name of the living trust.

A will does not deal with your spouse's share of any community property. Furthermore, a will cannot delay the distribution of an asset as a living trust can. Children's trusts and accounts set up under the Uniform Transfer to Minors Act (UTMA) are effective ways to protect the interests of your kids.

Checklist of Things to Do

1. List those assets that are not owned in joint tenancy or held in a living trust.
2. Find out if you live in a community- or separate-property state.
3. Decide with your spouse who is to inherit any assets not disposed of by your trust, joint tenancy, or by designated beneficiary (retirement accounts and life insurance).
4. Name a guardian if you have minor or incapacitated children.
5. If you are married, strongly consider naming your spouse as the executor of your estate. If you are single, choose someone you trust, preferably someone who is also an heir.
6. Contact the person you are naming as executor and make sure he or she is willing and able to serve.

CHAPTER 10

CONSERVATORSHIPS

CONSERVATORSHIPS ARE FOR people who are no longer able to handle their personal or financial affairs because of physical or mental incapacity. If this impairment is serious enough, the court will step in, declare incompetency, and place the person under the control of the probate court. This process, known as a conservatorship or probate guardianship, was designed to protect person and property. The idea was to stop someone from taking over or wasting the property of a person who lacked control.

The problem with a conservatorship is not its intent, but the practical aspects. Generally, people prefer a family member or friend take care of them, not the court. Nevertheless, if you are placed in a conservatorship, you and your family may lose all direct control. Even if a family member is named as conservator or guardian, the court will still control the purse strings. Most of your legal rights are also lost.

Without a living trust, avoiding a conservatorship for an incapacitated person can last only so long. If the person owns a bank or brokerage account, real estate, or other titled property, sooner or later money will probably be needed or the asset sold. If you are the only one who is authorized to sign on the account, your spouse, relatives, and friends cannot sign your name unless the court steps in, you had a durable power of attorney in place *before* the incapacity, or there was a living trust. (Durable powers of attorney are described in a later chapter.)

You may be physically and mentally able to still sign your name, but a court may find that you are not of sound mind. In any case, the probate court can declare you incompetent, place you in a conservatorship, and require that *its* agent sign on your behalf.

In the case of jointly owned property, the chances of a probate conservatorship increase; if just one of the co-owners is judged incompetent, the other owner(s) cannot sell or refinance the property without court involvement. This is true in all cases except certain joint *bank* accounts. These bank accounts are set up so that each owner can independently make deposits, withdrawals, or close the account.

Signatures on a jointly titled asset, with the exception of certain bank accounts, require all signatures before there can be a sale or refinancing. If there is an incapacity and there was no durable power or living trust, only the court can sign for that owner. The other co-owners will now find that they have a new partner: the probate court. Once involved, the court stays on until the person recovers or dies. There are three steps that must be taken before a conservatorship can occur.

The Steps Involved in Setting Up a Conservatorship

First, the court is petitioned so that proceedings can begin to determine if there is incompetency. This action could be brought by someone acting with your best interests in mind, or by a greedy relative. Usually an attorney is hired by the person(s) bringing the action. In some states, the person who is allegedly incompetent does not even have to be notified of the hearing.

The second step is to advertise the notice of the proceedings in a local newspaper. This lets creditors and other people who might have a claim against you come forward and present their case to the court. Unfortunately, this also makes your situation quite public.

Next, a hearing is held to determine competency. As previously mentioned, some states allow the judge to make a decision based solely on the written reports and testimony of others; you may not even be present. If the judge decides that you are incompetent, most of your legal rights are lost—and so is your financial freedom.

If incompetency has been declared, the judge will appoint a conservator to handle your affairs and make sure you receive proper care. The conservator is usually a spouse or adult child, but there is no guarantee that the appointed person will be a family member. Conservators are entitled to be compensated for their services; they must also post a bond. An attorney will be appointed to take care of the necessary paperwork. All of these expenses are charged to you.

One of the first things the conservator will do is take an inventory of all of your assets and liabilities. This documentation, along with a proposed budget for your living expenses, is then submitted to the court for approval. Depending upon your financial well-being, certain assets may have to be liquidated or sold at public auction to help pay conservatorship expenses.

The conservator is an agent of the court and is under its supervision. Depending on how crowded the court is, monitoring the actions of the conservatorship may be strict or quite lax. In the case of strict supervision, the conservator needs to account for every single expense; even receipts for food and clothing are required. The annual financial report submitted by the conservator must be audited and approved by the court. This process may take months and is certainly costly. If supervision is lax, usually owing to a lack of resources on the part of the court, your assets may either disappear or be squandered away.

Not only is a conservatorship expensive to set up and administer, it is also costly to end. If there is a recovery, the court is petitioned and you must prove your competency. An attorney is hired on your behalf. Often a psychiatrist or psychologist is also hired to help prove that you are, once again, competent and able to take care of yourself.

No matter how old you are, there is always the possibility that something could happen to cause you to be placed in the supervision and control of the court—a court that might not have the resources to properly monitor the conservatorship. Fortunately, there is an alternative: a living trust that includes the proper provisions.

The "Appointment of Conservatorship" section of your living trust identifies the individual who is to be responsible if you and your spouse become incompetent. Once identified, it is this person's responsibility to ensure the safety and financial well-being of the person placed in the conservatorship. The person you name in your trust to be your conservator should be someone you completely trust. Alzheimer's, multiple sclerosis, or some other disease or circumstance may require the named conservator to place you in a nursing home or obtain other help.

A living trust allows you to predetermine who will take care of you if you are unable to *and* what type of care you will receive. Without proper wording, your kids or spouse may have something else in mind. After all, these future heirs may decide on their own that there is no point in depleting your assets (the estate they will someday inherit) on a fancy facility since "Mom and/or Dad won't know where they are." These loved ones may not end up being so loving. They may decide that you will be just fine living in a tent in the backyard with an occasional delivery from the local Pizza Hut.

All of this can be prevented by choosing someone trustworthy and specifically describing the quality of health care you want if you cannot make your own decisions. As an example, your trust document could state that if medical help were needed you "want to be placed in a nursing home in La Jolla, California; one that overlooks the ocean. And in no case should less than $4,000 a month be spent on my housing and care (to be adjusted for inflation, naturally)."

Disadvantages of Conservatorships and Durable Powers

Conservatorships are a relatively expensive and cumbersome way of managing an incapacitated person's business affairs. Court authorization is usually needed for the purchase or sale of investments, entering into leases, and borrowing money. However, in these areas the court may give the conservator the power to act independently.

Inventories and periodic accounts are required, even if the court grants the conservator a great deal of independence. In sharp contrast to this, a trustee or attorney-in-fact (durable power of attorney) may act without such supervision, thereby saving time and money. In such cases, court supervision is available *only* if requested by the attorney-in-fact or trustee.

Durable powers of attorney are an inexpensive device that allows the personal representative to care for an individual's financial and/or personal needs. No transfer of titles is necessary, administrative requirements are simple, publicity is avoided, and so is any embarrassment.

A court-appointed conservator may revoke or amend a durable power with a court order. It is for this reason that you should consider nominating the same person as conservator and attorney in fact.

A disadvantage of a durable power of attorney is that you do not know to what degree a bank, securities firm, insurance company, or other institution will honor the document. This concern can be countered by contacting these institutions before an incapacity occurs and find out exactly what their position is. Unlike living trusts, the laws regarding durable powers vary from state to state.

100 YOUR LIVING TRUST

Summary

Naming a conservator is one of the most valuable things you can do for yourself. This is just one of the many beneficial aspects of a living trust and how it can aid you while you and your spouse are alive. If the unfortunate time ever comes when you need a conservator, save your family the agony of trying to choose one child or another or one friend over another. Most important, by selecting a conservator now, you will prevent the court from later choosing whom they *think* is best.

Checklist of Things to Do

1. Talk to your spouse about each of you being the conservator of the other.
2. Even though most spouses name each other, always list a successor; you can never be certain that your mate will not predecease you or become inactive.
3. Determine which of your children will act in lieu of your spouse; consider the child's geographic location, work habits, and family responsibilities.
4. Make it clear to the other children that only one person can be selected and that the choice had nothing to do with love or favoritism.
5. If there are no immediate family members able or willing to serve, think about asking a neighbor or friend you are close to. Make sure that this person is compensated.
6. Verify with your attorney that provisions dealing with conservatorships are included for both you and your spouse.

CHAPTER 11

GUARDIANSHIPS

ONE OF THE most important decisions a parent can make is the selection of a guardian for a minor or an adult handicapped child. Parents have certain goals and dreams for their children. Those hopes and objectives can be carried on, even if something happens to both of the child's parents if the right guardian is chosen. If both parents die without having appointed a guardian for their minor or handicapped adult children, the court must make the selection—often without knowing the wishes of the parents. As you will learn, there are several other ways in which a guardianship is court-imposed, but only one way to avoid the delays, frustrations, and expenses of this formal process.

A guardianship may occur whenever there is something owned by a minor. Since minors cannot legally sign their names, the probate court must get involved so that the child's interests are protected. Like a conservatorship, a guardianship requires court intervention since only the court, not the child's parents or relatives, may sign for the child. Often, this occurs only if property needs to be sold or refinanced. Sometimes the court gets involved before the child's name is added to an account title or money is received.

Guardianships are often triggered unintentionally. If your minor child or grandchild inherits titled property, such as real estate, stocks, bonds, automobiles, becomes a joint owner of titled property, or is the beneficiary of life insurance or a retirement account, the court may become involved. This is true even if one or both of the child's parents are both alive. There are four ways in which children can be placed in a guardianship: (1) if both parents die, (2) a children's testamentary trust, (3) if the child inherits assets, or (4) is made a joint owner.

Death of Both Parents

Upon the death of you and your spouse, the court will usually go along with the person named as guardian in your will. The approved guardian will look after and raise the children, but the court will control any inheritance through a probate guardianship. If you die without naming a guardian in your will or trust, the court first looks to the child's other natural parent, even if there had previously been a divorce. You may not have wanted anything to do with your ex-wife or ex-husband, but the probate court does not know this. This means that there is a good likelihood that someone you lost respect or trust for will end up managing assets and raising your children, all against your wishes.

Avoiding Probate or a Court-Appointed Guardian, But Not Both

Sometimes a children's trust is used by the parent(s) in order to prevent intervention by the court. If the trust is part of a will, it can be validated only through the probate process. Assets with beneficiary designations, such as the proceeds from life-insurance policies or retirement accounts, can avoid the probate process, but other assets will not. All other titled assets will have to be probated. More important, if you become incapacitated your will cannot be probated since you are not dead: no probate, no children's testamentary trust. There are also no beneficiaries. Therefore, if both of the the child's parents are incapacitated, the child will most likely end up with a court-appointed guardian.

Inheritances

An inheritance is the third way in which a guardianship may unknowingly be created. Minor children who inherit property must be protected. This protection is not free or necessarily voluntary. The court wants to make sure that no one takes advantage of the child financially. This means that an attorney will have to represent the child in court. Furthermore, life-insurance companies will not pay benefits to minors without proof of a court-approved guardian. This is also true with retirement accounts; the custodian of the decedent's account(s) wants the same proof in order to avoid potential legal problems.

Joint Owners

Property titled with a minor as a co-owner must go through the probate court before the asset can be sold or refinanced. Remember, the child does not have legal capacity yet to sign his or her name. A sale requires the signatures of all listed parties. Since a minor's signature would have no legal effect, a court-appointed guardian must do the actual signing.

The Steps Involved in Setting Up a Guardianship

A guardianship for a child is set up in a fashion similar to that of a conservatorship. The court-appointed guardian hires an attorney, posts a bond, and submits annual reports detailing all expenses and investments. All of this costs money; money that comes from the child's inheritance.

There are not only financial costs, there may be emotional problems. The court may take issue with expenses proposed by the guardian. The guardian may feel that the child should go to a certain school, take a trip, or own a car. If the court disagrees, it could lead to a great deal of disappointment for the minor child.

Guardianships continue until the child reaches the age of majority. A child is considered an adult at age 18 in some states and age 21 in others. No matter how immature or irresponsible the child might still be, the court has no choice but to turn everything over to this new adult. Guardianships cannot continue after the child has reached legal age.

An Alternative

As in the case of a conservatorship, you have a choice. A properly worded living trust can avoid all of the delays, frustrations, and expenses described above. The Appointment of Guardian provision, when placed within a living trust, protects the child even if you become incapacitated or die. This provision is used for minor children or handicapped individuals, regardless of age.

Summary

As in other aspects of estate planning, you have a choice. If there are minor children in your family or an adult child who is incapacitated, then they need special attention. A conservator can take your place after you are no longer able to act. By choosing a conservator who has similar views about education, discipline, love, and religion, you can provide those children with some continuity if something were to suddenly happen to you. People rarely think about their own mortality or deterioration, yet we all read about such occurrences every day in the newspaper.

Checklist of Things to Do

1. Sit down with your spouse and reach an agreement as to who will take care of your minor or incapacitated children if both of you are unable to.
2. Talk to your children, perhaps in an indirect manner, and find out what they think about your "replacement."
3. Talk to the potential guardian and find out if he or she is willing to accept the responsibility.
4. Find out if this person shares values with you that you and your spouse deem important.
5. Make sure your attorney knows of the status of your children so that a guardian is named in your living trust.

PART III

CHAPTER 12

THE DURABLE POWER OF ATTORNEY

A POWER OF attorney is a document signed by one person, authorizing another to act for him or her. The person who creates the power is known as the principal. Any competent adult who has not been convicted of certain felonies can create a power of attorney. Throughout this book the terms "incompetent" and "incapacitated" are used interchangeably. A finding of incompetency is usually made by one or more doctors. The most common causes are strokes, heart attacks, degenerative diseases, serious injury from an accident, mental illness, and drug or alcohol abuse.

The person you name to act on your behalf is called the attorney-in-fact or agent. Any competent adult can be your agent; the named person does not have to be a lawyer or related to you. There are four different powers of attorney: (1) conventional, (2) durable, (3) springing, (4) financial, and (5) health care.

Conventional Power of Attorney

A conventional power of attorney is something you might use to give someone the right to manage all or a specific part of your portfolio. Often this type of power is limited to one transaction (e.g., "to sell my stocks while I am on vacation"). You can be very creative with this and other types of power of attorney, giving someone the ability to represent you at IRS hearings, banking transactions, or paying bills. A conventional power of attorney automatically terminates when one of the following occurs: (1) the time specified in the power lapses, (2) the principal (you) becomes incapacitated or dies, or (3) the principal revokes the power. It is for some of these reasons that a *conventional* power is not recommended for *estate-planning* purposes.

Durable Power of Attorney

A durable power of attorney is effective even if the principal becomes incompetent; a durable power does end when the principal dies. Broadly speaking, it can be written so that the agent is able to make financial and medical decisions for you. It is valid from the date signed and remains in effect until the principal dies or revokes it. One of the advantages of a power of attorney is that it does not require court review, legal intervention, or notification to any special agency; it can be very private.

You can include almost any restrictions, qualifications, or limitations you choose. A durable power of attorney can be a very important estate-planning tool and is almost always included as part of any living-trust package. In short, it allows for the management of your affairs if you are unable to speak or act for yourself.

Springing Powers
A "springing" power is a special kind of durable power of attorney; it becomes effective only if the principal becomes incapacitated. If you so desire, any durable power of attorney can be structured as a springing power.

Durable Power of Attorney for Finances
A financial durable power of attorney provides for the management of your financial affairs without court proceedings or any other outside approval. This type of power can be drafted so that it goes into effect immediately or it can be "springing." The power normally allows the agent to (1) pay bills, (2) buy and sell securities, (3) deposit checks, (4) reinvest CDs, (5) pay taxes, and (6) maintain a household.

The financial durable power of attorney can be drafted so that it is effective if and when the principal becomes incapacitated. If you or a loved one may be entering a nursing home or a long-term-care facility, then one of these powers should be considered. It may even be possible for the agent to act so that the principal's assets are not depleted for medical or housing costs. Such action would then entail public assistance and would in turn help to preserve the estate for the principal's family.

Durable Power of Attorney for Health Care
As the name implies, a durable power of attorney for health care allows the attorney-in-fact, the person you name as agent, to make medical and health care decisions if you are unable to. This power can be very specific, requesting the use of certain doctors or facilities. It can also be used to require the use, or non-use, of life-sustaining procedures and equipment under certain circumstances. This power of attorney is an important part of a complete estate plan.

If you decide to draft a durable power of attorney for health care, you will first need to see if your state requires that a specifically worded form be used. The statutory states are: California, Georgia, Idaho, Kansas, Nevada, New York, Oregon, Rhode Island, Texas, Vermont, West Virginia, and Wisconsin. If you live in one of these states, you must use the exact wording required; each state's form is a little different.

If you live in Alaska, California, Colorado, the District of Columbia, Georgia, Idaho, Illinois, Kansas, Maine, Massachusetts, Michigan, Nevada, New Mexico, New York, North Carolina, Ohio, Oregon, Pennsylvania, Rhode Island, South Dakota, Texas, Vermont, Washington, West Virginia, or Wisconsin, then your state has expressly authorized durable powers of attorney for health care. Some of these states are silent on the issue of whether or not the agent has the authority to withhold or terminate life-sustaining equipment or procedures.

If you live in Arizona, Arkansas, Delaware, Hawaii, Indiana, Iowa, Maryland, Minnesota, New Jersey, Utah, Virginia, or Wyoming, then you live in a state that not only allows this type of power, but also gives the agent the power to make life-and-death decisions.

If you live in Alabama, Connecticut, Florida, Kentucky, Louisiana, Mississippi, Missouri, Montana, Nebraska, New Hampshire, Ohio, Oklahoma, South Carolina, or Tennessee, then you should definitely see a lawyer before you attempt to draft a durable power of attorney for health care. These states have special requirements, limitations, and/or other uncertainties.

Why You Need Two Separate Powers
Estate planning necessitates that you have two separate durable powers of attorney: one for health care and one for financial matters. You may name the same person to be the attorney-in-fact, but have two different powers drafted for two reasons: laws in your state may be different for each type of power, and a few states (not California) re-

quire the health-care power to be renewed every seven years.

Revoking a Power of Attorney

A competent principal may revoke any power of attorney, including durable powers, at any time. The principal does not have to have a valid reason and does not have to hire counsel to draw up some special document of revocation. Additionally, the named agent can also be changed at any time by the competent principal.

Court-Appointed Conservatorships

By drafting durable powers of attorney in advance, court proceedings can usually be avoided. As an incentive for you to strongly consider getting these two powers, let us see what happens if the court instead steps in. We will be looking at how the court goes about determining whether a conservatorship, known as a curatorship, custodianship, or guardianship in some states, should be used to manage the financial and/or personal affairs of the conservatee.

A great deal of freedom is lost under a conservatorship. The person deemed to be incompetent—the conservatee—may lose the right to vote, control money, decide where to live, travel, drive a car, or make medical decisions. The process begins when someone files a petition with a court located in the county of the conservatee. The process is usually initiated by the person's spouse, children, other family members, close friends, or by someone who wants to be under a conservatorship. The person filing the petition, known as the petitioner, alleges that you can no longer manage your own affairs. A date is then set for the hearing. The alleged conservatee, spouse, other family members, and close friends are formally notified of the hearing.

You are entitled to your own lawyer at the hearing. Witnesses and physical evidence can be introduced by both sides. A judge then determines if you are incapacitated, and if so, who will be your conservator. If no one opposes the petition, the proceedings can be simple and relatively inexpensive. The judge will usually let the conservatee appoint his or her own conservator, provided it is felt that you have at least a certain amount of competence and that the chosen one will act in the conservatee's best interests. If you are not allowed to select the conservator, state laws provide a recommended priority list. Generally, the spouse is the first choice, followed by an adult child, parent, and brother or sister of the conservatee.

The court may rely on a priority list for a conservator to manage your personal affairs and select a completely different person to handle your financial matters. The person appointed could be someone you or your family has never met before. Each of these conservators is entitled to a fee; these costs are borne by the conservatee. Speaking of costs, the named conservator will need to post a bond, paid by you, and have the conservatee's property appraised and inventoried, again at your expense.

From time to time, the conservator may find it necessary to go back to the judge for guidance or permission. Periodically, reports must be prepared and filed with the court. Even routine matters can be contested by almost anyone. All of these things involve the time of the court, conservator, and lawyers; time that is paid for by you.

As mentioned at the beginning of this section, all of this frustration, embarrassment, time, and expense can be avoided if you have already drafted and signed a durable power of attorney for health care and a separate durable power of attorney for finances. A court proceeding may still be necessary for one or more of the following reasons: (1) you do not know of anyone you trust enough, (2) a bitter fight by family members is anticipated, or (3) the person named as conservator refuses to serve.

How to Establish a Durable Power of Attorney

There are 9 steps involved in setting up one of these powers; the first 3 are required, the remaining 6 are recommended. While reading these steps, keep in mind that state laws vary somewhat.

The first step is to get a form or hire an attorney to draft the power. Sample forms are provided in the next two chapters. Second, the agent must be named along with a specific or general description of his or her powers. Third, you must date and sign the document.

Although not required by the laws of most states, you may find that some of the remaining steps are required by the persons or institutions who may be presented with the document. Therefore you should consider: (1) having the document typed, word processed, or using a standard form, (2) having the document notarized, particularly if real estate, finances, or health care are involved, (3) recording the document with the county recorder of deeds office, thereby adding more credibility to the powers, (4) having the powers signed by witnesses, (5) keeping the document in a safe place, and (6) reviewing the document once every few years.

Do You Want to Be an Agent?

There may be a time when the shoe is on the other foot; that is, you may be asked to be the attorney-in-fact. Before you say yes, consider the following. First, determine if you have the time to carry out the responsibilities of the job and to write the reports that need to be kept. Second, make sure you trust the principal and that his or her family will be supporting you. Third, you may have to make some very difficult and emotionally trying decisions, such as concluding when life-sustaining proceedings or equipment should be stopped. Finally, make sure you are fully informed of the legalities involved. For example, in some states such as California, when the agent signs a notarized document on behalf of the principal, a certain type of notary acknowledgment must be used.

You cannot be forced to take the job. If you do decide to accept the position, you may be entitled to compensation. The amount you are paid can be based on an hourly rate or a flat fee; in either case, if challenged, it must be considered "reasonable."

Legal Requirements of the Agent

The agent, also referred to as the attorney-in-fact, is legally required to (1) act in good faith and be able to justify his or her decisions, (2) avoid conflicts of interest, and (3) never commingle the principal's funds with his or her own.

Summary

A power of attorney comes in several different forms. Each type can be an important part of your overall estate plan. A power of attorney can be helpful when you are not able to act, owing either to incapacity or to being away on a trip. The form you will need to use to establish one or more of these powers should first be reviewed by your attorney. Different states have different requirements. In order to save money, you may wish to purchase a standardized form from your local stationery store. These stores often sell a wide range of blank forms that are useful if a power needs to be created quickly.

Checklist of Things to Do

1. No matter how old you are, get a durable power of attorney for health care and one for finances.
2. Telephone your attorney and find out how much he or she will charge you for the drafting of these two documents.
3. Go to a stationery store and see if the forms they have will serve your purpose.
4. When you have your living trust prepared, make sure that these two powers are included.
5. Find out from your attorney how long your durable power of attorney for health care is valid before it must be renewed.

CHAPTER 13

THE DURABLE POWER OF ATTORNEY FOR FINANCES

ALMOST EVERY COMPETENT adult can benefit from having a financial durable power of attorney. If you are over 40, have a serious health condition, suffer from a severe disease, will soon have a complex operation, or are about to embark on an extended trip, then you should have one of these powers. They just make common sense for anyone concerned about estate planning.

If you become incapacitated, someone needs to take care of your financial needs. Bills and premiums must be paid, property, including a personal residence, needs to be maintained, investments looked over, and business interests protected. For most people, the best protection for such matters is a durable power of attorney for finances.

Every state allows some form of a durable power of attorney for finances. The problem is that there are three different sets of rules. Your state of residence has approved one of these forms. If you live in Alabama, Arizona, California, Colorado, the District of Columbia, Delaware, Hawaii, Idaho, Indiana, Kansas, Kentucky, Maine, Massachusetts, Michigan, Minnesota, Montana, Nebraska, New Mexico, North Dakota, Oklahoma, Pennsylvania, Tennessee,

Utah, Vermont, West Virginia, or Wisconsin, then your state has adopted the Uniform Durable Power of Attorney Act and you can use the form at the end of this chapter.

If you live in Alaska, Connecticut, Iowa, Maryland, Nevada, New Jersey, New York, Ohio, Oregon, Rhode Island, South Dakota, Washington, or Wyoming, then your state has adopted the Uniform Probate Code, which authorizes durable powers of attorney. As far as durable powers are concerned, this code is almost identical to the Uniform Durable Power of Attorney Act. Thus, if you live in one of the states listed in this paragraph, you are probably on solid ground if you use the sample form at the end of the chapter. Since some of these states have slightly different regulations, it is a good idea to review the document with your lawyer.

If you live in Arkansas, Florida, Georgia, Illinois, Louisiana, Mississippi, Missouri, New Hampshire, North Carolina, South Carolina, Texas, or Virginia, then you should consult with an attorney. Laws in these states are not clear-cut and legal counsel can be helpful.

Standard and "Springing"

Whatever state you live in, you have two choices as to the *type* of power you can use: standard or springing. A standard financial durable power is effective as soon as you sign it; that is, your agent has whatever power(s) described in the document. A springing financial durable power is effective only if you become incapacitated. Since there is no exact definition of incapacity, your best protection will be written into the actual document. Your springing durable power can state that a certain doctor or that two doctors must be in agreement that you can no longer handle your financial affairs. Most married couples name their spouse as their attorney-in-fact (agent) for all durable powers of attorney.

Living Trusts and Joint Tenancy

In the event of incapacity, standard language in most living trusts provides for the management of all property and financial matters by the spouse who is competent. Since a living trust may not cover all of your assets or financial dealings, a durable power is still recommended. Accounts owned in joint tenancy may settle the issue of deposits and sometimes withdrawals, but checks, sales of property, gifts, or transfers of titled assets cannot be accomplished without both signatures. That is why a durable power is recommended even if everything you own is in joint tenancy.

Limits on Power

Your durable power of attorney for finances *can* give your agent, either immediately or upon your incapacity, the power to pretty much do everything financially that you used to do. The attorney-in-fact can be empowered to pay school expenses for your kids, send checks to your parents, pay your bills and tax liabilities, settle medical bills, make investment decisions, or run your business. If all of this sounds like there is too much power, do not despair. Your doc-ument can be as limiting as you like. As an example, your durable power may only allow the named agent to pay bills and write checks for up to a certain dollar figure. Or the provision dealing with the scope of power may restrict investments to mutual funds and annuities. While you are competent, the choice is always yours.

A durable power of attorney cannot be used to give an agent authority over your children; such powers are reserved for you or a guardian. The attorney-in-fact may have the power to manage your assets to pay for the child's needs, however. Furthermore, your agent cannot be given the power to have you marry, adopt a child, or have a will drafted on your behalf. All powers of attorney end when the principal dies. The attorney-in-fact has no right to make burial or funeral arrangements, much less attempt to transfer or distribute assets to your beneficiaries.

Sample Form for a Durable Power of Attorney for Finances

Before reviewing or using this sample form, make sure that it is valid in your state of residence (see beginning of chapter). Whatever form you end up using, you will want to make sure that it is acceptable to the financial institutions that you deal with. Therefore, it would be a good idea for the respective branch manager of such entities to review the document and to perhaps keep a copy on file. This would be advisable whether you use a standard or springing power of attorney. Make a list of everyone you give an original or copy to; you never know when you might want to revoke or amend the power. The sample form below is the standard (not springing) variety.

One final bit of advice: If you live in Alaska, California, Connecticut, Illinois, Minnesota, New York, or North Carolina, your state has statutory wording that has been approved. You are better off using such a form (or exact wording). This will make the document even more likely to be accepted.

FINANCIAL DURABLE POWER OF ATTORNEY

I, _____ , intend to create a financial durable power of attorney upon the signing
      (your name)
of this form. This power shall not be disrupted or affected in any way by my subsequent mental
or physical incapacity. It shall remain in effect until revoked by me in writing. This durable power
of attorney shall become effective as of the date of signing.

I, _____ , appoint _____ , who resides at
      (your name)   (name of your agent)

_____ as my attorney-in-fact; to act
      (his/her address)
on my behalf and in my name. If this appointed person ceases to be my attorney-in-fact, I appoint

_____ , who resides at _____
     (name of alternate agent)   (his/her address)
to be my attorney-in-fact.

Except as noted in this paragraph, I grant my attorney-in-fact full power and authority over all of
my personal and real property and authorize him/her to perform every act which I as an owner or
co-owner of said property could do.

My attorney-in-fact has no authority to:

(1) _____ ,

(2) _____ ,

(3) _____ or

(4) _____ .

The powers conferred on my attorney-in-fact in this document shall be exercisable by his/her
signature alone and shall have the same effect as if I were personally present, competent, and
signing my own name.

No person, organization, or entity who relies on this durable power of attorney or representation
by my attorney-in-fact concerning his or her authority shall be liable to me, my estate, heirs,
successors, or assignees due to such reliance(s).

This durable power of attorney for finances is entered into on _____ and signed at
         (date)

_____ .
   (city and state)

principal _____
      (your signature)

The undersigned are witnesses to this signing.

_____
(his or her signature)

_____
(name of first witness)

residing at _____
       (his or her address)

_____
(his or her signature)

_____
(name of second witness)

residing at _____
(his or her address)

Notarization

State of _____ , County of _____

On _____ , before me, a Notary Public of the state of _____ ,

duly commissioned and sworn, personally appeared _____ ,

whose identity is known by me either personally or by satisfactory evidence, to be the person whose name is signed on this document and acknowledged to me that he/she executed the same.

In witness whereof, I set my hand and affix my official seal in the state of _____ on the date set forth above in this certificate.

_____

(notary seal)

state of _____

My commission expires _____

Summary

A durable power of attorney for finances allows someone to sign your name and transact business on your behalf. These powers are recognized in all 50 states, although some states require different wording. The amount of discretion you give your agent depends upon how the document is worded. You can request your lawyer to severely limit the powers (e.g., "Kate Jones can sell my IBM stock while I am away on my trip during the month of November, 1992") or grant quite a bit of latitude.

Powers of attorney, not just for financial matters, are recommended because your living trust and will do not begin to cover all of the situations that could arise. The cost of having a durable power of attorney drawn up by your lawyer is nominal. Financial powers do not have to be renewed periodically. If the power is durable, it will be recognized even if you become incapacitated. As a competent adult you can create or destroy a power of attorney whenever you like.

Checklist of Things to Do

1. Talk to your spouse about the benefits of a durable power of attorney for finances.
2. See how much your attorney would charge to draft such a document.
3. Go to a stationery store and see if their forms will serve your purpose.
4. When you have your living trust prepared, make sure that this power is included.
5. Contact the person you have chosen, making sure that he or she knows of your selection and the responsibility involved in the event of an emergency.

CHAPTER 14

THE DURABLE POWER OF ATTORNEY FOR HEALTH CARE

Like "incapacity," there is no standard definition of "health care." A well-known description used by one state defines it as "treatment, service, or procedure to maintain, diagnose, or treat an individual's physical or mental condition." The decisions you would make as a patient, or your attorney-in-fact could be empowered to make, include the right to refuse, accept, or have existing treatment discontinued. In some states, an agent's powers in this area are less than the patient's.

In 1990 the Patient Self-Determination Act was passed. It applies to all hospitals and nursing homes that receive federal aid such as Medicare or Medicaid, which means that most health and medical facilities must adhere to it. The legislation requires these facilities to give each admittee written information about his or her rights, including the right to accept or refuse medical help. The institution must honor durable powers of attorney for health care and living wills. If such documents are presented, then copies must be placed in the patient's file. The institution must provide ongoing education to the staff and the community regarding durable powers and living wills and adhere to its state's policy concerning living wills.

If medical personnel or staff refuse the authority of your attorney-in-fact, counsel will then be needed. Once your attorney and the lawyer representing the facility or doctor meet, the powers will probably be honored. At this point, the health-care provider is looking at an expensive court battle and the strong possibility that further medical costs will end up being paid for by the provider.

Making It All Legal

Try to make your durable power of attorney for health care as specific as possible. The clearer the wording, the more likely that it will be honored by your doctor, hospital, or nursing home. You will also need to decide if you want a standard or springing durable power. A standard power becomes effective upon your signing; a springing power is effective only if you become incapacitated. Your document can specify that incapacity must be determined by one or two doctors. If you are currently in good health and not planning on having any major surgery in the foreseeable future, you will probably be better off with the springing variety.

The powers you convey upon your attorney-in-fact can be extremely broad or narrow. There are some limitations, however. States will not generally allow your agent to authorize certain procedures, such as lobotomies and abortions. Surprisingly, some of these same states will allow the attorney-in-fact to make life-sustaining decisions. If you live in California, Georgia, Idaho, Kansas, Nevada, New York, Oregon, Rhode Island, Texas, Vermont, West Virginia, or Wisconsin, then you must use a specific, statutory form. If you are a resident of one of these states, do not attempt to use the sample form below or draft your own document.

Despite national regulations that cover federally assisted facilities, each state has its own laws concerning durable powers of attorney for health care. If you live in Alaska, California, Colorado, the District of Columbia, Georgia, Idaho, Illinois, Kansas, Maine, Massachusetts, Michigan, Nevada, New Mexico, New York, North Carolina, Ohio, Oregon, Pennsylvania, Rhode Island, South Dakota, Texas, Vermont, Washington, West Virginia, or Wisconsin, then your state has adopted the Uniform Durable Power of Attorney Act and you can use the form at the end of this chapter.

If you live in Alaska, Connecticut, Iowa, Maryland, Nevada, New Jersey, New York, Ohio, Oregon, Rhode Island, South Dakota, Washington, or Wisconsin, then your state has authorized and accepts the attorney-in-fact; most of these states even allow your agent to withhold or terminate life-sustaining procedures and equipment.

If you live in Arizona, Arkansas, Delaware, Hawaii, Indiana, Iowa, Maryland, Minnesota, New Jersey, Utah, Virginia, or Wyoming, then your state has not expressly authorized such durable powers, but other legislation generally permits the use of these documents.

If you live in one of the remaining states, consult your attorney. There are certain problems and concerns unique to each of these remaining states.

No matter what state you live in, make sure you follow these steps: (1) use the correct form, (2) sign the document and have it notarized, (3) check with the doctor, hospital, and any other health-care provider you might be using in the future and make sure your power is something they will accept, (4) store the original in a safe place, (5) give your doctor a copy of the powers so that it can be placed in your medical files, and (6) make sure the power is reviewed at least once every several years; some states require that this type of durable power of attorney be renewed every 7 years.

Sample Form

Shown below is a sample standard durable power of attorney for health care. As you may recall, "standard" means that the power is effective as soon as you sign the document. This form can be used unless you live in a state that requires the use of a statutory form.

Once your document has been completed, you should sign it in front of a notary; although not generally required, it is still a good idea. Some states require witnessed signatures. A place on the sample form has been added for two witnesses. The witnesses can be of value if the powers are later questioned or challenged. The witnesses must be competent adults, preferably persons who live near you and have not been named as an attorney-in-fact.

Statutory forms, which must be used in California, Georgia, Idaho, Kansas, Nevada, New York, Oregon, Rhode Island, Texas, Vermont, West Virginia, and Wisconsin, may include a "Warnings" section. This warning must be included and should stand out from the other text. The "Warnings" show doctors, hospitals, and other providers that you knew the ramifications of the document when you signed it. The sample below, which cannot be used in any of the above states, does not include such a warning.

DURABLE POWER OF ATTORNEY FOR HEALTH CARE

I, _____, a competent adult, intend to create, by this document, a durable
(your name)

power of attorney for my health care; designating _____ , who resides at
(name of your agent)

_____ , as my attorney-in-fact to make health-care
(his/her complete address)

decisions for me. This power shall remain effective even if I become incapacitated. If this person

ceases to serve as my attorney-in-fact for health care, then _____ ,
(name of your alternate attorney-in-fact)

who resides at _____ , shall be my attorney-in-fact
(his/her complete address)

for health care.

This durable power of attorney shall be effective as of the date I sign it. My attorney-in-fact shall
have all authority permissible to make health-care decisions for me, including, but not limited to,
consent, withdraw consent, refuse treatment, service, procedure, or equipment that will maintain,
diagnose, or treat my physical and/or mental condition, except:

        (add any exceptions you like, including life-sustaining treatment)

Subject to any limitations in this document, my attorney-in-fact has the power and authority to (1)
request and review any written or verbal information regarding my condition, including all medical
and hospital records, (2) execute on my behalf any forms that may be required to obtain such
information, (3) disclose any such information to others, and (4) execute on my behalf any and all
documents dealing with "refusal to permit treatment," "leaving hospital against medical advice,"
and "waiver or release from liability."

This durable power of attorney for health care shall remain in effect until I revoke it in writing or
die.

This document is executed on _____ at _____ .
(date)   (city and state)

principal _____
(your signature)

WITNESSES

I declare the following: (a) that I personally know the principal, (b) that he/she acknowledged this
document, including its contents, and signed it in front of me, (c) it appears that the principal was
of sound mind and was not acting under any form of duress or fraud, (d) I am not related to the
principal by blood, marriage, or adoption, (e) to the best of my knowledge, I am not entitled to any
part of his/her estate.

_____ residing at _____
(signature of first witness)   (address of first witness)

_____ residing at _____
(signature of second witness)   (address of second witness)

Notarization

State of _____ County of _____

On _____ , before me, a Notary Public of the state of _____ ,

duly commissioned and sworn, personally appeared _____ ,

whose identity is known by me either personally or by satisfactory evidence, to be the person whose name is signed on this document and acknowledged to me that he/she executed the same.

In witness whereof, I set my hand and affix my official seal in the state of _____ on the date set forth above in this certificate.

_____

(notary seal)

state of _____

My commission expires _____

Summary

A durable power of attorney for health care allows someone to make medical decisions for you in the event you are unconscious, physically impaired, mentally diminished, or for some other reason unable to speak. These powers are recognized in all 50 states, although some states require different wording. The amount of discretion you give your agent depends upon how the document is worded. The powers can be restricted so that your attorney-in-fact can make medical decisions only while you are on the operating table for a specific procedure. At the other end of the spectrum, the power can be as far-reaching as to allow the agent to request that life-sustaining equipment be turned off if there is no chance of a meaningful recovery.

The health-care power is something that should be used in conjunction with a living will. One document is not considered a substitute for the other. In several states, a durable power of attorney must be renewed every several years.

Checklist of Things to Do

1. Talk to your spouse about each of you having a durable power of attorney for health care. Explain how it can be useful for things other than just life-and-death situations.
2. See how much your attorney would charge to draft such a document.
3. Contact your doctor and local hospitals; find out which forms they recognize.
4. When you have your living trust prepared, make sure that this power is included.
5. Contact the person you have chosen, making sure that he or she knows of your selection and the responsibility involved.

CHAPTER 15

REVOKING A POWER OF ATTORNEY

MOST OF THE time, a power of attorney, whether conventional, standard, springing, or durable, can be revoked by a principal, so long as he or she is competent. The revocation should always be in writing. To be effective, the written revocation should be given to the following person(s): the attorney-in-fact (your agent), persons or institutions whom the attorney-in-fact has dealt with, and persons or institutions your agent may be likely to deal with in the future.

The best way to revoke any power of attorney is by using a form called a Notice of Revocation. Like the original power, revocation is serious and filled with potential legal and financial consequences if not done properly. If a third party is not aware of the revocation, you may be liable for the acts of your agent. This is true even if your attorney-in-fact is aware of the revocation. After all, it would not be fair for business associates, friends, vendors, etc., to rely on something they thought was valid, when in fact it had been revoked. The legal burden is on you to be sure everyone knows that the power has been revoked.

Shown below is a sample of a Notice of Revocation. To make sure that your revocation is legally effective: (1) sign and date the notice, (2) have your signature notarized, (3) have the revocation recorded if the power was recorded, (4) deliver a copy to the attorney-in-fact and all others who have dealt with or are likely to deal with this agent in the future. The notice does not have to be witnessed, but this is probably a good idea. Recording the revocation should also be done, even if it is not required.

Sample Form

The sample form below can be reproduced and used in any state to revoke a general power of attorney, a durable power of attorney for health care (standard or springing) and a durable power of attorney for finances (standard or springing).

NOTICE OF REVOCATION OF POWER OF ATTORNEY

Recording requested by and when recorded mail to:

_____
(your name)

_____
(street address)

_____
(city, state, and zip code)

I, _____ , of _____ ,
    (your name)   (street address)

City of _____ , County of _____ ,

State of _____ , hereby give notice that I have revoked, and do hereby revoke,

the power of attorney date _____ , 19_____ given to _____ ,
                                                       (name of attorney-in-fact)

empowering said person to act as my true and lawful attorney-in-fact, and I declare that all power and authority granted under said power of attorney is hereby revoked and withdrawn.

Dated: _____ , 19_____

principal _____
         (sign your name here)

_____
(type your name here)

WITNESSES

_____ residing at _____
(signature of first witness)   (address of first witness)

_____ residing at _____
(signature of second witness)   (address of second witness)

Notarization

State of _____ County of _____

On _____ , before me, a Notary Public of the state of _____ ,

duly commissioned and sworn, personally appeared _____ ,

whose identity is known by me either personally or by satisfactory evidence, to be the person whose name is signed on this document and acknowledged to me that he/she executed the same.

In witness whereof, I set my hand and affix my official seal in the state of _____ on the date set forth above in this certificate.

_____

(notary seal)

state of _____

My commission expires _____

Summary

You once gave someone the power to do something. That power may or may not have been exercised by your agent, also known as the attorney-in-fact. You now want to strip these powers away, owing to changed circumstances, to the fact that you no longer trust the person, or because you have found a better substitute. To make sure that you are protected financially and/or medically, a power of attorney needs to be revoked. By using the form provided above, along with proper notification, you can stop any current or future actions by this agent. Surprisingly, revoking a power of attorney is more difficult than creating one.

Checklist of Things to Do

1. If you want to revoke a power of attorney, copy the included form and fill it out.
2. Contact your lawyer and tell him or her your proposed course of action. An attorney may be able to give some additional valuable information.
3. Send registered letters, return receipt requested, to those individuals and companies you think your agent has contacted in the past or is likely to contact in the future. Such entities would include places where you bank and conduct securities transactions (in the case of a power of attorney for finances); hospitals, nursing homes, and doctors (in the case of a power of attorney for health care).
4. Keep copies of this correspondence, noting any telephone conversations and dates.

CHAPTER 16

LIVING WILLS

A LIVING WILL, valid in most states, sets out your desires regarding the use of life-sustaining procedures. A living will deals only with life-and-death issues; it is not as broad in scope as a durable power of attorney for health care. And, despite its name, a living will has nothing to do with the distribution of your estate.

At first, living wills were the answer for someone wishing to stop the use of life-support systems when there was no chance of recovery. With the introduction of the durable power of attorney for health care, you now have two choices. Because state statutes vary and the idea of "pulling the plug" is still relatively new, you should use both. Fortunately, both of these documents are part of most attorneys' living trust packages, meaning that you will not be paying any more for this additional layer of protection.

Why You Need a Durable Power and a Living Will

There are several reasons why you should express the same wishes in both of these documents. First, a living will is a "pre-written" letter to your doctor; usually, a living will cannot be used to appoint someone to see to

it that your wishes are carried out. Second, some states will honor a living will only if it is executed after you have been informed of having a terminal condition. Third, a number of states require that you use a statutory-approved form that may not give you the latitude you are looking for. Fourth, living wills deal only with a terminally ill situation; you cannot use this form for other health-care decisions. It is for all of these reasons that a durable power of attorney for health care should also be used. The durable power solves all four of these concerns. It is also something that is recommended by the American Medical Association.

Living wills are valid in the following states: Alabama, Alaska, Arizona, Arkansas, California, Colorado, Connecticut, Delaware, the District of Columbia, Florida, Georgia, Hawaii, Idaho, Illinois, Indiana, Iowa, Kansas, Kentucky, Louisiana, Maine, Maryland, Minnesota, Mississippi, Missouri, Montana, Nevada, New Hampshire, New Mexico, North Carolina, North Dakota, Oklahoma, Oregon, South Carolina, Tennessee, Texas, Utah, Vermont, Virginia, Washington, West Virginia, Wisconsin, and Wyoming. By the time you read this book, there is a fairly good chance that most of the remaining states will have enacted living-will statutes.

Sample Form

The exact wording your living will needs to contain varies depending upon your state of residence. If you are a California resident, you are in luck. Printed below is a copy of a living will that is acceptable in California. If you live in a state other than California, contact The Society for the Right to Die (250 West 57th Street, Suite 323, New York, NY 10107) by writing or telephone (212) 246-6973. This nonprofit organization, which accepts donations, will send you a copy of the living will that can be used in your specific state.

CALIFORNIA LIVING WILL AND DIRECTIVE TO MY PHYSICIANS

Directive made this _____ day of _____ , 19_____ .

I,_____ , residing in the County of _____ , State of _____ ,
   (your name)

being of sound mind, willfully and voluntarily make known my desire that my life shall not be artificially prolonged under the circumstances set forth and do hereby declare:

1. If at any time I should have an incurable injury, disease, or illness certified to be a terminal condition by two physicians, and where the application of life-sustaining procedures would serve only to artificially prolong the moment of my death and where my physician determines that my death is imminent whether or not life-sustaining procedures are utilized, I direct that such procedures be withheld or withdrawn, and that I be permitted to die naturally.

2. In the absence of my ability to give directions regarding the use of such life-sustaining procedures, it is my intention that this directive shall be honored by my family and physician(s) as the final expression of my legal right to refuse medical or surgical treatment and accept the consequences from such refusal.

3. If I have been diagnosed as pregnant and that diagnosis is known to my physician, this directive shall have no force or effect during the course of my pregnancy.

4. I have been diagnosed and notified at least 14 days ago as having a terminal condition by

_____ , M.D., whose address is _____ , and whose
   (your doctor's name)

telephone number is _____ . I understand that if I have not filled in the physician's name and address, it shall be presumed that I did not have a terminal condition when I made out this directive.

5. I understand the full impact of this directive and I am emotionally and mentally competent to make this directive.

Dated: _____ , 19_____

_____
(sign your name here)

_____
(city, county, and state of residence)

This declarant has been personally known to me and I believe him or her to be of sound mind.

_____
(signature of first witness)

Residing at _____
(address of first witness)

_____
(signature of second witness)

Residing at _____
(address of second witness)

Summary

A living will is valid in most, but not all, states. Its sole purpose is to determine if life-sustaining procedures are to be used to keep the patient alive. The type of equipment and/or procedures that are to be used (or not used) can be specified in the document. This is a document that you must have drawn up and sign before your incapacity. No one has the right to make such a life-or-death decision for you unless this right was given to them by you in the form of a living will or durable power of attorney for health care.

Checklist of Things to Do

1. Talk to your spouse about each of you having a living will. Bear in mind that this is a very sensitive issue and deals with one's upbringing, religion, and current quality of life.
2. See how much your attorney would charge to draft such a document.
3. Contact your doctor and local hospitals; find out what form they recognize and its limitations.
4. When you have your living trust prepared, make sure that this power is included.

CHAPTER 17

PREPARING FOR A MEETING WITH THE ATTORNEY

ONCE AN ATTORNEY or law firm has been selected, you will need to prepare for the initial meeting. This preparation will save you time and may save you some money. You should bring the following items to the meeting:

- net-worth statement or estimate of your holdings
- a list of all your life-insurance policies (death benefits, company name, telephone number, and address of policy owner and designated beneficiary)
- schedule of all titled property, how it is owned, and who the other co-owners are,
- a breakdown of how the estate is to be distributed after your death and the death of your surviving spouse, if you have one
- listing of your co-trustee (if any), successor trustees, executor, power of attorney designees, conservator of your person, guardian (if you have a minor child); the names, addresses and phone numbers of each of these persons should also be included
- copies of your most recent will, trust, and any deeds of trust
- your spouse and checkbook.

Each of these items is described in detail below.

Net-Worth Statement
Calculating your net worth is a way to determine if (1) you need a living trust, (2) your estate may be subjected to estate taxes, and (3) whether insurance policies should be placed in an irrevocable life-insurance trust.

If your gross estate is worth $60,000 ($30,000 in some states) or more, then you should have a living trust. If your estate is less than $60,000, then you may still be a candidate. Calculate the projected value of your estate at death. It should easily double in value every 12 years, particularly if you own real estate or common stocks. A male age 65 has a remaining life expectancy of at least 15 years, a female age 65 has a life expectancy of at least 18 more years.

How an Estate Increases in Value Because of Inflation
If the net value of your estate (gross value minus debts, liabilities, mortgages, final medical expenses, and funeral costs) is expected to be more than $600,000 and you have a life-insurance policy, you are a candidate for an irre-

6% Average Inflation Rate		8% Average Inflation Rate	
current value	$100,000	current value	$100,000
value in 12 years	$200,000	value in 9 years	$200,000
value in 24 years	$400,000	value in 18 years	$400,000
value in 36 years	$800,000	value in 27 years	$800,000

vocable life-insurance trust. This type of trust will remove your life insurance out of your estate, thereby reducing its value and eliminating or cutting down any estate-tax liability.

If you are married and the combined net estate of you and your spouse is expected to exceed $1,200,000, then you should ask your attorney about an A-B and A-B-C Trust as part of your living-trust package. As you review the chapters on the A-B and A-B-C Trust, you will see that there are other reasons why such trusts could be important parts of your overall estate plan.

Listing of Life-Insurance Policies

One of the documents that your attorney can prepare for you is nonlegal in nature. It is a listing of all of your life-insurance policies. This is done to ensure that your beneficiaries receive the death benefit. Another reason why such a listing is made is to help determine the value of your estate. Life-insurance proceeds are not subjected to probate, but they are included as part of your net worth for estate-tax computation purposes. Depending on the size of your net estate, it may be wise to have your attorney include a separate trust, an irrevocable life-insurance trust.

Schedule of All Titled Property

The next step is to determine the ownership of all of your *titled* assets. Reviewing account registrations, brokerage-firm statements, and copies of deeds will show you if an asset is owned in joint tenancy, individually, or in community property. If you live in a community-property state and you trust your spouse (or are certain that you will die before she or he does), then property held in joint tenancy

should be retitled as community property. It is just as easy to put community property in a living trust as it is to add separate or joint tenancy. If you do not want to go to the trouble of retitling every jointly owned asset into community property, your attorney can provide you with a blanket form as part of your trust package.

Distribution Schedule After Your Death

Most married couples leave everything to the survivor; after the death of the second spouse, all remaining assets are divided among the children. Even with these commonly used provisions, there are still two decisions that need to be made. First, what will happen if a child predeceases you. The deceased child's share can either go to his or her spouse and/or children or it can be used to increase the shares of your other children. Second, you need to decide when the distribution are to be made. As an example, you may want your daughter to receive her share outright but have your son's share distributed at staggered intervals.

Whatever the distribution schedule, your attorney will need to know the full name of each beneficiary, the date of birth of any minor children, and how each beneficiary can be contacted.

Listing of Members of Your Trust Team

One of the most important decisions to be made is determining who will be acting for you once you are no longer able; fortunately, it is also one of the easiest decisions. The *successor trustee(s)* should be someone you trust. If there are several people you trust, then choose the one you feel has the greatest investment skills. The successor trustee can be your spouse, adult child, brother, mother, banker, or financial advisor. The *executor* of your pour-over will also has to be named; the executor is often the same person who is named as successor trustee.

If you have any minor children or incapacitated adult children, then a *guardian* needs to be elected. The guardian should be someone you feel would raise the child the way you would have; this person does not have to have a strong background in finance or psychology. The *durable powers of attorney* will probably be the same person as the successor trustee. If the trustee is good enough to manage your affairs, he or she should be good enough to make financial and medical decisions. *The conservator of your person* is someone who may never be called upon, but the person chosen should be trustworthy beyond reproach and possibly someone who does not have a financial interest in your estate.

Married couples usually name each other to fill each and every one of the positions described in the two paragraphs above. If both spouses are unable to act, then the successor trustee(s) is frequently selected to act in all of these capacities. The choice is always yours; you are free to choose whomever you want. You and your spouse may even disagree when it comes to successor trustees, powers of attorney, executors, and conservatorship of your person. In such a case, each spouse could end up having different people fill these spots.

The persons selected should be listed on a piece of paper, along with their addresses and telephone numbers.

Copy of Any Existing Wills, Trusts and Deeds of Trust

Your attorney may wish to review your existing will or trust to see if there are parties or provisions that should be included in your new living trust package. A copy of your deed of trust is important so that your lawyer can make sure that title is properly transferred into the name of the trust. Assets not titled in the name of the trust can end up being subject to probate.

Your Checkbook and Spouse

It is important to bring your husband or wife to the meeting. After all, he or she is going to play an important role if you become incapacitated or die. It is also likely that the trust is going to contain property belonging to both of you. If you plan on naming your spouse as co-trustor, then his or her signature is required on the trust document.

Most attorneys want a deposit or to be paid in full before they begin drafting any documents. This is only fair. The only thing an attorney has to sell is advice and time.

The Actual Meeting

The early part of the meeting will consist of the attorney asking you a number of questions. She will want to know about your current and former marital status, if there are children from any of these marriages, if you have any separate property, and what property is titled as joint tenancy. At this point the lawyer may want to know if you wish to make a gift of your separate property to the "community" for future tax benefits. If you live in a community-property state, your attorney will explain the pros and cons of titling property in this manner. The attorney will also want to know the approximate value of your assets, any major indebtedness (i.e., a home mortgage), whom you want to inherit your property, and when such distributions are to be made.

Once the lawyer has a good grasp of your situation, she can determine if any special trust should be included, such as an A-B Trust, A-B-C Trust, irrevocable life-insurance trust, minor's trust, or charitable remainder trust. At this point it is appropriate for you to ask your questions.

You will want to know exactly what will be provided, the expenses involved, the amount to be charged for any special provisions or trusts, and if there are any miscellaneous transfer fees. If there are discrepancies between what you were originally quoted and are now hearing, bring up the issue. Fees are a very sensitive issue. You do not want to think that you were intentionally misinformed. A special rate may have been originally quoted since you were a seminar attendee, existing client, or a referral from a mutual friend. The attorney you are now meeting with may have forgotten this or was never informed of special circumstances.

Once the fees have been agreed upon, the attorney will want to either be paid in full or have you pay a retainer of several hundred dollars. At the end of the first meeting if you are not certain about going forward, do not write a check.

If you proceed, another appointment should be scheduled for the review and signing of the trust documents. Depending on your schedule and that of your attorney's, the follow-up meeting is usually two or three weeks after the first interview. The first meeting should take an hour and a half or less. The second meeting will probably take less than an hour.

Second meetings often include a review of the different sections of the trust. Signature(s) will need to be notarized. If you are married, your spouse should be at the signing. Chances are that he or she is either a co-trustor or will be granting powers in one of the supporting documents.

Some attorneys will mail you a copy of the trust before the second meeting. In theory this sounds good, but is not usually wise. A living trust contains terms and phrases that you may not be familiar with; a face-to-face meeting can answer these questions.

The purpose of the second meeting is to go over the entire document, making sure it reflects your desires and that names have been correctly spelled. If you feel that a close review is needed, you can still sign the documents and then take them home for close inspection. This makes sense for two reasons. First, you will at least now be covered in case there is an auto accident, stroke, or unexpected death. Second, this speeds up the trust process. A mailing may delay the actual signing, particularly if you do not read the documents in a timely fashion. If, upon further

review, you discover that a mistake has been made, contact the attorney. Law firms will correct any mistakes they have made for free.

Your living trust will also contain instructions on how property should be retitled and how assets should be purchased in the future. Other than deeds of trust, you will be able to make all of the name changes for free. Recording deeds of trust requires experience and a small fee for the county recorder's office. Your attorney will probably charge you $50 to $100 for each retitled parcel. The reconveyance takes anywhere from four to 12 weeks, depending upon how busy the recorder's office is.

The second meeting should end with (1) a check for any remaining balance, including real-estate title changes, (2) a clear understanding of what the trust and any ancillary documents can do for you and your family, (3) your knowing what still needs to be done, and (4) who is responsible for these final tasks. What remains is usually only the transfer of accounts and property into the name of the living trust. Once the trust has been signed and notarized, you should leave with an original and copy of the trust. If the original is lost, your attorney can provide you with another copy; the replacement will be made either for free or for a nominal charge.

Transferring Assets to Your Living Trust

There is a strong likelihood that the only thing remaining is for you and/or your financial advisor to change the ownership of titled assets from the name of a person or couple to that of the trust. Grant deeds must be recorded in the county where the property is located. If you own properties in several different counties, each will have to be notified in person or by mail. If you do not know where the county recorder's office is located, look in your telephone book or call information. Instructions for titling all of your assets, including real estate and personal effects, are included as part of your trust package. If you cannot find these instructions or are having difficulty, telephone your attorney for help.

The lawyer who prepared your living trust wants things to go smoothly; after all, you may be a potential source for referrals (i.e., your parents, brother, sister, next-door neighbor, fellow workers).

Your Ongoing Responsibilities

Once all of the documents have been signed and properties transferred into the trust, you will need to do the following: (1) make sure that future purchases of titled property are done in the name of the trust, (2) list personal property, that is, property not formally titled, on your Assignment of Personal Property sheet, (3) review the trust whenever there is a change in your family's status, (4) renew your Durable Power of Attorney for Health Care every 7 years, and (5) renew the Directive to Physicians (your living will) every 5 years. Some law firms will have you under a "tickler system" wherein you are automatically sent a notice, or the actual form or forms, before their expiration.

Making Changes to Your Documents

There may come a time when you will want to change your trust owing either to something that has happened to you or your family or because of tax legislation. The last major change in estate planning that necessitated a review and amendment was over a decade ago. Your attorney's tickler system should be set up so that you are sent a notice if such sweeping changes are made in the law. It is a good idea to question your lawyer as to when, if ever, you will be contacted.

Changes to the actual trust or pour-over will should be made only by your attorney. You should not attempt to prepare an amendment or codicil without advice of counsel. The last thing you want to do is save a $50 or $100 fee only to later find out that part or all of the trust or will is now invalid because of illegal or contradictory changes. Input from your attorney will give you a sounding board to bounce ideas off of. Changes to other documents can be made by you without an attorney.

Summary

The estate-planning attorney you meet with can end up saving you tens of thousands of dollars and future grief. A talented practitioner can give you guidance as to what provisions should be included in your living-trust package and why. Your lawyer may be able to save you both income and estate taxes. He or she can also expose you to ancillary documents that may be ideal for your particular situation.

Perhaps most important, the attorney you meet with can provide you with objective advice as to how your estate should be distributed and when. He or she has probably had a great deal of experience in this area and can help you avoid pitfalls that are not described in any seminar or book. One cannot put a price tag on these life experiences.

Checklist of Things to Do

1. Prepare the information listed at the beginning of the chapter.
2. Consider interviewing a couple of attorneys to compare competency, price, and approach.
3. Bring your spouse and be prepared to write a check after your first meeting.
4. During your meeting, schedule a final meeting for the trust signing.
5. Have your spouse present at both meetings if he or she is to be part of the trust.
6. After the trust signing, make sure you read the trust documents carefully for content and proper spelling of names.

PART IV

CHAPTER 18

THE A-B TRUST

A LIVING TRUST can come in one of three forms: (1) the basic revocable trust, (2) an A-B Trust, and (3) an A-B-C Trust. All three trusts can ensure that your assets will go to the named beneficiaries. The A-B and A-B-C trusts can end up reducing or eliminating estate taxes. If you are certain that your *net* estate, even factoring in the effects of inflation, will never exceed $600,000 *and* that any surviving spouse will leave his or her assets to your loved ones, then you can skip this chapter *after* you have read the definition of a "net estate" below. You can also avoid this chapter if you are not married.

Your net estate is determined by adding up the current value of everything you own (home, car, boat, bank accounts, retirement plans, mutual funds, stocks, tax-free bonds, face value of any life insurance, etc.) and subtracting any debts (mortgages, personal loans, auto loans, etc.). For estate-tax purposes, your net estate includes any life-insurance policies in which you have any "incidents of ownership," not just those policies that you are shown as owner. Incidents of ownership include those policies which you pay premiums on or on which you have the right to change the beneficiary, borrow against, or assign.

This means that any policy provided by your employer should probably be included in your computations as an asset.

An A-B Trust is designed for married couples. In some respects it is like having two trusts in one. When the first spouse dies, the "master" trust is automatically split into two separate trusts: one for the survivor and one for the estate of the deceased. The attorney who drafts your will and trust can include an A-B Trust with little additional effort.

To make things easy to understand, think of **Trust A** as the "above-ground" trust (for the sole benefit of the surviving spouse) and **Trust B** as the "below-the-ground" trust (for the benefit of the survivor and children). To better understand how the A-B Trust works, look at the illustration below. It assumes that the value of a couple's estate is worth $1,200,000 just prior to the death of the first spouse. As you can see, there is $1,200,000 worth of assets titled under the "master" living trust. As far as the IRS, courts, and other parties are concerned, you have only one trust until a spouse dies. *Until that death, the A-B Trust is identical to a simple revocable living trust.*

A-B Living Trust

living trust
$1,200,000

Trust A
(surviving spouse)
$600,000

Trust B
(deceased spouse)
$600,000

beneficiaries receive
$1,200,000
free of probate and no estate taxes

In this example, when the first spouse dies, the $1,200,000 is evenly split into two separate trusts. Six hundred thousand dollars' worth of assets and/or cash are placed in Trust B in order to make sure that each spouse's estate avails itself of the $600,000 exclusion. Since there is now a decedent's trust, "Trust B," a separate tax-identification number must be obtained from the IRS. The surviving spouse's trust, "Trust A," can maintain its original tax-identification number, which is the social security number of one of the spouses, unless that number was that of the decedent's. If your spouse's social security number was listed on the "master" living trust, then you will need to begin using your social security number for tax and identification purposes.

The Survivor's Trust

The surviving spouse's trust, "A Trust," is now the sole property of that survivor. He or she can do anything they want with the money and property placed in this trust. The surviving spouse can use the money for trips, gambling, gifts, food, investments, etc. No court or prospective heir has any right to know or even question what goes on in the A Trust. Like other trusts, the A Trust is completely private. The survivor's only obligation is to make sure that his personal income tax return includes any taxable activity that goes on in Trust A. All income, interest, dividends, rents, royalties and capital gains that take place in the survivor's trust must be reported for tax purposes, using the social security number of the survivor.

The Decedent's Trust

The decedent's share of the "master" trust is transferred into a new trust, the B Trust. By law, the surviving spouse is entitled to any and all income from the B Trust. For most couples, the chief concern is providing for the survivor, not saving estate taxes that will later benefit the kids or someone else. It is for this reason that most married couples include two additional provisions, making it easy for the surviving spouse to invade the cash, real estate, or personal property that is in the B Trust.

The first provision allows the survivor to invade the B Trust for "health, education, support, or maintenance." This phrase is defined very liberally. Let us look at each of these components individually.

"Health" would include having the B Trust pay for any medical bills, hospitalizations, doctors visits, or routine checkups. The care can be provided by a local hospital, specialist, or international clinic.

"Education" includes pursuing a high school, college, or graduate degree. Money could also be used to pay for courses of general or special interest that do not lead to a degree or designation. You could even use the money for correspondence or trade school. The educational facility does not have to be a recognized public or private institution.

"Support" would include money for food, clothing, and shelter. This could mean eating out at the most expensive restaurants every night of the week or simply groceries for the home. The clothing tastes of the survivor would determine how much was spent on a monthly or annual basis. The survivor can shop at a department store or specialty boutique. There is also a wide range of possibilities when it comes to shelter. The survivor may have lived with the decedent in a tent somewhere in the desert. Now alone, this person may decide that she would like to live in Beverly Hills and rent a condominium or purchase a lavish home.

The final part of the phrase, "maintenance," is the catch-all. We may be in agreement that cosmetic surgery is not a necessary "medical" expense. However, it can certainly be defined as "maintenance." The survivor may be used to taking an exotic cruise several times a year or leasing a Rolls-Royce. Both of these expenses would fall under the heading of maintenance. After all, the surviving spouse is simply maintaining the life-style the two of you were accustomed to.

As you can see, the surviving spouse can get at anything in the B Trust for just about any reason. What cannot be done with the assets in the B Trust? Well, you probably could not use the money for a gambling spree in Las Vegas or Atlantic City. Similarly, money and assets could not be gifted away. This may mean that when you hop on the Orient Express, you cannot pay for the fares of your closest friends.

Assets can be easily withdrawn from the B Trust. The trustee simply writes a check or sells a piece of real estate or personal property from the B Trust. There is no court or attorney intervention. The ultimate beneficiaries, usually a child or children from one or both of the spouses, are not contacted or involved. The surviving spouse contacts the trustee and makes the request. In the vast majority of A-B Trusts established, the surviving spouse is also the trustee of the B Trust. This makes things very convenient; you simply say to yourself "Trustee, I'm going to the Bahamas next week to learn about local customs, write me a check." This would be considered either "education" or "maintenance" and the request would naturally be granted—by you.

Is there a chance that the beneficiaries of the B Trust would become concerned and try to stop the survivor from wiping out whatever might be left on the B side? Yes, but keep in mind the following: (a) they would first have to learn about what is going on (they have no right, short of obtaining a court order, to examine the books or be put on notice as to what is going on), (b) it is not very likely that a child would try to prevent his or her parent from spending what, in all fairness, was prob-

ably that survivor's to begin with, (c) a great deal of time and expense would be involved on both sides; the "winning side" would probably not be able to collect attorney's fees or get reimbursed for their time, and (d) there is only a small likelihood that the court would side with anyone other than the surviving spouse.

The second clause that can be added to the A-B Trust allows the survivor to annually deplete the B Trust of $5,000 or 5% of the value of the trust, *whichever is greater*, for any reason. This means that if this provision is added, the surviving spouse, if he or she wanted to, could completely wipe out the B Trust in about 20 years (less if $5,000 represents more than 5% of the value of the B Trust). These withdrawals do not have to be justified; money taken out within these guidelines can be used by the survivor for anything: gambling, clothes, to buy a boat, or to make a gift.

These two options, the 5%–$5,000 yearly withdrawal and the health, education, support, and maintenance provisions, do not have to be included. This is something that has to be agreed upon by both spouses. Obviously both spouses must be alive if either or both of these clauses is to be included in the A-B Trust.

Experience has shown that most surviving spouses do not suddenly change their lifestyle or intentionally try to deplete the assets of the B Trust (the decedent's share). Two other questions remain: How much should be put into the B Trust and, if necessary, which trust should be used up first?

Deciding How Much Should Go into Each Trust

The amount that each trust should be funded with depends on the size of the estate. As a general rule, for estates under $1,200,000 (what might be the "master" trust), the first $600,000 should be placed in the A Trust and the balance, up to $600,000, would go into the B Trust. By making this division, the couple will have effectively used both of their

$600,000 exclusions and the entire estate will pass free of federal estate taxes.

Assets are not actually divided or earmarked for either trust until the first spouse dies. The decedent's lifetime exclusion is used up when assets are transferred to the B Trust at death. The survivor receives the other $600,000 with no strings attached. At the death of the second spouse, his or her estate passes free of federal estate taxes to the extent that it totals $600,000 or less at death. If the survivor's net estate exceeds $600,000, then that excess amount will be subject to estate taxes (unless the surviving spouse remarries and leaves his or her entire estate, minus up to $600,000, to the "new" spouse).

Estates That Are Larger Than $1,200,000

Some married couples have estates that will exceed $1.2 million at death. In such a case, it is usually best to transfer $600,000 into the B Trust when the first spouse dies and leave the balance to the survivor, no matter how large that balance might be. This strategy takes full advantage of the decedent's lifetime exclusion of $600,000 and the unlimited marital deduction. However, there are alternate strategies that may be more beneficial for estate-tax purposes.

By reviewing the estate-tax table, you can see that the initial rate is 37% and climbs to as high as 55%. If the surviving spouse is not expected to live for more than a few years, and the expected estate taxes on the survivor's estate will be in the 50% range, it may make sense to subject the A Trust to some estate taxes. This strategy would effectively cause some assets to be taxed at "only" 37% instead of a higher rate at the death of the second spouse.

This strategy makes sense only if the survivor has a short life expectancy. This is because the original plan, putting everything but $600,000 in the A Trust, would allow taxation to be deferred on these assets. It makes much more sense to have whole dollars (assets) compounding estate-tax-deferred in the A Trust instead of being compounded at only 63-cent dollars (one dollar minus 37 cents in taxes). Although most couples do not have a combined estate that is greater than $1.2 million, let us go through an example and see how this compounding of whole versus partial dollars works.

Let us suppose that you and your spouse have an estate that you expect will have a net value of $2,600,000. The two of you set up an A-B Trust. One of the reasons you set up this trust is for estate-tax savings. If the B trust is

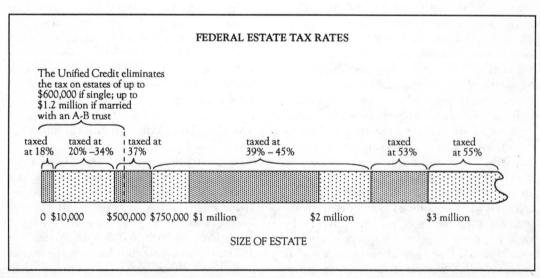

FEDERAL ESTATE TAX RATES

The Unified Credit eliminates the tax on estates of up to $600,000 if single; up to $1.2 million if married with an A-B trust

taxed at 18%   taxed at 20% –34%   taxed at 37%   taxed at 39% – 45%   taxed at 53%   taxed at 55%

0    $10,000 $500,000 $750,000 $1 million $2 million $3 million

SIZE OF ESTATE

to later be funded with $600,000, upon the death of the first spouse, $2,000,000 will pass outright to the survivor. The surviving spouse receives this money free from estate taxes, because of the unlimited marital deduction. We will assume that this $2,000,000 continues to grow; the survivor is able to reinvest part of the earnings and/or makes some good investments. A few years later, the surviving spouse passes away, leaving an estate worth $2,500,000 (the $2,000,000 grew by 25%). The *tentative* tax on this amount is $1,025,800. This amount is reduced by $192,800 (this is a credit which is equivalent to an exemption of $600,000 which everyone is entitled to). The actual tax due is $833,000 ($1,025,800 minus $192,800). Phrased another way, the net taxable estate, $2,500,000, minus the lifetime exemption, $600,000, equals $1,900,000; this $1,900,000 estate is taxed at an effective rate of 44% ($833,000 divided by $1,900,000).

Assuming the same estate, let us see what happens if more than $600,000 were transferred into the B Trust. Let us now suppose that $1,250,000 is put into the B Trust. This would trigger an estate tax event immediately. The tentative taxes on the $1,250,000 would be $448,300; by taking this figure and subtracting the $192,800 credit (which is equal to the $600,000 exclusion), the actual taxes due at the death of the first spouse would be $255,500. With $1,250,000 going into the B Trust, the survivor (the A Trust) would receive $1,350,000 ($2,600,000 minus the $1,250,000 transferred to the B Trust). Assuming the same growth rate of 25%, the $1,350,000 grows to $1,687,500 by the time the surviving spouse dies. The tentative tax on the survivor's estate is $640,175. This figure would be reduced by the survivor's credit of $192,800, resulting in an actual tax of $447,375.

By using this alternate strategy, this couple has spent a total of $702,875 ($447,375 plus $255,500) instead of $833,000, which would have been the total amount due when the *second* spouse died. This savings of over $130,000 could be increased even

further by making certain assumptions and projections.

How Assets Are Taxed in the B Trust

We now know that the survivor's trust is subject to estate taxes to the extent that it exceeds $600,000. What has not been discussed is what happens to those earnings that are generated in the B Trust.

Taxable income generated from the B Trust is taxed to the trust. The amount left over, like the principal, can be left to grow. *No matter how large the B Trust is when the surviving spouse dies, there are no estate taxes due when these assets are then distributed to the beneficiaries.* The reason for this is that the U.S. Constitution says that you cannot tax someone (or an estate) twice. The government taxed, or at least tried to tax, the B Trust when it was first funded. As previously discussed, to the extent that the B Trust was funded with less than $600,000 there were no taxes due. It is true that income taxes may be due on the subsequent earnings or growth of the B Trust, but there will be no more estate taxes on this trust.

As you can see from this description of the A-B Trust, it can be an extremely effective estate-planning device, allowing a married couple to leave substantial amounts to children or others without having the estate diminished. For large estates, a tax may be due on the death of the second spouse, or it may be decided that overall estate taxes would be lower by having part of the B Trust taxed when the first spouse dies.

Using an A-B Trust to Protect All of Your Heirs

As mentioned in an earlier chapter, one of the advantages of a revocable living trust is that either spouse usually has complete control over everything in the trust when either spouse dies or becomes incapacitated. There may be a disadvantage to such uncontrolled power, however. As co-trustee, once one spouse is out of the way, the other spouse can deplete the entire trust. This situation is not very likely, but the odds increase if the survivor remarries and/or has children from a previous marriage or with the "new spouse." Maternal and paternal instincts can be quite strong. Sometimes these feelings are much stronger than those between the two mates. With the traditional living trust, the surviving spouse could eliminate your children as beneficiaries and name children from another marriage. This same spouse could also drop the kids and name anyone else as the beneficiary(s). There is a way to prevent this.

The A-B provision in your living trust makes it impossible for the surviving spouse or co-trustee to make any changes without your permission. If you are dead or incapacitated, no such alterations can be made. Under these circumstances, the A Trust is not protected; remember, it was originally designed for the person "above ground," the surviving spouse. But the B Trust is completely protected. Keep in mind that the B Trust can end up being partially or fully depleted, depending upon whether or not you include one or both of the provisions described in a previous section (by using the "health, education, support, or maintenance" and/or the "$5,000–5%" clause).

The only other way in which the B Trust could be affected before your death is if you became incapacitated. If this were the case and you had given your spouse a durable power of attorney (discussed in another chapter), then this spouse, or whoever you had given the power to, could sign your name to financial and legal documents, including amendments to the trust. There is one more advantage to the A-B Trust: protecting the B Trust if the survivor incurs large medical expenses.

Insulating the Estate From a Catastrophic Illness

Protecting the estate from a catastrophic illness can take place only if there is an A-B Trust and one spouse has already died. Thus, we are dealing with a very specific set of circumstances: a surviving spouse who has been afflicted with an illness or disease that threatens to wipe out more than what is in the A Trust and that survivor is not the trustee of the B Trust. If these circumstances exist, and the trustee of the B Trust was originally (while *both* spouses were alive and competent) given discretion to distribute income and/or principal from the decedent's trust, then the B Trust can be protected.

Since the trustee of the B Trust can decide not to make any kind of distribution to the remaining, now ill, survivor, these assets cannot be considered available to pay for medical or hospital expenses. Government benefits could then be used. Almost everything in the A Trust would have to be "spent down" before such assistance would kick in, but at least the B Trust could remain intact, even if it had been funded with tens of millions of dollars. Is there a possible way to protect the assets in the A Trust (the survivor's portfolio)? The answer is yes.

State and federal government assistance programs often depend on the net worth of the injured or ill party. These programs do not include the person's personal residence when making a determination of ability to pay. In other words, the house would not have to be mortgaged, refinanced, sold, or in any way "spent down" to qualify for public assistance. This is true if your house, co-op, or condominium is worth $10,000 or $10,000,000.

In order to preserve as much of the estate as possible for the kids, a house is often remodeled or cleared of any indebtedness before the hospital and medical bills begin. By paying off the mortgage(s), or even selling the existing home and buying a more expensive dwelling, the individual or couple can then pass on a valuable asset, intact, to children or other family members. Clearly, this could be a situation where someone was "dirt (house) rich and cash poor."

Summary

An A-B Trust can (1) reduce or eliminate estate taxes, (2) provide support for the surviving spouse, (3) be structured to protect your children, (4) be allowed to grow so that Trust B pays no estate taxes, and (5) protect part of a portfolio from being wiped out in the event of a catastrophic illness.

We have now explored all of the nuances of the A-B Trust. Let us now explore the pros and cons of the A-B-C Trust (don't worry, there isn't an A-B-C-D Trust). Enough groundwork has been laid so that the description of the A-B-C Trust will be brief and easy to understand.

Checklist of Things to Do

1. If your estate is worth more than $1,200,000, sit down with your spouse and explain the benefits of an A-B Trust. Be sure to emphasize that assets in both trusts can be easily invaded.
2. Talk to your estate-planning attorney to see if part of your estate can be later protected in the event of large medical bills.
3. Calculate how much should be placed in the B Trust. In certain cases, it may be wise to subject part of the B Trust to estate taxes now for larger savings later.
4. Since assets placed in the B Trust are subject to a potential estate tax only when the first spouse dies, try to place property in the B Trust that is likely to appreciate.
5. Put income-producing assets into the A Trust so that the surviving spouse will be afforded the greatest current income possible.

CHAPTER 19

THE A-B-C TRUST

IF YOU ARE married and the value of your and your spouse's estate is expected to be $1,200,000 or greater on the date of either spouse's death, you should read this chapter. The purpose of an A-B-C Trust is twofold: (1) to postpone paying estate taxes and (2) to provide you with further estate-planning control and flexibility.

Like the A-B Trust, the A-B-C will allow *each* spouse to use his or her lifetime equivalent exemption of up to $600,000, thereby having up to $1,200,000 pass free of estate taxes and probate fees. With an A-B-C Trust, a married couple can have a C Trust that can be funded with unlimited assets. Whatever is in the C Trust will avoid estate taxes until the surviving spouse dies. For practical purposes, the C Trust is usually limited to being no greater than the decedent's share of the estate.

The advantage of this delay in paying estate taxes is that it allows that much more money to grow and compound. Without the C Trust, there would be some estate taxes immediately imposed on that portion of the estate that did not pass outright to the surviving spouse if it exceeded $600,000. Obviously, it is better to have, say, $100,000 compound in value over a number of years instead of $60,000 (which is

the approximate figure you would have if the $100,000 was subjected to estate taxes immediately upon the death of the first spouse). This compounding of "whole" dollars or assets continues until the second spouse dies.

The beauty of this program is that assets in the C Trust, as well as the B Trust, can be used by the surviving spouse if needed. Income and/or principal from the C and B Trust can be used. The A Trust is always owned by the surviving spouse outright, as soon as the first spouse dies. If assets from the C Trust *are used*, this may mean that the entire estate may be worth less by the time the second spouse dies. This reduction in value means that less estate taxes will be paid.

The other advantage of the A-B-C Trust is that it allows you to keep control of your share of the estate, no matter how big or small your share is. An example of how the A-B-C Trust works may be helpful.

Let us assume that a married couple has a net worth of $2,000,000 and that each spouse's share represents $1,000,000. An A-B-C Trust can be structured so that when the first spouse dies, his or her share is divided as follows: $600,000 in the B Trust (to take full advantage of the lifetime exclusion) and $400,000 in the C Trust (which would not be subject to estate taxes until the surviving spouse died). The remaining $1,000,000 does not belong to the first spouse and therefore remains under the control of the second spouse.

The survivor is entitled to the income from the B *and* C Trust, whether you like it or not. Provisions can also be added to allow the second spouse the ability to receive parts of the principal under certain circumstances. These circumstances could be as broad or narrow as you like; after all, at least in theory, the assets that are going to fund the C Trust are either part or all of your separate property or your share of the community property.

There is one more benefit to an A-B-C Trust and, again, this feature can also be included in an A-B Trust (but not a standard living trust). If the surviving spouse contracts a catastrophic illness, disease, or is involved in a serious accident, the A-B-C Trust can be written so that the assets in the B and C Trust cannot be touched. However, the income from the B and C Trust, which the survivor is entitled to until his or her death, will be included as part of the spouse's assets when the government determines if public assistance should be afforded.

The A-B-C Trust is sometimes called a "Q-TIP Trust," which stands for "qualified terminable interest property." The survivor has at least some interest in the C Trust; at a minimum he or she is entitled to take out up to all of the income generated by this trust. This interest or right does not last forever. When the surviving spouse dies, he or she cannot transfer this right onto someone else, hence the term "terminable interest."

Summary

An A-B-C Trust can (1) reduce or eliminate estate taxes, (2) provide support for your spouse, (3) be structured to protect your children, (4) grow without paying any estate taxes on the B Trust after the death of the first spouse, (5) protect part of an estate in case either you or your spouse incurs large medical bills, and (6) postpone estate taxation on everything placed in the C Trust.

You have now been thoroughly introduced to living trusts, A-B Trusts, and A-B-C Trusts. Let us now turn to some of the other documents that you may wish to consider. All of the documents mentioned in the remaining chapters are separate from your trust and will not affect its ongoing operation or final disposition in any manner.

These provisions and documents are simply things that make up what our firm calls "The Great Estate." Other attorneys sometimes refer to these documents as something that, when combined with a living trust, is a "complete estate plan." Let us examine some of the other documents that we will probably want to include in our estate planning package.

Checklist of Things to Do

1. Review the "checklist of things to do" at the end of the last chapter.
2. Place those assets that you believe will appreciate the most into the C Trust, since this is the only way you can postpone estate taxes when the first spouse dies.
3. Remind your spouse that until one of you dies, the B and C Trusts do not have any effect or bearing on your ability to spend, save, invest, gift, sell, encumber, or transfer anything you own individually or as a couple.

CHAPTER 20

SPENDTHRIFT TRUSTS

A SPENDTHRIFT TRUST is one in which the beneficiary is unable to voluntarily or involuntarily transfer his or her interest in the trust. Creditors are unable to collect future income or capital, and the beneficiary cannot sell or give away these rights. This type of trust is created to provide for the maintenance of someone while protecting this person from his or her own actions. Spendthrift provisions are valid in most but not all states. They can be part of a living-trust package.

Spendthrift trusts, or provisions, are allowed because, if the trust is worded properly, the beneficiary (donee) has no right to the property. If someone has no right to something, it is only fair that his or her creditors do not either. The trustor (donor) owns the property and should have the right to determine what a beneficiary receives, when it is received, and under what conditions.

There are no special words that are needed to create a spendthrift trust; the trustor's intent to limit the beneficiary's power to transfer his or her interest is sufficient. As an example, you could say, "John is to receive the income from all of my rental properties; the trustee, Mary, is to manage these rental units and distribute the net proceeds *only to*

John and to no other, not even creditors or others who may have authority." The guidelines that the trustee must act within can include voluntary and/or involuntary transfers.

You cannot create a spendthrift trust for yourself. That is, you are not allowed to put your own property in a trust that is beyond the reach of creditors and others. This protection can possibly be found in an irrevocable trust, but not in a trust in which you have retained interests or powers.

In the majority of states where a spendthrift restraint is valid, no enforceable transfer is allowed. If the beneficiary attempts to transfer, encumber, sell, or gift his trust interest to another person or entity, the assignee cannot enforce the assignment over the beneficiary's later objection.

Creditors are generally barred from reaching the beneficiary's interest in the trust. However, once monies are actually paid to the beneficiary from the trust, they are no longer protected. If the beneficiary receives the money, creditors can then go after the distribution, just as they could on any other asset owned by the beneficiary. Bear in mind that the beneficiary does not own assets titled in the name of any trust, including one that contains spendthrift provisions.

Limited Restraints

Several states, including California, limit the effectiveness of spendthrift restraints. Some of these states will allow only the trustee (or trust) to insulate amounts necessary to provide support to the beneficiary. The definition of support is based on the beneficiary's accustomed standard of living for support and education. This means that the income protected could end up being substantial. In the minority of states that narrowly limit the effectiveness of spendthrift provisions, you can protect the beneficiary by including a provision that allows the trustee to accumulate excess income. Surprisingly, federal bankruptcy laws honor spendthrift trusts as they apply to the beneficiary's state of residency.

Gaps in Protection Found in All 50 States

Most of the states that recognize spendthrift trusts will still allow certain types of creditors to "break through" and reach the beneficiary's interest. Thus, spendthrift provisions are usually not effective when it comes to (1) the federal or state government (taxes, penalties, and/or interest due), (2) spousal or child support, and (3) anyone who furnishes the necessities of life to the beneficiary. A few states, including California and Minnesota, may still not allow a spouse, ex-spouse, or child to break through the trust in order to satisfy their support claims. There are even some cases in which the furnisher of necessities could not go after the trust's assets.

An Alternate Way to Protect the Trust's Assets

A discretionary trust may accomplish what a spendthrift trust cannot. A discretionary trust gives the trustee (the person you name) discretion over distributions of income and/or principal. If given the power in the trust document, the trustee can decide to withhold distributions to one or more beneficiaries or give extra amounts to another beneficiary.

The discretionary trust is frequently used in jurisdictions that do not allow, or significantly restrict, spendthrift trusts. Still, if a trustee of a discretionary trust has been notified of an assignment or attachment of the beneficiary's interest, the trustee would become personally liable if he or she were to then make a distribution directly to the beneficiary. In such a situation the trustee may still be protected if a valid spendthrift restraint was also in place.

Summary

A living trust that contains spendthrift provisions is something that should be considered by anyone who is concerned about a loved one's ability to manage money. You cannot set up your own spendthrift trust and place your assets in it with the hope of shielding yourself from creditors or lawsuits (an irrevocable trust may be the solution if that were the goal). However, you can protect your heirs in this way.

The coverage afforded by a spendthrift trust varies from state to state. If your lawyer advises you against such an instrument, ask her about the use of a discretionary or irrevocable trust. In any case, these types of trusts and provisions do not normally have any effect until both you and/or your spouse are deceased.

Checklist of Things to Do

1. Carefully weigh the advantages and disadvantages of spendthrift provisions: potential creditor protection and checked spending versus the beneficiary's inability to have access to the principal and any accompanying humiliation.
2. See your attorney and get additional input.
3. Inform counsel that the spendthrift provisions are to apply only to certain beneficiaries.

CHAPTER 21

THE IRREVOCABLE LIFE-INSURANCE TRUST

THERE ARE THREE reasons why people own life insurance: (1) to provide security for loved ones in the event of an untimely death, (2) to pay estate taxes, or (3) for current or future income needs while the insured is still alive. Whatever reason people have for owning life insurance, few realize that its proceeds are usually included in the decedent's estate to determine estate-tax liability. Insurance proceeds avoid probate, but without proper estate planning the death benefit may be reduced by estate taxes.

An irrevocable life-insurance trust lets your beneficiaries receive the death benefit intact by keeping the policy outside of your estate. This is done by transferring ownership of the policy from you to a life insurance trust that is *irrevocable* (a completed gift or transaction). If you do not own the policy and retain no "incidents of ownership" (described below), then it cannot be considered part of your estate by the IRS.

You will find this chapter beneficial if: (1) you own life insurance, (2) the projected value of your estate at death will be worth over $600,000 ($1,200,000 if you are married), and (3) you want your estate to pay the least amount of taxes possible.

Life Insurance

If you have any life insurance and possess "incidents of ownership" in the policy, the proceeds from the policy will be considered part of your estate when determining your estate-tax liability, even though you are not the beneficiary of the policy. Incidents of ownership include: (1) the right to borrow against the policy, (2) the ability to change beneficiaries, (3) the right to surrender or assign the policy, and (4) the ability to obtain any economic benefit from the policy. Successfully transferring a life-insurance policy (i.e., getting rid of any incidents of ownership) will still result in having the death benefit included in your estate if the policy was transferred within three years of your death. However, insurance owned by a third party (your children, parents, siblings, etc.) and made payable to the insured's revocable living trust will not be included in your estate.

You are always free to sell, gift, or transfer ownership of your life insurance to someone else. However, in such a situation you could not be sure who would survive whom or if the new owner might cancel the policy, change the beneficiaries, or forget to pay the premiums. As an example, if you were to name your wife or husband as the owner and they somehow died before you did, the cash value of the policy, even though you were the insured, would be included in the deceased's estate. Ownership would also revert back to you, leaving you where you started.

The person you transfer your policy to may be someone you trust now, but what about later? If there is a divorce, the court will most likely treat the transference as a gift by you to your spouse, thereby taking community or *your* separate property and making it the separate property of your spouse. This would mean that you would not be entitled to even half the cash value of the account when the estate was divided up. Naming your children does not provide any greater assurances. The cash value in the policy may have to be used to settle a creditor's claim or lawsuit against the child. The new owner may get involved with drugs or alcohol and take on a new personality. There is even the chance that your son or daughter will marry a dominant partner who convinces your child to cash in the policy. Fortunately, all of these things can be avoided by having an irrevocable life-insurance trust.

Making It Work

There are four things you should make sure of when setting up one of these irrevocable trusts: (1) the trust's instructions should be worded so that the trustee is able to purchase the policy, (2) the policy should be written so that you are the insured and the trust is the owner, (3) premiums should be no more than $10,000 per year ($20,000 if you are married), (4) you should make a gift of the premium payment to the trust, and (5) you should not name yourself as the trustee.

As you recall from previous chapters, the trustee must act within the confines of the trust document. By narrowly defining these powers when you have the trust set up, including the right to buy life insurance, you increase the likelihood that your wishes will be followed.

The purpose of an irrevocable life-insurance trust is to make sure that there is some economic benefit when *you* die and that the benefit will not be included in your estate. This is why it is important that the trustor name the trust as owner and you as the insured. It is also a good idea to name the trust as the beneficiary. By doing this, the insurance proceeds will go into the trust and then be distributed or managed for the beneficiaries. This means that there will be no probate, income taxes, or estate taxes.

There is another important estate-planning reason why the trust should be named the beneficiary. Your trust can be worded so that the trustee can use the insurance money to purchase illiquid or difficult-to-market assets from the living trust and put them into the life-insurance trust. This would prevent a "fire sale" of assets if money were needed by the living trust to satisfy estate taxes. Think how much your estate could shrink in value if it was forced to sell stocks right after a crash, or a piece of depressed real estate. A 25% "correction" or "adjustment" in price is almost commonplace in today's markets.

Before moving on to the issue of gifting, there is one more reason that these trusts are so important and why the trust should be named beneficiary. When you die, if one or more of the beneficiaries is a minor or incompetent, it is highly unlikely that the insurer will pay such a person directly. In order to protect itself from any kind of liability, the insurance company will look to the court for direction, perhaps requesting a court-appointed guardian or conservator. This means extra costs, delays, and the naming of someone you may not have liked or trusted. Naming the trust as beneficiary means that the trustee *you chose* can use the proceeds to take care of the child or incapacitated adult.

When you purchase life insurance, you should have your financial advisor shop for quality and price. Some policies are better than others, depending upon your circumstances.

Whatever policy you buy, try to make sure that the annual premiums are less than $10,000. As you may recall from the chapter on gifts, if you make a gift of more than $10,000 per year, you must file a gift-tax return and either pay some gift taxes or reduce your lifetime exclusion of $600,000. If your spouse joins in on the gift, the two of you could gift the trust up to $20,000 per year. The gifted money would then be used to pay the annual policy premiums. You want to make sure that you do not gift more than the premiums due.

To make everything legal, the trustee must notify the beneficiaries that a gift has been made (by either you and/or your spouse) and that each beneficiary has a right to demand his or her share of such gift. When the beneficiaries decline the gift, they forfeit any right to the money. This notification must be in writing.

If the annual premiums on the life-insurance policy are greater than $5,000 or 5% of any beneficiary's share of the insurance trust, an additional section must be added. This section would divide the insurance trust into shares, one for each beneficiary. The trust assets (the premiums and later the death benefit) would then be allocated among the shares. By doing this, any excess gift turned down by a beneficiary turns into a gift to the person who turned down the money, not the trust or other beneficiaries. This then eliminates any gift-tax concern. The ability to gift up to $10,000 does not apply when one beneficiary makes a gift to another beneficiary.

If the paragraph above sounds a little confusing, do not worry. The only thing you have to remember is to alert your attorney that possibly the irrevocable life-insurance trust may need to be divided into shares for gift-tax purposes.

Whatever the dollar figure of the premiums is, make sure your gift is to the trust and not directly to the beneficiaries or someone else. One of the reasons for setting up this type of trust, along with your living trust, was to maximize estate-planning opportunities. If you make a gift to someone or something other than the trust, there is no assurance that the donee will use the money to pay the insurance premiums.

The final point to making this thing work is to name someone other than yourself as the trustee. If you name yourself as the trustee, then the IRS will claim that you still possess incidents of ownership and include the insurance proceeds as part of your estate. Do not worry about losing control. After all, you can still name anyone you want as the trustee, as long as he or she is competent and an adult. And, as an added safety measure, you can word the powers of the trustee very narrowly.

What to Do If You Already Own Some Life Insurance

The irrevocable life-insurance trust is still a good idea, but the strategy must now be a little different *if you already own a policy*. The biggest concern is the cash value of the policy (or the alternate way the IRS measures the policy's worth). If it has a current worth of $10,000 ($20,000 if you are married) or more, you have two choices. One, you can gift partial-ownership interests into the irrevocable trust over a period of years (i.e., if the value was $50,000, you would gift $10,000 of the cash value to the trust each year). The gifting could take the form of a policy loan. Insurance-policy loans reduce the cash value dollar for dollar. Two, you could gift the entire policy to the trust. If the policy's value at that point was worth more than $10,000 ($20,000 if you were married at the time of the gift), then you would have to file a gift-tax return and eat into your lifetime exclusion.

Assuming you follow these guidelines, there is one more thing necessary for the irrevocable life-insurance trust to work (if the policy is being gifted into the trust). This final requirement is known as the "3-year rule," something you have little control over. The IRS says that if a *life-insurance policy* is gifted away within 3 years of the donor's death, such gift will be considered invalid for estate-tax purposes. This means that the whole purpose of the insurance trust would be worthless and the death benefit would be included in the decedent's estate.

Second-to-Die Life Insurance

Survivorship—sometimes called second-to-die—insurance is written on two lives, usually a married couple's. Nothing is paid out until the second death. Premiums on second-to-die policies can be significantly less than premiums on a similar policy designed for a single person. The risk is spread over two lives. Say there is a one in 10 chance you will die within the next 10 years, and a one in 10 chance your spouse will die in 10 years. But, barring a common accident, the odds that you will both die in the next 10 years is something like one in 100. So there is only a 1-in-100 chance that the insurance company will have to pay off that soon. That translates into a lower premium.

Survivorship policies are a strong candidate for a couple who own a closely held business or a lot of real estate. These are the kinds of assets that can appreciate and generate a lot of estate tax, but they are not liquid. The insurance proceeds provide the cash needed to pay the tax, leaving the property intact for the heirs. No need for distress sales in unfriendly markets. This type of policy also comes in handy if you want to pass along a family business to some of your offspring without disinheriting the others. It could provide the cash for the ones in the business to buy out the outside siblings.

While considering second-to-die policies, keep in mind the following: (1) life insurance solely for liquidity purposes is not appropriate if you expect the value of your net estate to be $600,000 or less when you die ($1,200,000 or less if you are married) and (2) be realistic about the cash and projected values shown in the policy illustrations: sometimes these "future" values are based on unrealistic assumptions. Speaking of the value of your estate at death, try to gauge the size of your spouse's estate. Without the use of an A-B or A-B-C Trust, a second-to-die policy could be appropriate if you think her or his estate will exceed $600,000.

The Next Step

If you think an irrevocable life-insurance trust might be for you, ask the opinion of your estate-planning attorney and insurance advisor. Your lawyer can tell you if such a trust makes sense. The insurance expert can help you shop price, quality, and features. Your advisor may even be able to get the insurance company to provide the trust free of charge.

One last point. This type of trust is irrevocable (and must be for estate-tax purposes); once you sign the document you cannot later change your mind. However, you always have the freedom of not making (gifting) the actual policy transfer or annual premiums.

Not for Everyone

This type of trust is not for everyone. Several financial planners recommend that individuals and couples in their mid-40s or younger postpone the establishment of such an irrevocable trust for several reasons. First, you may later need the cash value from the policy. Second, you may want to change beneficiaries because of divorce or something else unforeseen. Not all of these events are negative; you may later discover that one child needs the money less than another. You lose the flexibility to do any of these things if the policy is owned by the irrevocable trust.

On a more positive note, this type of estate planning can be quite powerful. If a person places a life-insurance policy in an irrevocable trust and gives up ownership, it is not subject to state or federal estate taxes if ownership was relinquished at least 3 years before the former owner dies. According to one expert, "The trust contains powerful leverage and tax judo."

Usually, a life-insurance policy has a very low value for gift-tax purposes. Yet it has a value of many times that for beneficiaries when the donor dies. Life insurance is often an easier gift for a client to part with on a psychological basis than real estate or stocks. This is because most policies do not produce current income. It is also an asset that is thought of only as something that will benefit the insured's survivors after his or her death.

Life insurance is not the only way to use an irrevocable trust. You should also consider buying municipal bonds or low-dividend-paying growth stocks as an alternative. The decision between insurance and some other investments comes down to which product would produce the better return. If you die early, life insurance wins easily. If you die at your life expectancy, an investment in tax-free bonds would be about equal to the insurance proceeds.

To give you an idea of the possible federal estate-tax savings from transferring a $500,000 life insurance policy into an irrevocable trust, look at the table below. These examples assume that (1) there has been no prior use of the $600,000 lifetime exclusion, (2) no gift taxes were due on the annual insurance premiums, and (3) the previous owner, who is still the insured, lives at least 3 years after the policy was transferred to the irrevocable trust.

Size of Estate (excluding life insurance)	Estate-tax Savings
$250,000	$55,000
500,000	153,000
1,000,000	210,000
1,500,000	225,000
2,000,000	245,000
3,000,000	275,000

Source: Arthur Anderson & Co.

The "estate-tax savings" shown above is what happens when the irrevocable trust, and not the decedent, owns the policy. This is in addition to the beneficiary(s) receiving the $500,000 death benefit.

Irrevocable Trusts

There are only two advantages an irrevocable trust has over a revocable trust. First, since assets placed in an irrevocable trust cannot be taken back, a completed gift has been made and any income generated from such assets will then be taxed to the new owner, the beneficiary, or the actual trust. Furthermore, the asset is no longer part of your estate and therefore cannot be used in computing whether or not there is an estate-tax liability.

The second advantage of an irrevocable trust is that it protects your loved ones against senility, lawsuits involving the trustors, remarriage of the surviving spouse, or extravagances of either spouse while both are still alive. This is because assets in an irrevocable trust cannot be touched by you or your spouse, even though one or both of you is alive and well. Once assets are in this trust, they no longer belong to you and/or your spouse. Either or both of you may have administrative and management control, but neither of you has access to the principal.

As you can imagine, the primary disadvantage of an irrevocable trust is your loss of control over the property placed in the trust. A secondary problem is that by making such a gift, there is not any type of step-up in basis on any of the property when either you or your spouse dies. A living trust is given a 100% step-up in basis upon the death of either spouse if the property was described as community property or the separate property of the decedent.

Summary

An irrevocable life-insurance trust should be considered only if very specific criteria are met. You must have a good-sized estate, own (or plan to buy) life insurance, plan on benefiting someone other than your spouse exclusively, and understand that once the trust is funded, the gift cannot be taken back. This is an *irrevocable* trust.

The sole purpose of this type of trust is to reduce the size of your estate. If you and your spouse have no incidents of ownership, then the policy's proceeds will not be considered part of your holdings for estate-tax purposes. Setting up and funding the trust are two important steps, but shopping for the right *type* of policy is just as important. Once you have selected the right kind, then you and your agent can shop price and quality. You may be surprised to learn that some of the best-known companies offer policies that are not competitively priced and are not as financially secure as some of the lesser-known insurers.

The easiest way to set up an irrevocable life-insurance trust is to first establish the trust and then fund it. By making annual gifts (to pay policy premiums) to the trust, you are always free to suspend or stop the program at any time.

Checklist of Things to Do

1. If your estate plan will benefit from one of these insurance trusts, contact your investment advisor and insurance agent and find out the best way to proceed.
2. Make it clear to the person doing the shopping that you are most interested in quality first, coverage second, and price third.
3. Request several quotes, using different insurance companies.
4. Once a company is selected, see if it provides a free irrevocable life-insurance trust if you purchase a policy through them. Otherwise consult with your attorney.

CHAPTER 22

THE CHARITABLE REMAINDER TRUST

H OW WOULD YOU like to make a gift of appreciated property, avoid paying any capital gains or estate taxes on the gift, and get some write-offs at the same time? Well, this is exactly what can happen with a charitable remainder trust. This type of trust works best if someone wants to benefit a specific charity, although any charitable group recognized by the IRS will do.

If you have real or personal property that has appreciated, you are in a high tax bracket, and want to benefit a charity, then you should read this chapter. There are other advantages to a charitable remainder trust, such as getting a lifetime income, receiving public recognition, and the enjoyment of helping others, but the points mentioned in the preceding paragraph are the ones that motivate most people.

The charitable remainder trust is a popular and effective estate-planning device. This type of trust allows you to take appreciated property (real estate, stocks, bonds, artwork, etc.) and convert it into an income stream for the rest of your life (and the life of your spouse, children, parents, etc.). This conversion also means that you will not have to pay any taxes on the appreciation, and the asset will be permanently removed from your estate. Finally,

the fact that you have made a gift means that you are also entitled to an immediate tax write-off.

Why the IRS Allows This
The logic behind this form of gift giving is that the government wants to encourage you to make gifts to groups and organizations they deem worthy: in short, those recognized and approved by the IRS. The approved list includes hundreds of nonprofit groups but does not include political parties. The encouragement from the IRS and Congress comes in two forms: estate- and income-tax savings.

Once accepted by the charity, you are given an immediate write-off equal to the "present value" of the gift (this concept is discussed below). Oftentimes the charity is able to sell off the asset, take the proceeds, and invest them in the name of the organization. Income produced from these investments is passed on to you. The income you receive is fully taxable but is not taxed to the nonprofit group since a qualified charity does not pay taxes. Sometimes the asset is not sold off and/or the charity has no money to "purchase" it from you. In such a case, the gift will still entitle you to immediate tax benefits but you will not be getting any current income.

What You Need to Do

The first step is to contact an IRS-recognized charitable group. The nonprofit group you are thinking about benefiting will be able to tell you if they are recognized as a charity in the eyes of the IRS. If you are in doubt, contact the IRS and find out what status they have given the organization.

The second step is to meet with the charity's planned-giving coordinator. The charity's representative will be able to tell you if the gift is something it will accept and whether or not it is willing to provide you with an immediate income stream or wait until the asset sells. Lastly, the coordinator can tell you if the group will pay part or all of the costs of having a charitable remainder trust drafted.

The third step is to contact your tax preparer and investment advisor and find out the income- and estate-tax benefits. One or both of these advisors can give you some valuable insight into how many live(s) the income stream should last (see "present value," below). Your advisor can also tell you if the property you are donating is the best choice. The financial planner may be able to give you a sense of direction as to who should draft the charitable remainder trust if the charity will not pay for the needed legal services.

Assuming the first three steps have been dealt with satisfactorily, the final step is to sign the trust (which names one or more charities as beneficiary), transfer title of the property from you to the trust, have the trustee sell the asset and use the proceeds to purchase income-producing property (bonds, utility stocks, leasing program, rental property, etc.). Once an asset is placed in the charitable trust, there will be no capital-gains tax due when the sale occurs. No taxes are paid on any gains from the "new" property (whatever the proceeds went into). As income flows into the trust, the trustee can then write you checks

each month from the trust's checking account.

The Income You Will Be Receiving

The frequency of the income stream is something you decide on when having the trust drafted. It will be part of the "powers of the trustee" section.

Some people want monthly checks; others prefer quarterly or annual distributions. The income lasts until the time specified in the trust lapses. Your trust can be drafted so that income is provided until one, some, or all of the following die: you, your spouse, parents, children, grandchildren, relatives, and friends. What is commonly done is to have the checks continue until the donor and his or her spouse are both dead. The second-most common arrangement is for the income to last until both spouses and all children are deceased.

The wording of the trust can be quite liberal. As an example, a person could require the trustee to make distributions as long as his disabled brother was alive. Tax benefits decrease the longer the distribution is expected to last. Income for your life will produce a write-off of X. Income for your life and the life of your spouse (son, friend, parent, etc.) will produce a write-off of X minus Y. This calculation is more fully explained in the "present-value" section, which follows.

Once a fair value is assigned to the property, you need to determine over what period the income stream will last. This is done by having your investment or tax advisor look at life-expectancy tables and then using IRS-published guidelines for determining present value. Let us examine both of these points.

How Present-Value Tables Affect Your Deduction

If you donate something to a qualified charity, you are entitled to an immediate deduction. The deduction you receive is based on the fair market value of the gift at the time of the donation. The fair market value of marketable securities (e.g., IBM stock, GM bonds, U.S. government obligations) and cash is easy to determine. A donation of artwork, jewelry, and real estate is a little more tricky. An independent appraisal is necessary to substantiate the value. This is not necessary if the personal property or real estate is first sold by the trust (instead of being given to the charity). The fair market value in such a situation is simply the amount of money *netted* from the sale; the sales price minus any selling fees or commissions. Now let us look at what happens when the gift is "delayed" or "qualified."

If you donate something to a charity but tell them that they are not going to benefit from the gift until a certain amount of time has lapsed (i.e., 5 years, 30 years, until you die, until you and your grandchildren are all dead), then the value of the gift is diminished. This is because of the effects of inflation and what is referred to as "lost-opportunity costs."

As an example, would you rather have someone give you a dollar today or a dollar in 10 years? The answer is obvious. By having the dollar today you can invest it and begin to reap the benefits of the investment immediately. Or you could use the dollar to purchase something needed. If instead you received the same dollar in 10 years, the item you wanted would almost certainly cost more (probably two or three times as much). If the money was earmarked for an investment, you would have received all of the income and/or appreciation for the previous decade.

The IRS understands both of these concepts and makes adjustments accordingly, using "present-value" tables to discount the value of a gift to be received in the future. Even though you have set up a charitable trust, funded it, and sold the property, the reality is that the charity will not really benefit from any of these until they have use of the proceeds or property. An outright gift to a charitable group is *presently* worthless if the charity must turn around and pay you some kind of regular income.

Generally, the discounting, or present value table, used by the IRS has a lot to do with current and projected rates of inflation. When inflation is running particularly high, the value of your gift may be discounted by 8–12% a year. At another time, inflation might be running at 3–4% and the discounts would be adjusted accordingly.

The Value of the Tax Write-off

The write-off you will receive is based on the value of the asset multiplied by a present-value factor (some number less than 1.00). This deduction can be used to offset up to 50% of your adjusted gross income (30% in some cases) for the year in which the contribution is made. If the dollar figure of the write-off is greater than 50% of your adjusted gross income, the excess can be carried forward for up to 5 more years.

As an example, let us suppose you bought $14,000 worth of stock several years ago and it is now worth $200,000. Further assume that the charitable remainder trust was set up so that the income stream would end upon your death (and the asset would then go to the charity). Finally, assume that after looking up your life expectancy and then using IRS guidelines, the discounting factor was .80. You would be entitled to a $160,000 charitable deduction (80% of $200,000). This same year, you had adjusted gross income of $100,000. Assume the donated property and charity chosen meant that you qualified for a deduction "up to 50% of adjusted gross income." This means that you would be able to use only $50,000 of the $160,000 deduction (your taxable income for the year would drop from $100,000 to $50,000). The remaining $110,000 write-off would be carried forward to the next year. The same rules would apply for that year. Any excess would be rolled over into the following year. The "carry-forward" would last until all of the $160,000 was used up or for 5 years after the year of the initial deduction, whichever comes first.

Before moving on to the next section, an

additional comment needs to be made about the write-off. Your first priority should be to provide for your family. If this means having the income last for the lifetime of several people, so be it. As you will see below, the benefits of a charitable remainder trust are sizable, even if the immediate deduction is not.

How Much Income You Can Expect to Receive

The amount of money you will receive from the trust depends on how the money is invested. Junk bonds throw off more income than government securities. GNMAs usually offer a higher yield than money market accounts. The actual investing is largely determined by the discretion of the trustee, within the confines of the trust. As an example, you can write your charitable trust so that the trustee can invest only in tax-free bonds, a leasing program, or a short-term global income fund. All three of these investments produce a healthy amount of current income but little or no appreciation potential. Trust powers limiting the investments to these three areas would be good for the income beneficiaries (you, your spouse, children, etc.) but not the charity. The charity would end up receiving an asset that had little or no growth to offset the effects of inflation during the income period (which might end up being a couple of years or several decades).

There are two ways to structure the income stream: either as a percentage of the value of the trust or as a fixed amount. By selecting a percentage figure, the value of the trust property is revalued each year, and your income stream may go up or down each year (a bond portfolio worth $200,000 giving you a 9% return could turn into a $230,000 bond portfolio next year, giving you 9% on that higher figure). As an optional provision, your trust can include what is known as a "make-up" clause. This means that if the trust is unable to give you, say, 9% one year, the shortfall will be made up and added to next year's distribution (assuming that the value of the portfolio

has increased). This type of trust is known as a charitable remainder *unit trust*.

Your second option is to receive a fixed amount instead. There are advantages and disadvantages associated with a fixed annual or monthly income stream. Since the amount does not change, even though the trust's assets may have dramatically dropped during one or more years, you are protected against adverse market conditions. On the other hand, you will not benefit from the good years. Historically, with investments such as stocks, bonds, and real estate, the good years have greatly outnumbered the bad. Equally important, a fixed amount will not provide you or your family with a hedge against inflation. The amount you receive each year will stay the same, but the prices of the goods and services you use continue to go up.

What Most People Do

Most people who set up a charitable remainder trust opt for a percentage. The variability of the principal (the trust assets) can be controlled by the types of investments made by the trustee. Provided the trust powers include flexibility in investment selection, the trustee could invest in growth-oriented assets during periods of high inflation and then change the portfolio to more predictable investments when markets looked uncertain or when the economy was experiencing very low levels of inflation.

Your "suggestions" to the trustee will be decided by your risk level and time horizon. The trustee is free to listen to your ideas or completely ignore them. Remember, the charitable remainder trust is an irrevocable instrument. Once the gift is made, you cannot take it back or force the trustee to act in a certain manner. The trustee must always act within the confines of the trust document. Fortunately, the trust document is something that you have a hand in designing.

No matter how your income is determined, you are always free to have it deferred. By having income reinvested into the trust, the value of the account will grow (9% reinvested for 8 years results in the account doubling in size). If your trust property is well managed and you have opted for a percentage figure, deferral means that the trust will be able to give you more money each year when you begin needing it.

What Is Good for You Is Bad for the Charity

As you can see from the previous section, there is somewhat of a conflict of interest. Some investments are designed for growth, others for income, and still others can provide modest levels of current income along with some growth. The more "income-oriented" the investment, the greater your checks will be each month. The more "growth-oriented" the investment, the greater the value of the investment when it is eventually received by the charity.

For most people the decision is easy: choose an investment, or series of investments, that produces the greatest amount of current income. The charitable-tax deduction will not be affected by what the trustee invests in. Your first responsibility should be to you and/or your loved ones. And finally, the charity should be thankful that they are getting anything.

A good case for the charity can also be made. First, the donor might be so wealthy that neither she nor her family needs any more income. Second, maybe the donor's real love is a charity and she would rather see it enjoy the gift to its fullest extent. If either of these is the case, the donor is always free to make an outright gift to the charity and just accept the tax deduction. If there is no concern or need for the income, you do not need a charitable remainder trust.

What Property Should You Transfer into the Trust?

Given the choice, you will want to fund your charitable trust with the most highly appreciated asset(s) you have. This could mean real estate, stocks, art, or antiques. When sold by the charitable trust, appreciated property will avoid paying any capital-gains taxes, something you would not have been able to accomplish on your own.

A Word About Capital Losses

Under no circumstances should you gift an asset that has declined in value. The tax code works both ways: capital gains *and* losses are not recognized by the trust or trustor. If you have property that is now worth less than you paid for it, you are better off selling the asset. Take a capital loss. Uncle Sam wants to share in your profits. Not many people know that he will also share in your losses. Capital losses can offset your capital gains dollar for dollar (assuming both such events are outside of the charitable trust). There is no limit to this offsetting. If you have $10,000,000 worth of losses, you can offset up to $10,000,000 worth of gains. "Offsetting" means that your taxable gains are either reduced (if the losses are not as great as the gains) or eliminated (if losses equal or exceed the gains), thereby saving you tax dollars.

You never lose your losses. This means that if you cannot use up all of the losses in one year, you can carry them forward to the next. If, in the following year, you are still unable to use the remaining losses, then you carry them forward to the next, etc. The IRS requires you to use your losses any year there is a gain; you do not have the option of saving your losses for a year in which you are in a higher bracket. Thus, carrying forward losses means that you do not have enough capital gains.

Besides offsetting capital gains dollar for dollar, capital losses can also be used to offset what is known as *earned income*. This is money you have received as salary, tips, bonuses, or commissions; in short, compensation from your job. Unlike capital-gains offsetting, there is an annual dollar limit for earned income. Capital losses can offset only up to $3,000 of earned income each year. This offsetting will reduce your taxable income, dollar for dollar, up to $3,000 per year. Instead of paying taxes on, say, $42,000 of adjusted gross income, you will now be paying taxes on $39,000 of taxable income. Any remaining losses are carried forward to offset capital gains and/or earned income in future years. Let us go through an example to see how capital losses work.

An Example of a Capital-Loss Carry-Forward

Assume the following: (1) you have some stock you paid $50,000 for and it is now worth $10,000, (2) you also own some gold that has increased in value from $12,000 to $21,000, (3) you work for the XYZ company and earn $78,000 a year, and (4) you are in a 28% income-tax bracket. By selling the stock and gold and offsetting your salary, you end up with the results shown on the chart that follows.

A Commonly Made Mistake

You never want to create losses, but if they exist, do not ignore them. Sure, a stock you paid $30,000 for that is now worth $7,000 may go back up to $30,000 (or higher), but it may drop even more. In many cases one would be better off selling the stock for a $23,000 loss, using the loss to offset a gain now or in the future as well as offsetting earned income now and in the future. The

$7,000 that remains (the proceeds from the stock sale) can be used to go into another investment that may increase in value at a faster rate than the stock you just sold.

One of the most common investment mistakes people make is refusing to sell something because it has taken a beating under the mistaken belief that: (1) the investment will definitely go back up in value, (2) an alternate investment will not do just as well or better during this same "recovery period," and/or (3) there is really no loss as long as the asset is not sold. Do not be fooled by any of this. Your net worth is based on the market value of *all* of your holdings, not just the proceeds from some sale. If you do not think you have lost money by holding on to a stock or bond that has dropped in value by several thousand dollars, then you should not think that you have made a gain if a different stock or bond goes up thousands of dollars.

Determining Who the Trustee Will Be

Your choice of trustee may be limited by the charity chosen. Some charities do not like outside trustees and will assign one of their own people to oversee your trust. This is not recommended for most people. The charity's trustee is employed by the organization and

	Selling the Stock and Gold	Selling the Gold Only
loss from the stock	$40,000	—
gain from the gold	9,000	$9,000
taxable gain or loss	−31,000 loss[1]	9,000 gain
taxes due from sale	0	2,520 (28% of $9,000)
salary from work	78,000	78,000
using the capital loss	− 3,000 (of the $31,000 loss)	—
net taxable salary	75,000	78,000
taxes due on salary	16,573[2]	17,413
total tax liability	16,573	19,993 (17,413 + 2,520)
income-tax savings	3,360[3]	

1. This loss can be carried forward to future years.
2. Based on 1991 federal income-tax tables. No adjustments have been made for deductions, exemptions, or credits.
3. Plus you have $28,000 in losses that can be carried forward ($40k − $9k − $3k)

owes his or her allegiance to the employer. This often means that the trustee will not maximize your income, deciding instead to give you an "acceptable income" plus as much growth as possible for the charity. As previously mentioned, you cannot have maximum growth and maximum income: something has to suffer. If the charity gives you the greatest possible income stream, then they are going to see very little, if any, appreciation in the donated property.

If possible, choose your own trustee. Preferably this should be someone other than you, and someone who is well versed in the area of investments. You do not want to be the trustee in case the IRS ever questions the workings of the charitable trust. A person who knows the ins and outs of investing can help you (actually the trust) select securities and/or real estate that produces high levels of income and possibly some growth to help you and the charity out later.

The trust controls everything in the charitable remainder trust. The trustee must follow the instructions drafted by you and your attorney. If you become dissatisfied with your trustee, fire her and hire a new one. As in the case of revocable living trusts, you never have to have a reason to get rid of a trustee. If the charity becomes too pushy, your original charitable trust document can be worded so that the beneficiary can be removed and replaced by another charitable organization.

How Valuable a Charitable Remainder Trust Can Be

To give you an idea of how a deduction and a high current income, from "whole dollars" (see below) can be a better deal than selling the appreciated asset, paying taxes, and then investing the net proceeds, let us go through an example.

Suppose the following facts: (1) you bought some real estate for $100,000 twenty years ago, it is now worth $1,100,000, (2) you are in a 30% tax bracket (state and federal brackets combined), (3) the combined life expectancies of you, your wife, and two children is 50

years, (4) inflation for the next many years is projected to average 4%, (5) money safely invested yields 9%, and (6) your estate will be large enough to be subjected to a 50% estate tax after you and your wife die. Let us first see what would happen if you sold the real estate and invested the proceeds in an income-producing asset for the next 50 years.

$1,100,000		value of real estate
−	300,000	taxes due on the gain ($1,100,000 − $100,000 basis × 30%)
	800,000	left to invest
×	9%	the return received on the new investment
	72,000	annual income you and your family will receive
×	50	the number of years you and your family will live
$3,600,000		total amount received (and spent) over the 50 years

Now let us see what happens if a charitable remainder trust is established, the real estate is placed in the trust, sold, and the proceeds are invested in the same 9%-yielding asset.

$1,100,000		value of real estate
−	0	taxes due on the gain
	1,100,000	left to invest
×	9%	the return received on the new investment
	99,000	annual income you and your family will receive
×	50	the number of years you and your family will live
$4,950,000		total amount received (and spent) over the 50 years

As you can see, you and your family will receive an additional $1,350,000 by using the charitable trust. However, it is also true that the real estate cannot be passed on to your kids or grandchildren; instead, it belongs to the trust and will be turned over to the charity when the income beneficiaries are all dead (you, your wife, and two children in this example). Is the charitable trust still a good idea? Yes, for three reasons: (1) you had use of this extra annual income while you and your wife were alive ($99,000 a year vs. $72,000), (2) your kids or grandchildren were not going to inherit $1,100,000 after paying half that amount in estate taxes (we assumed your estate was large enough so that it was subject to a 50% estate tax); instead, they would have ended up with $550,000 (which at 9% would have given them $49,500 per year), and (3) the "lost" real estate can be substituted with something much better—cash in excess of $1,100,000 (see next section).

Making Up the "Lost" Property

So far our example has looked at everything but the immediate tax deduction you are going to receive. Based on the value of the real estate ($1,100,000), the life expectancies of you and your family (50 years combined), and a projected inflation rate of 4% (this is important to know so we know what present-value table should be used), you would be entitled to a $155,100 deduction. A $155,100 deduction translates into a tax savings of $46,530 for someone in a 30% bracket ($155,100 × .30).

This "windfall" of $46,530 is something you would not have gotten unless the real estate had been donated to a charity. By using the $46,530 for a single-pay, second-to-die life insurance policy (you are buying a paid-up life insurance policy in which no future premiums are due; the policy will pay off when you and your wife are both dead—hence the phrase "second-to-die") to obtain a death benefit in excess of $1,100,000.

To ensure that your kids get the entire $1,100,000 (remember, the example assumes that you are in a 50% estate-tax bracket), set up an irrevocable life-insurance trust and fund it with the $46,530. The trustee will then use these monies to purchase the insurance policy, naming the trust as owner and the children as beneficiaries.

Why It Pays to Be Generous

Let us list all of the benefits that were obtained in this example by setting up a charitable remainder trust and an irrevocable life-insurance trust:

- The family will be receiving $17,000 extra each year for 50 years.
- You did not have to pay any capital-gains taxes.
- Your estate was not subjected to taxes on the inherited property.
- Your kids will inherit more.
- You and your family are getting a "guaranteed" income stream.
- You no longer have to worry about the management of the property, and
- A charity(s) of your choosing received a nice piece of real estate (or cash).

Who says nice guys (and gals) don't finish first?

A Simpler Approach

Depending on the value of the intended donation(s), you and your financial advisor may deem it more appropriate for the assets to be donated to a "pooled account." These accounts are frequently used by charities. By making your gift directly to the charity, the proceeds are placed in a general account managed by the charity. This is a great way to go if your gifts are small or you want to make a series of contributions over a number of years.

Pooling income funds are similar to your own charitable trust except: (1) you do not have to pay to have a trust drafted and/or whatever fees may be charged by the trustee and (2) you have little, if any, say as to how much income you will be receiving.

If the contemplated gift is in the $50,000 range or higher, you are better off gaining the maximum flexibility (and income) possible by having an attorney draft a customized charitable remainder trust.

Summary

A charitable remainder trust can be like having your cake and eating it too. Think about it. You bought some real estate years ago that is now worth a small fortune. As income-producing property you have been receiving tax benefits from this improved property for years. You are now ready to sell the property and Uncle Sam is eagerly waiting for his share. Almost as if by magic, your estate-planning lawyer shows you how the IRS gets nothing, you get an income stream for life, and the government will also pay you, in the form of an up-front deduction, to make such a choice. There is just one little catch.

A charitable remainder trust is irrevocable; once established and funded, you cannot change your mind later. A gift has been made to one or more charities. True, they may not receive any actual benefit from this gift for several decades, but there will come a time, perhaps at your death, the death of your spouse, children, or grandchildren, when all strings will be cut, the income will cease, and the charity will keep whatever is left.

Since most individuals and couples will be income-oriented when they reach a point of wanting to make charitable gifts, try to establish your own trust and select your own trustee. The powers of the trust and discretion used by the trustee can have a great bearing on the amount of income you and your spouse (and possibly children and/or grandchildren) will receive for years to come.

When selecting a charity, verify that it is recognized as a nonprofit organization in the eyes of the Internal Revenue Service. If possible, fund the trust with assets that have already appreciated greatly. Assets that are commonly used are real estate, common stocks, and art.

Checklist of Things to Do

1. Eliminating an asset from your estate can be a sensitive issue. Consult with your spouse, explaining what you believe are the pros and cons.
2. See your attorney and get additional input.
3. Contact your favorite charity or charities and see what plans or options they offer.
4. In most cases it should be made clear to the charity that you want to select the trustee.
5. Make sure that the trustee's powers are broad enough to take advantage of future growth and/or income-oriented investments.

CHAPTER 23

THE CHARITABLE LEAD TRUST

A CHARITABLE LEAD trust is designed for someone who wants to benefit a charity now, receive tax benefits now, and eventually get back the donated property. In some ways it is almost the opposite of a charitable remainder trust. However, there are also similarities. First, you are still entitled to an immediate charitable income-tax deduction. Second, the trustee sells the asset and reinvests the proceeds into income-oriented investments. Third, income taxes are saved.

If you understand how a charitable remainder trust works, you will have no trouble seeing how a charitable lead trust operates. After the trust is set up, assets are transferred to it, preferably highly appreciated property. The trustee sells the asset and you avoid having to pay any capital-gains taxes. The income from the "new investment" goes to the charity. The charity continues to receive distributions until the trust ends. The duration of the trust depends upon how your trust document is drafted. You can have the charity receive money for a specific period (e.g., 3 years) or for the life of someone. As an example, your charitable lead trust could say, "The XYZ charity will receive monthly distributions of income until my mother, age 83, dies. The principal is to then revert back to me or my family, if I am no longer alive."

As you can see from the brief example above, the donated property eventually comes back to you (or your family). The amount of money the charity will receive depends on how the proceeds from the property are invested and on the powers given to the trustee. Your immediate deduction is based on the "life expectancy" of the program. As an example, if the charity were to receive income from $100,000 until your mother died, there is a real value to that gift—income for so many years. This is money that will be going somewhere else, to a charity. If your mother, according to life-expectancy tables, was expected to live for 8 more years, and the IRS was using 5% tables, the math would look like this:

	$100,000	amount invested
×	9%	the rate of return that the charity will receive
	$9,000	the amount of money given to the charity each year
×	8	the number of years Mom is expected to live

	$72,000	expected cumulative value of all charitable distributions
×	.677	factor used (8-year time horizon)
	$48,744	present value of the income streams

As the donor, you would be entitled to an immediate write-off (subject to the 30% or 50% adjusted-gross-income cap described in the previous chapter) of $48,744. Any amounts not used would then be carried forward.

Not Commonly Used

The charitable lead trust is so named because the charity "leads off" in the benefit. In a charitable remainder trust, the charity gets the "remainder" after you and your family are done receiving income. The charitable lead trust is not nearly as popular as the charitable remainder version. Most people want to enjoy income now and possibly leave something to a charity or someone else later. The remainder trust allows you to do this, the lead trust does not. Still, the advantages of a lead trust can be more attractive than one might initially imagine. Let us go through a complete example and see all of the pros and cons to this type of trust.

Example

Assume the following: (1) you own some stocks that are now worth $350,000 and you paid $50,000 for them, (2) you are in a 25% tax bracket (state and federal combined), (3) money can be safely invested for a 9% return, (4) your life expectancy is 22 years, (5) the IRS is using present-value tables based on 4% inflation, and (6) the life expectancy of your grandchildren (your heirs) is 72 years (50 more years after your death). Let us see what happens if a lead trust is *not* used.

	$350,000	value of stocks
−	75,000	taxes due on the gain ($300,000 net gain × 25%)
	275,000	left to invest
×	9%	the return received on your new investment

	24,750	annual income received from the new investment
×	72	remaining life expectancy of you and your grandchildren
	$1,782,000	total amount received over the 72 years

Let us now see what happens if a charitable lead trust is used. As you will see, there are two benefits. The example assumes that the charity will have use of the property for 22 years. First, the beneficiaries will be able to invest a larger amount since there are no taxes to erode the principal. Second, you will be getting some tax benefits immediately.

	$350,000	value of stocks
−	0	the charitable lead trust pays no taxes on your gain
	350,000	left to invest
×	9%	the return received by the grandchildren after your death
	31,500	annual income received from the new investment
×	50	life expectancy of grandchildren after your death
	$1,575,000	total amount received over the lifetime of your grandchildren

At this point it does not look good for the lead trust from a purely financial perspective. By not having the lead trust, an additional $207,000 in income will be received ($1,782,000 − $1,575,000). Let us now add the immediate tax benefits that were created when the stocks were transferred to the charitable trust.

	$350,000	amount available to invest by the charitable lead trust
×	9%	the return the charity will receive each year
	31,500	what the charity will receive each year
×	22	the number of years the charity will receive the income
	$693,000	the cumulative amount to be received by the charity before the asset reverts

		to your beneficiaries (the grandchildren)
×	.422	the present-value factor
	$292,446	present value of the 22-year income stream (your deduction)
×	25%	your tax bracket
	$73,112	dollar value of the deduction (amount saved in taxes)

By adding $73,112 to $1,575,000 (the amount your grandchildren will receive) you end up with a total dollar benefit of $1,648,112 (vs. $1,782,000 if the trust was not set up). Does this mean that the charitable lead trust is not a good idea? No.

In this example, the charitable lead trust is a good idea for the following reasons:

· You get immediate tax relief.
· The "time value of money" concept means that the actual benefits are greater.
· Your grandchildren inherit more (no taxes were due from the sale).
· The grandchildren receive a safer asset (income vs. growth) and
· A charity benefited greatly from your generosity.

As you can see, these benefits are not as great as those found by using a charitable remainder trust. It is for this reason, and the fact mentioned earlier that people want to enjoy income now and not later, that makes the remainder trust more popular.

Summary

A charitable lead trust is an effective estate-planning device under the right circumstances. By having the "lead," the charity has use of the proceeds from the donated property for a set number of years or until an event occurs. Once the period ends, the trust property reverts back to you and/or your family. Any connection between the property, charity, and you ends at this point.

Most people who have a charitable lead trust drafted do so in order to benefit the charity first and themselves (or heirs) second. But a charitable *remainder* trust can be of tremendous benefit to you, your beneficiaries, and the nonprofit organization. Both of these trusts allow an appreciated asset to be sold without there being any income-tax liability to the owner, her family, or trust.

Checklist of Things to Do

1. First decide if you want to benefit a charity.
2. Determine which asset(s) would be donated. Your first choice should be those items that have appreciated the greatest.
3. Contact your favorite charity or charities and see what plans or options they offer.
4. Find out if the charity uses a pooled account and if it will pay to have the trust drafted.
5. Keep detailed records of the trust, what went into it, and the proceeds obtained from the sale of the property in case something happens to you before the asset reverts back.

CHAPTER 24

COMMONLY ASKED QUESTIONS

What if I don't have a will?
If you die without a will, or the will you have is found to be invalid, your state of residence will determine whom your assets are distributed to and in what percentages. Whom the state decides to give your property to and whom you had in mind may be completely different. This scheme of distribution applies only to assets left outside of a trust.

Are assets distributed differently under a will than they are with a trust?
That depends. A living trust can be structured for distribution the same way a will can, but not necessarily vice versa. This is because a will, once the probate process ends, must immediately make distributions. A living trust can be structured so that distributions are delayed until certain events occur (e.g., when the child reaches age 35, when a granddaughter finishes college, etc.). In short, a living trust is much more flexible in this regard.

Why hasn't my attorney told me about a living trust?
There are three possible answers to this question. First, your lawyer may not be familiar enough with your estate to make such a recommendation. Small estates may be better off

with a "summary probate." Second, since probate fees can be so high, the attorney may not want to miss out on the opportunity of being able to probate your estate and collect hefty fees. Third, there is a good chance that your attorney is not well versed in estate planning. Living trusts represent a somewhat specialized area. A lawyer generally has a narrowly concentrated practice that may be in trial work, contracts, personal injury, etc.

What if my estate is not probated?
Assuming that all of your property was held in joint tenancy and/or you had a living trust, probate is not necessary. If this is not the case, probate can still be avoided, but this would be a mistake. The beneficiaries would not be able to sell any titled asset that included your name. The major purpose of probate is to establish clear title. Perfected title is necessary before an asset can be sold.

What should I do if I replace my will?
Nothing. When your living trust and pour-over will are executed, any former wills are automatically revoked. You do not need to contact the lawyer who drafted the previous will or trust.

Do I need a trust if I have an estate worth less than $600,000?
Yes. The fact that your estate may not be subject to estate taxes has nothing to do with probate. The majority of states require that your estate be probated if (1) you do not have a living trust, (2) any real estate or interest in real estate is greater than $10,000, or (3) the value of all assets exceeds $30,000 ($60,000 in some states, including California).

What happens to assets not included in my living trust?
With a few exceptions, assets left outside a living trust must go through probate. A pour-over will does not prevent probate; its purpose is to make sure that those assets not in the trust, once probated, will be "poured" into the trust and distributed and/or managed according to the terms of the trust.

Why isn't joint-tenancy property treated like community property?
In the 8 states that practice community-property laws, the law says that a husband and wife each has an equal interest in the assets acquired during their marriage. This equality also means that each spouse has the right to take his or her assets and title those assets in any way desired, including joint tenancy. This is usually a bad idea, but it is your constitutional right to make a good or poor decision.

How is title affected once a property is transferred to the living trust?
Even though the trust now formally "owns" those assets placed in it, title, for purposes of divorce or death, is not changed. Property owned individually, in joint tenancy, community property, etc., maintains its identity. Thus, if your single property is transferred into the living trust and there is a divorce later, all of that single property still belongs to its original owner, you.

Are living trusts something new?
No. Living trusts have been around for over 1,200 years. The first *known* living trust used

in the United States was written by Patrick Henry. Some of the more famous people who had living trusts include President Kennedy, Bing Crosby, and Malcolm Forbes.

What happens to my living trust if I move?
Living trusts are valid in all 50 states and in all commonwealth nations. You do not have to have your trust amended or changed in any way because you have moved to another state or to the United Kingdom.

Will Congress eliminate living trusts?
Not likely. Many members have a living trust. Your elected officials understand the benefits a trust can offer them and their families. And from a legal perspective, it may not be possible for the federal government to do away with trusts. The U.S. Constitution grants states certain powers that the federal government does not have. One of these is the right to create a "legal entity" such as a partnership, corporation, or living trust.

Probate and conservatorship fees are not taxed and do not generate any revenue for the federal government. Estate taxes generate revenue, but it is unlikely that Congress will change these rules either. The average net worth of a person in Congress is $1,000,000; the federal estate-tax exemption for a married couple is $1,200,000.

What is the most commonly used title for a living trust?
If the name of your family is Addams, the most appropriate way to name your living trust would be "The Addams Family Trust, dated May 6, 1992, Frank A. Addams and June R. Addams, co-trustees."

Does my trust need to be registered?
This is one of the greatest misconceptions about a living trust. The document does not have to be registered *anywhere*. On the death of the person(s) who made the trust, known as the trustor(s), the only person who has a legal right to even see the trust document is the successor trustee. The trust cannot even be

seen by a court subpoena! When the trustor(s) passes away, the IRS is given only the *name* of the trust, and this is done only for tax-identification purposes.

How long does it take to get a living trust?
A trust can be created as fast as the attorney and client can gather the appropriate information (lists of assets, names of beneficiaries and successor trustees, etc.). It is quite possible to have a trust completed, signed, notarized, and effective within a few days. Unless there is a "rush order," you should expect the process to take a couple of weeks.

Can single people have a living trust?
Yes. Whether you are married or not does not exclude you from the benefits of a living trust. In the case of unmarried couples, the trust might be titled something like "The Hollingsworth/Shore Trust, dated June 3, 1991, Jill Hollingsworth and Steven Shore, co-trustees."

How long can a living trust last?
According to the law, a living trust could last as long as it does not violate the "rules of perpetuity." This law states that the trust must cease within 21 years after the death of the last potential heir.

Will I pay two fees to have an A-B Trust?
Most attorneys will not charge you an extra fee for an A-B Trust. This is because the A-B Trust is only one trust while *both* spouses are alive. Only when one of the spouses dies does the distinction have any importance.

Can I leave my estate to an unborn child or grandchild?
A living trust allows you to leave part or all of your assets to someone who has not even been conceived yet. The language of the trust can be structured so that as children and/or grandchildren later appear, they are to be provided for. A clause could also be included to state that if there are no children living upon the death of the trustor(s),

the estate will go to designated contingent beneficiaries.

What happens if one of my children dies before I do?
Usually, the deceased child's share will pass on to that child's children, your grandchildren. If your deceased child had no children, his or her share would be divided among your other remaining children. Your trust document can be worded differently.

What happens if my son or daughter gets divorced?
If you want to ensure that any gift or bequest to your child remains that person's separate property, you could: (1) carefully explain to that child that he or she should not commingle such assets with those of the spouse, (2) have your trust provide income only for the child and, upon his or her death, the assets would pass to your grandchildren, or (3) have your living trust make distributions of principal over a number of years (i.e., one-third at age 25, one-third at age 30, and one-third at age 35). This would increase the chances that part or all of the assets would either go to the child once divorced or that the marriage had survived for a number of years.

What happens if my daughter remarries and/or changes her name?
Nothing. Your trust identified your children as your children; they are still your children whether they keep the family name or not.

Can I make gifts to charity through my living trust?
Absolutely. You may designate a charity, trust, partnership, corporation, group, or other entity to inherit part or all of your estate. After all, it is *your* estate.

What if I have a handicapped child or incapacitated parent?
Perhaps the only way to ensure care and/or financial security for such an individual is through a living trust. In such a situation, you

will want to name a successor trustee to manage their share of your estate after you have passed away. Language in a trust can be included so that the beneficiary's share cannot first be depleted as a prerequisite for government assistance.

How do I prevent certain people from inheriting anything?
In the case of children and spouses, former or current, it is best first to acknowledge and identify such a person(s) and then state you leave them nothing or perhaps one dollar. Others are excluded by simply not referring to them in your trust documents.

Can I have my pets taken care of?
Yes. The person you choose to "inherit" your pet(s) should be someone who likes such pets; ideally, someone who is familiar with and has shown affection toward your pet. A monetary incentive can also be added.

What is my spouse entitled to?
The rights of your spouse depend to a large degree on your state of residence at death as well as other states you may have lived in while you were both married. Separate-property states do not have the same rules as community-property states. Management of your estate is decided on while you are still competent and alive. Even though you may decide that your wife or husband is to be the successor trustee, the powers of management and/or distribution can be very limited.

What can my surviving spouse do in the case of an A-B Trust?
Your spouse is entitled to everything that goes into the A Trust. Which assets end up in the A Trust are largely determined by you and your spouse when the trust was drawn up or later amended *by the two of you.* By law, the survivor is also entitled to the income from the B Trust. How the assets in the B Trust are invested will determine the level of such income. Bonds throw off more income than a low-dividend-paying common stock or mu-

tual fund. Language can be added, while both of you are alive and competent, that gives the survivor access to principal in the B Trust. Keep in mind, what is good for the goose is good for the gander. *You* may end up being the surviving spouse. If so, your rights to the B Trust become just as open or restrictive as you *thought* your spouse's *were going to be.*

Can one spouse step down as trustee and later reclaim her or his position?
Yes. Either spouse, assuming both are co-trustees, has the freedom not to act as a trustee at any time for any reason. This same spouse has the right to name someone to act in his or her place and then later "fire" this person, without just cause or reason, and reassume the position as co-trustee, successor trustee (after your death), or simply name someone else. This answer assumes that your spouse is competent when such decisions are made and that the trust is not worded to exclude the right to change trustees.

Can I make changes to my trust?
While you are alive and competent, you can alter, amend, or even revoke your living trust at any time. If it is your separate trust, your spouse's permission or knowledge is not needed. Typically, in a married situation, most spouses are named as co-trustees. In such a situation both spouses' signature and consent would be required.

How often do I have to update my trust?
You never *have* to update your trust. However, a review once every few years is suggested. Such a review might alert you to the fact that one or more of your beneficiaries or successor trustees is no longer married to you or is a child or other relative that has fallen from your favor.

Can someone change my trust after I have died?
No. The right to alter, amend, or revoke your living trust ends when you die. The successor trustee has a fiduciary responsibility to carefully follow the instructions and powers given

in the trust. Acts that are contrary to the trust could result in the acting trustee's being faced with a personal lawsuit.

What happens if I get divorced?

Usually, one spouse will revoke his or her interest in the trust and have those assets re-titled accordingly. The other spouse is free to continue the revocable living trust by retaining his or her share of the property in the name of the trust. All of this can be accomplished by executing what is known as a Disclaimer of Trust Interest form.

What happens if I remarry?

It depends on your age and wishes. If you are older and have finished building your estate, it may be wiser for you to maintain exclusive control. If you are younger, you may wish to include your new spouse as a co-trustee and/or successor trustee. You and your new bride or groom could then both add to the trust. Each person's property can be identified as separate property in the event of a subsequent divorce or death.

When does my living trust end?

Since you created the trust, you can destroy it at any time. The quickest way to revoke a living trust is to retitle all of the assets in the trust back to the original owners. Excluding revocation, a trust ends once all of its assets have been distributed. No special court order or attorney is needed to end or dissolve your trust.

Who should read my trust?

If you are transferring assets from your name to the name of the trust, then the brokerage firm, bank, or other institution might want to ensure the validity of such a retitlement. This means that they will want to see that: (1) you are the trustor and trustee, (2) the trustee's powers include making such a transfer or transaction, and (3) that the trust is valid, as evidenced by the signature page. Thus, the firm or entity you deal with needs only to have a copy of these three pages; it is none of their business who your successor trustee(s) are, who you are leaving your estate to or the extent of your holdings.

How much should my children know about my trust?

Your children should know that you have a trust and the general intent of the document. It is not recommended that they read your trust. This makes it much easier for you to change beneficiaries and reapportion distributions or successor trustees without offending or hurting anyone's feelings. Never lose sight of the fact that a living trust, first and foremost, is for the benefit of its creator: you.

What should I tell my successor trustee?

Since this is the person(s) who will take over once you become incapacitated or die, the successor trustee should know where your estate-planning documents are located, including the original or working copy of the living trust. It also makes sense to tell the successor trustee the name, address, and telephone number of the lawyer who helped you put together your trust. This information will be helpful if the trust document cannot later be found. The successor trustee could then get a duplicate copy from the law firm.

Should my child be my successor trustee?

A child must be an adult before he or she can be a successor trustee. Most individuals and couples name their adult children as successor trustees. Your decision as to whether an adult child should be the successor trustee should depend upon (a) how financially knowledgeable that child is, (b) whether the child is too "wild" (i.e., would he or she be likely to invest the trust's assets in the most aggressive investments allowed by the trust document?), (c) where the child lives (e.g., is the person difficult to reach because she lives in another country or travels extensively?), and (d) the child's workload (e.g., a doctor in residency might not have the time to run your estate).

Should I have a successor trustee or successor co-trustees?

There are advantages to having one person act as successor trustee. First, it is easier and quicker for decisions to be made. Second, a specific person can be looked to in the event someone decides to challenge the trustee's actions. Third, there is usually one adult child who has a greater interest in investments than the other children. Finally, there may be a problem reaching an agreement. If you have two successor trustees, what will happen if they disagree on something?

There are also disadvantages. First, the feelings of the other children may be hurt if they were not also chosen. However, you may not care about this, since no one will know until after your death or incapacity. Second, if successor co-trustees are used, a group decision may be more balanced. Input from multiple sources is usually better than the perspective of one person. Furthermore, successor co-trustees tend to monitor each other, making it more likely that your trust will be handled in the way you wanted. The trust can be written so that if there is a disagreement, a majority vote rules. If there is an even split (i.e., one says yes, one says no, or two say yes and two say no), then the trust could provide for an outside mediator to make the final decision.

Is there some government or legal entity that monitors living trusts?

No. One of the advantages of a living trust is that the trustee or trustees need no approval from anyone else. No one is watching over you, your spouse, or your adult children who may later be trustees.

Are there restrictions on how my spouse uses the estate?

As co-trustees either one of you can buy, sell, encumber, transfer, or gift away any asset(s) within the trust. You and your spouse are limited only by restrictions found in the section of the trust entitled Powers of the Trustee. If the trust says that the trustee can do "anything," then it is almost limitless as to what can be done with the trust property. Some trusts set up by married couples require that both spouses must agree to any act before it is set into motion. After you are dead or unable to make decisions, your spouse is still limited by the powers set forth in the trust.

How do I file my taxes if I get a living trust?

In 1981, Congress changed the filing requirements for a living trust. If you have a *revocable* living trust (virtually all living trusts are *revocable* living trusts), then a trust tax return does not need to be filed and in fact would not be accepted by the IRS. *For tax purposes*, the IRS assumes that the trust is you and vice versa. Therefore, once the trust is set up, your tax return is filed the same way it was before. You use the same social security number(s) you did before. Income-tax liability does not increase or decrease when you have a revocable living trust. The tax rates are no different and there are no special exemptions, deductions, or credits with or without a living trust.

What is the difference between the unlimited marital deduction and the lifetime exclusion?

The unlimited marital deduction can be used only by a married couple. It allows you to gift, will, or transfer any amount you want, all at once or over an unlimited number of years, to your spouse without filing a gift-tax return or paying any gift or inheritance taxes now or in the future. The lifetime exclusion is something every individual gets, no matter what your marital status is, or your age. For a number of years this exclusion has been $600,000. This means that you can cumulatively leave, in your will or trust, up to $600,000 to others without any estate-tax liability.

What is the difference between the annual and lifetime exclusion?

Each of us is entitled to make gifts of up to $10,000 per year. The person making the gift is referred to as the donor; the person receiving the gift is the donee. A donor can make an unlimited number of gifts without filing a gift-tax return or paying any gift taxes to as many people as he or she desires as long as no gift or gifts exceed $10,000 *per donee* per calendar year. This means that if you have, say, 3 nieces and 2 nephews, you may gift *each one* of them up to $10,000 without filing a gift-tax return. You could do this every year until you die. If your spouse joins in, the limit for each donee is doubled to $20,000 per calendar year. There are no dollar limits if the money is used for medical or educational purposes. In such a case, make sure that the check is made out directly to the doctor, hospital, or school and not to the donee.

The lifetime exclusion is in addition to the annual exclusion. You are entitled to a $600,000 lifetime exclusion whether you have used the $10,000 annual exclusion zero times or for the past 80 years. The lifetime exclusion is reduced each time the annual exclusion is exceeded. As an example, if you were single and gave your brother $28,000 worth of property during the year, you would have to file a gift-tax return and reduce your lifetime exclusion by $18,000, the amount in excess of the *annual* exclusion.

What is the difference between the lifetime exclusion and equivalent exemption?
Once your net estate has been determined (assets minus liabilities, charitable gifts, and funeral costs) and amounts given to your spouse are also subtracted, you then have a net estate subject to tax. This amount is also referred to as the "net taxable estate." Whatever this figure is, it is matched against the appropriate row and column on the estate- and gift-tax rate schedule, and the tax liability is determined. This figure is then reduced by the federal estate-tax credit. Your lifetime exclusion of $600,000 is equivalent to a federal estate-tax credit of $192,900. Tax credits offset tax liability dollar for dollar. An example may be helpful to understand what this means.

Let us suppose that you left a gross estate valued at $1,000,000. After subtracting the outstanding mortgage on your home, final bills, and funeral expenses, your estate looked like this:

	$1,000,000	gross estate
−	150,000	remaining mortgage on home
−	6,000	personal debts and credit-card balances
−	4,000	final medical bills and funeral costs
	$840,000	net estate
−	240,000	inheritance to your spouse
	$600,000	net taxable estate

The taxes due on a $600,000 estate are $192,800. This figure would be offset, dollar for dollar, by the $192,800 credit. That means, in this example, there would be no taxes due.

The only way in which the $192,800 credit ($600,000 equivalent exemption) can be reduced is if you had made gifts in excess of $10,000 ($20,000 if you were married) per calendar year while you were alive. *If there are no estate taxes due*, then there is no practical difference between the tax credit and equivalent exemption.

How would a Q-TIP (A-B-C) Trust help me or my estate?
A Q-TIP, also referred to as an A-B-C Trust, does not benefit either you or your spouse. It can benefit your children or other beneficiaries. If you are married, have an estate that will have a projected net worth of at least $1,200,000, and want to have someone other than your spouse inherit part of your estate, then you should consider an A-B-C Trust. This type of living trust will give the surviving spouse the option of postponing taxes on the C Trust. The major reason people set up an A-B-C Trust is for tax-deferral purposes. Taxes on the C Trust are due when the *second* spouse dies. The C Trust can also be structured to preserve assets for the ultimate beneficiaries (your children, parents, brother, sister, etc.).

Can a living trust reduce my income taxes?
No. The position of the IRS is that as long as the trust is revocable, no gift has been made and the assets in the trust, for tax purposes, are still yours. You, and your spouse if you

are married, will continue to file a Form 1040 Individual Income Tax Return.

If you have an A-B Trust, upon the death of the first spouse, part or all of his or her share goes into the B Trust ("B" for below ground) and becomes irrevocable. Since it then becomes irrevocable, the IRS considers this part to now be a special tax entity. A separate trust-tax return for the B Trust would then have to be filed for each year this trust remains effective. Depending on the *size* of the B Trust, it is possible, but not likely, that income taxes could be lower.

Will I lose any tax breaks by placing some or all of my assets in a living trust?
No. Not even your property taxes are affected by changing title from your name to the name of the living trust. The interest portion of your mortgage payments is also still deductible. The $125,000 lifetime exclusion is still available if you sell your personal residence and at least one spouse is age 55 or older. Your home will not be reappraised for property-tax purposes. Your social security benefits are not reduced either.

Can I deduct the cost of having a living trust prepared?
Yes, keeping certain restrictions in mind. First, the cost of the pour-over will must first be subtracted. Second, as an "estate-planning expense" this cost is categorized as a "miscellaneous expense." All such miscellaneous expenses (accounting fees, financial planning costs, etc.) for the year need to be added up. If they exceed 2% of your adjusted gross income, *then* that excess amount over 2% can be deducted.

How much will it cost to transfer title of my assets to that of the trust?
With the exception of real estate, there should be no cost in retitling assets into the name of the trust. Real-estate interests can be recorded for approximately $50 per deed. All other assets can be transferred by letter or form, free of charge.

Who transfers my assets into the name of the trust?
You can make all of the changes yourself. In the case of real estate, you should probably have someone recommended by your attorney make the title change(s). The reconveyance of real-estate deeds can be somewhat confusing to anyone who has not had previous experience in this area.

Can I take things out of the trust?
Yes. Unless you are mentally incapacitated, you can add or withdraw (retitle, sell, transfer, assign, encumber, or gift) whatever you like from the trust. If you are married and your spouse is the co-trustee, either spouse can make the same additions or deletions without telling the other spouse.

What should I do with the proceeds from the sale of a house?
If you sell a house or other valuable asset, the proceeds should be placed in an account that is titled in the name of your living trust. Such an account might be a checking, CD, money-market fund, or brokerage account. The subsequent purchase of another home, piece of real estate, stock, bond, mutual fund, etc., can also be made under the name of the trust.

Once set up, how do I make purchases in the name of the trust?
Buying personal property or real estate is easy. Instead of taking title to that house, expensive automobile, boat, or mobile home as "Mary Johnson," you will take title as "Mary Johnson, trustee of the Mary Johnson Trust, dated 9/4/92."

What shouldn't be in my trust?
Checking accounts and automobiles that will never exceed $30,000 should be kept out of the trust. The only reason you may not want to retitle these assets in the name of the trust is that some vendors are still unaware of a living trust and may not accept your check if it is in the name of the trust. There is no need to register a car worth less than $30,000 in the

name of the trust since it is exempt from probate under the jurisdiction of the motor vehicle code.

Personal property, including cars worth less than $30,000, may still be considered worthy candidates for your trust in order to ensure that they are still managed and/or distributed according to your wishes.

Do my assets have to be appraised when they are placed in the trust?
No. This would not accomplish anything. When you die, all property should be revalued for estate-tax purposes and so that there will be a step-up in valuation for income-tax purposes (if property is later sold).

Should my personal effects, furniture, and art be included?
Yes. Even though these items are not formally titled, they should still be listed on an assignment form, which is part of your trust package. This listing will avoid future arguments as to who should inherit or manage such assets. Your safe-deposit box should also be titled under the name of the trust. There is always the chance that, when combined, your untitled personal property, furniture, and contents of your safe-deposit box will exceed $30,000. If this is the case, then the assignment form is necessary to ensure that such items will not go through the probate court.

Can I use trust assets as collateral for a loan?
Yes. In such a situation you would be pledging specific assets, not the living trust itself.

Should my life insurance be part of the trust?
Insurance proceeds are not probated unless you and the beneficiary die simultaneously. You cannot insure a living trust, but you should list the trust as the beneficiary of all life-insurance policies. Including your life-insurance policy(s) also makes future changes easier. When you want to change a beneficiary, you will need to change only one document, the trust. The only way to make sure that the beneficiary(s) does not receive the insurance proceeds all at once is through a living trust.

Your trust can provide for the immediate inheritance of any insurance policy or any asset, but you may want the distributions staggered over a number of years (e.g., one-third to John when he reaches age 30, one-third when he reaches age 40, and the final third when he becomes 50) or upon the completion of an event (e.g., Mary is to get one-half of her inheritance when she receives her undergraduate degree and the other half when she buys a house).

Should my retirement accounts be in my trust?
No. A living trust cannot be the owner of any retirement account, including IRAs, Keoghs, pension plans, 401(k)s, 403(b)s, etc. The trust can be the beneficiary or contingent beneficiary, however. As beneficiary, your retirement accounts could then be managed and/or distributed according to your wishes. By naming the trust as the *primary* beneficiary of a retirement account, your spouse will not have the option of rolling over the proceeds into another retirement plan when you die. Therefore, if you are married, you should probably name your wife or husband as primary beneficiary and the trust as contingent beneficiary.

Will assets in a revocable living trust be exempt from lawsuits?
No. However, if you feel that at the death of either you or your spouse there might be a lawsuit filed (you are sued by a customer, client, partner, etc.), then leaving some assets outside of the trust could be beneficial since it would trigger a probate. Even though one of the objectives of a living trust is to *avoid* probate, this is the one time when it might be wise to have *part* of your estate probated.

Lawsuits can be long and expensive. By having the matter resolved in the probate court after your death, you accomplish the following: (1) reduce court and legal costs, since the suit will most likely be resolved within four months and without a jury, and (2) put a time cap on when a suit can be brought against your estate. Claims against the estate (you) must be formally made within a few months after notice has been given of the probate. If this is not done, prospective litigants are out of luck.

Do assets have to be sold in order to make distributions?
No. Ideally, you do not want your successor trustee(s) to sell assets. The reason for this is that you might want certain sound investments to continue and want to avoid any selling fee or commission.

After I die, how long will it take to settle my estate?
This calls for a two-part answer. First, assets *in the trust* can be distributed to their intended beneficiaries by simply having certified copies of the death certificate and a copy of the trust. There is no special waiting period. Your estate could literally be distributed within a couple of days after your death. The actual settlement of your estate is a different matter. The executor of your estate will need to make sure that a final income-tax return is filed and that no estate taxes are due.

How large should my estate be before I get a living trust?
All gross *estates* over $60,000 are subject to probate. The key word here is "gross." If you have a house that has a fair market value of $120,000 and it has an outstanding mortgage of $115,000, your estate may go through probate. A gross estate does not consider any outstanding loans, mortgages, or other encumbrances. Although it may not sound fair, even though there is only $5,000 of equity in this particular example, the probate fee in many states would exceed $5,000, leaving your heirs with a "negative estate."

Can I be the trustor, trustee, and beneficiary of my trust?
Yes. In such a case, you will need to name a successor trustee and contingent beneficiary.

Without such alternates, who will manage your affairs if you become incapacitated or die? Furthermore, who will inherit your portfolio after you die?

Does my spouse, former or current, have to be the co-trustee?
No. As far as your own assets are concerned, you do not have to list anyone you do not want to as trustee, co-trustee, successor trustee, or beneficiary. Jointly owned property does not require co-trustees either. Your spouse can agree to not be included in the trust or later drop his or her name from the document.

What are the disadvantages of a revocable living trust?
If you take out a mortgage or refinance any property, including your personal residence, many lenders will require that the property be titled under an individual or couple's name. Once the financing is in place, the property can be legally titled into (or back into) the name of the trust.

The second disadvantage of a living trust has already been discussed: claims or lawsuits filed after your death. Probate limits such claims to 4 months after the executor has published notice of your death.

The third disadvantage of a living trust is if you have an A-B or A-B-C Trust. After the death of the first spouse, when the assets have been titled under the name of the B, or B and C, Trusts, separate tax returns must be filed for these "secondary" trusts. The IRS considers the B and C Trusts to be taxpaying entities, separate from the surviving spouse. The surviving spouse would continue to file income taxes, using Form 1040. The B Trust would file a Form 1041. A separate set of books must be kept for each trust after the death of the first spouse: one set for the survivor (a regular tax return is filed for this A Trust), one for the B Trust, and one for the C Trust (if an A-B-C Trust was set up and funded). Most people do not need an A-B or A-B-C Trust. They are designed for married couples with estates in excess of $1,200,000.

Can I include jointly owned properties as part of my trust?
Yes. Your share of property that is partially owned by another co-owner can be placed in your living trust, whether that owner is a joint tenant, partnership, corporation, or other trust.

Can a person have more than one trust?
Yes, although it is not common. If so desired, a spouse could have a living trust for his or her separate property and another trust with their mate for property owned jointly.

What is separate property?
Anything you acquired before you were married or after you are legally separated is considered to be separate property. Income or proceeds from the sale of such assets are also generally separate property. What may surprise you is that if you receive an inheritance or gift while you are married, that item is also separate property if that was the donor's intent. Separate property can become community or jointly owned property only by the actions of its owner.

As an example, if you owned some separate property, sold it, and then placed the proceeds in a joint checking, savings, or brokerage-firm account, that could be interpreted to mean that you intended to make a gift to the "community." As the owner of separate property, you are always free to gift it to your spouse at any time. Certain items can be gifted orally, no written conveyance is necessary.

What is community property?
If you live in one of the 8 states that recognize community property, then this question-and-answer is important to you. Property acquired during marriage is community property. "Property" in this context includes your salary, contributions to a retirement plan, proceeds from the sale of community assets, and all income, interest, and dividends generated from community assets. There are two exceptions to this definition: (1) income or proceeds from separate property to the extent that "community efforts" were not used for the special management of that property and (2) if one spouse wishes to gift his or her share of a community-property asset to the other spouse as separate property.

What is "basis"?
"Basis" is important to know if you plan to trade, sell, or inherit an asset. For most assets, it is the original cost of the item, including any commission or fee. Basis can be adjusted upward or downward. It will increase if the asset is added to (a room addition, spending money to fix up an antique car, etc.). Basis can also be decreased, but only for those items that can be depreciated (buildings, other than your personal residence, office equipment, etc.). These adjustments are made to determine the taxable gain or loss of the property when it is sold or exchanged. The capital gain, or loss, is calculated by taking the basis and subtracting it from the sales price, less certain adjustments (selling costs, fix-up expenses, brokerage fees, etc.).

What is a stepped-up basis?
A step-up in basis occurs when one of the property's owners dies. The surviving owner's interest is given a stepped-up basis. This reduces or eliminates any subsequent tax on the gain; it also increases the likelihood of loss *for tax purposes.* The capital gain or loss is then determined by this new basis. Community property is given a 100% step-up in basis when either spouse dies, but only a 100% step-up on the *decedent's* share in the case of property held in joint tenancy (even though the co-owners are husband and wife). The amount a piece of property is stepped up depends on how it was titled at death.

If you have an A-B or A-B-C Trust, there is a step-up in basis for the B (and C) Trust when the surviving spouse dies. The A Trust received a step-up when the first spouse died, so it is not entitled to a second increase when the survivor dies.

How can I change property from joint tenancy to community property?
There are two conditions that must be met before this can be done: (a) you must be married to the co-owner and (b) you must live in a community-property state. If both criteria have been met, then there are three ways to make the change: (1) change the title on the property from joint tenancy (jtwros) to community property (c/p)—this can be accomplished easily by letter or form signed by both owners, (2) have your executor petition the court to set aside the joint tenancy (unfortunately, this would also trigger a probate), or (3) put the property in a living trust that includes a community-property agreement— this is the best of both worlds: probate avoidance and a 100% step-up in basis.

What can single people do about a step-up in basis?
When a single person dies, all of his or her property automatically gets a 100% step-up in basis for estate-tax and, later, income-tax purposes. Property owned by a single person in joint tenancy will result in *one-half* of the property getting a step-up in basis upon the death of either co-owner.

Are assets in my revocable living trust protected from creditors?
No. A living trust can avoid probate, conservatorship, and a court-appointed guardianship. It can eliminate or lower estate taxes. But it will not help you when it comes to creditors. If creditor protection is a concern, you should look into setting up a family partnership or having an irrevocable trust.

How will a divorce affect a living trust?
A living trust will not help or hurt you in a divorce; how title is held inside the trust will. Property retains its separate, joint-tenancy or community-property status, even inside a living trust.

Can a couple living together have just one living trust?
Yes. You do not even have to be living with the other person. Your only limitation is that you cannot change separate or joint-tenancy property into community property.

Will signing a new will revoke my trust?
No. A will, new or otherwise, will have no impact on assets in a living trust. A new will revokes the pour-over will in most cases, but this is just one part of your estate plan.

If I have a will, do I need a living trust?
Yes. A will does nothing to help your estate avoid probate, conservatorship, or a court-imposed guardianship. It will not help you minimize or eliminate estate taxes either.

If I have a living trust, do I need a will?
Yes. No matter how careful you are, there is a strong likelihood that something will not be titled in the name of the trust. A pour-over will is needed to make sure that those assets left outside the trust will be "poured into" the trust after your death. A will is also the proper place to name a guardian for any minor or incapacitated children.

Does a will control the inheritance of property in joint tenancy?
No. No matter how specific your will is in naming or describing the asset and whom it is to go to, property held as automatically passes to the surviving owner(s). If all parties agree, there is a procedure to set aside a joint tenancy. Such a procedure would take time, cost some money, and possibly subject the asset to probate joint tenancy.

Does a will decide who gets my life insurance or retirement accounts?
No. These types of assets have designated beneficiaries written into the policy or plan. The only way a will can dictate who gets the

proceeds from your insurance or retirement plan is if you name your estate as the beneficiary.

Does a will decide who gets some or all of the assets in my estate?
A will designates your beneficiaries and what they are entitled to only if you do not have a living trust that includes a pour-over will.

What is an unfunded living trust?
A living trust that is not funded is also known as "invalid." Some states allow unfunded trusts, others do not. In order to make sure that your trust is legal and valid, transfer at least one asset into the name of the trust. This is often done by the attorney drafting the trust agreement. This way, at least one of your assets will avoid probate.

What are the ongoing fees associated with a living trust?
None. The only reason to change your trust is if you want to amend the powers of the trustee or replace beneficiaries. Trust law and estate-tax rates change very infrequently. You do not have to pay the state or federal government, the courts, or your attorney any type of annual fee.

Who keeps a record of what goes on in the trust?
The trustee, who will probably be you while you are alive and competent, keeps record of any transactions that go on in the trust. There are no special reporting requirements to the IRS, successor trustee(s) or beneficiary(s).

What is the difference between a co-trustee and a successor trustee?
A successor trustee steps in once *both* co-trustees either die or become incapacitated. On the other hand, a co-trustee has equal power with you. After your death, the co-trustee will have complete power alone unless a provision has been added to have a successor co-trustee take your place.

What should I do if my children do not get along with each other?
If your children appear to continually fight or dislike each other, you should strongly consider naming just one of them as the successor trustee or selecting an independent, such as a bank or financial planner, as successor trustee.

Can a living trust be challenged in court, just like a will?
Yes, but a successful challenge is not nearly as likely. Your trust was drawn up and acted upon while you were alive and competent. Chances are that the trustor, you (the person who created the trust), lived with the trust a number of years before death or alleged incapacity. Courts are not likely to go along with any challenge under such circumstances. A will, on the other hand, may have been drawn up under duress or when the decedent was in poor mental health. However, successful challenges of a will are not very common either.

An estate or person can be sued by anyone for just about anything. A *successful* suit is another matter. As an example, a court will not set aside a will or trust simply because a person is unable to identify a friend or family member.

A more important point needs to be added when talking about a trust being challenged. It is cost-effective for a will to be challenged during probate; in fact, hiring counsel may not even be necessary. A living trust is a different matter. Since there is usually no probate proceeding, a claimant would have to go through "regular channels" to contest a trust, assuming he or she found out about your death to begin with. Furthermore, the costs could be prohibitive for the person bringing the suit. The person would first have to identify the assets in the trust, a difficult task since, unlike a will, this information is not public and a cause of action would have to be brought against each beneficiary who had received contested property.

Can a trust protect unborn children?
Yes. It is common to include language in the trust that after both spouses have died, all remaining assets will be divided among children then living. This would include children who had not been conceived at the time the trust was executed. A subsequent birth, while either parent was still alive, would not even require an amendment or alteration to the trust.

What happens if one of my children dies before I do?
Living trusts can take this possibility into account and provide for distribution upon your death in one of two ways. The trust can be worded so that assets are equally distributed among the remaining beneficiaries (or children). Or it can include a provision calling for the deceased child's portion to go to your grandchildren.

How do I disinherit someone?
Your pour-over will can mention your children and state the names of those who are to be disinherited. Failure to include the name of the child in the will or trust might indicate to the court that you simply forgot to name the child, and that child could be successful in challenging the will and living trust. As a backup measure, some attorneys suggest that you send a handwritten note to your attorney, stating why you are disinheriting someone who is "the natural object of your bounty."

How old should someone be before he or she considers having a trust?
Once someone becomes an adult, the decision of having a living trust should depend on the size of the estate and/or if this person is married and has children. Most adults should have a living trust.

When are estate taxes payable?
Assuming there is an estate-tax liability, Uncle Sam wants his money within 9 months from the date of death. The IRS does not care that a special asset or piece of property must be sold to satisfy taxes, nor do they care that the stock, art, or real-estate market happens to be depressed when the "forced" sale occurs.

An estate-tax return, Form 706, is filed within 9 months of death if the net estate is worth more than $600,000. This figure jumps to $1,200,000 if you are married and property is evenly divided between the two spouses.

Does a living trust increase my chances of an audit?
No. While you are alive the IRS is not aware that you have a living trust, nor do they care. After the death of the first spouse, the IRS treats an estate in trust just as if no trust existed. Chances of an audit greatly increase at death, but this has nothing to do with having a will or living trust.

Can the trust be changed by the successor trustee or co-trustee?
Your co-trustee can change the trust only if you agree. A successor trustee can never make changes to your trust.

What happens if one co-trustor wants to change the trust but the other co-trustor does not?
If both trust makers (co-trustors) do not completely agree to the change, the living trust will remain unchanged. Either co-trustor (if you are married, then this would probably be you or your spouse) can revoke the *entire* living trust at any time without the consent or knowledge of the other co-trustor.

If I replace my old will or trust, is there anything special I must do?
No. In order to avoid future confusion, it would be a good idea to destroy all copies and originals of the old will and/or trust.

What happens if I move?
Nothing. Your living trust is recognized in all 50 states and by the District of Columbia.

Can property located outside of my state of residency be included?
Yes. The only requirement you face will be to comply with that state's transfer requirements. Personal property located in another state is rarely a problem; however, you may wish to hire an attorney to retitle real estate located in another state.

What is a "community property set aside"?
This is an alternative to a normal probate proceeding. It can be used only by a married couple living in a community-property state. It is not a substitute for a living trust.

If I own my house in joint tenancy, can the other joint tenant move in?
Yes. The joint tenant—your spouse, ex-spouse, child, relative, or friend—is a co-owner and has just as much right as you do to occupy the property. It is unimportant that you were the original or former sole owner. The joint tenant can also sell his or her interest to anyone else without your permission or knowledge. Creditors of a joint tenant can place liens against the property.

Why is joint tenancy usually only a postponement of probate?
Property held in joint tenancy will not be subjected to probate. However, when the final owner of the property dies, the asset will be subject to probate. The only way to ensure that a probate would not occur at this point would be for the survivor to add a new joint owner to the property title before death.

How are stocks, bonds, mutual funds, and partnership interests changed?
All positions held at your brokerage firm, what is referred to as "street name," can be placed in the name of the trust by filling out and signing a new account form.

Does a will help you avoid probate?
No. A will may be an "invitation" to probate. How assets are titled determines if there will be a probate and the extent of such proceedings.

What is an inter vivos trust?
Technically, this is a trust that is created during your lifetime. This is in sharp contrast to a testamentary trust, which becomes effective only upon death. A *testamentary* trust does not avoid probate. Living trusts are a form of inter vivos trust.

What is a "durable power of attorney for health care"?
This document is separate from your living trust but is often included as part of a trust *package*. This power appoints another person to make health-care decisions for you if you are unable, owing either to physical or mental limitations. The person you name makes all medical decisions and has access to your medical records, subject to the limitations that were set down by you and your attorney when the document was drafted and signed. Another reason to include such a document as part of your estate planning is to avoid possible burdens on family or friends. Any adult who is mentally competent can obtain a durable power of attorney for health care.

What is the difference between a power of attorney and a durable power of attorney?
There is only one difference between these two powers: a durable power remains in effect even if the maker becomes incapacitated; a regular power becomes void under such an occurrence. Either type of power can be revoked or amended by its maker.

What is a "durable general power of attorney"?
This document is also commonly found as part of a trust package. It applies to all non-health-care decisions. People often grant this power to the same person named under the durable power of attorney for health care. This type of power does not have to be renewed or acknowledged periodically.

What happens to the 7-year time limit if I become incapacitated?
The durable power of attorney for health care remains intact until capacity is regained. Once the person becomes legally competent again, assuming that 7 years have now lapsed since the document was originally signed, it lapses immediately and a new one should be signed. In some respects, the incapacity freezes the 7-year clock.

What effect does a durable power carry while I am still competent and able to speak?
None. If you are competent and speak for yourself, no one is able to make health-care decisions for you without your consent. A durable power can be revoked in writing or orally by contacting the person you gave the power to or the health-care provider.

Are there any health-care rights I cannot waive or relinquish?
Yes. By law, the person you select to make health-care decisions cannot (a) have you committed to or placed in a mental hospital, (b) require convulsive treatment, (c) request sterilization, (d) force you to have an abortion, or (e) ask for neurosurgery.

What about the use of life-sustaining equipment and a durable power?
Your durable power of attorney for health care can provide for the appointed person to "have the plug pulled," even though that will end your life. This would be the case only if (1) it was included within the scope of the power, (2) your doctors felt that the situation was irreversible or that there was an incurable disease or terminal condition, and (3) there was no reasonable hope of long-term recovery or survival.

Does the durable power of attorney for health care need to be notarized?
This power must either be notarized or signed by two people you know and who were present when you originally signed the document.

The person you give the power to does not qualify to be one of the witnesses.

Is there a final probate when my trust is dissolved?
No. After all of the assets named in the trust are distributed, the living trust just ceases to exist. No formal filings, meetings with an attorney, or court appearances are needed.

In some states probate fees are negotiable. Do I still need a trust?
Yes. The fact that you live in a state where such fees are negotiable is unimportant. "Negotiable" may end up meaning that your estate will pay more than one settled in a state with a statutory fee schedule. Fees are just one of the several benefits afforded by a living trust.

How do I find a qualified attorney to prepare my living trust?
Your living-trust package, along with an ancillary documents, should be prepared by someone who is experienced in this particular area. An estate-planning specialist may also be less expensive. A large portion of a living trust is already stored in your attorney's word processor. This information may have been specially tailored and written by your lawyer or she may have purchased a living-trust software package. In either case, this is documentation they are familiar with; this intimacy should translate into a time-and-cost-saver for you.

Are all trusts the same?
No. Conceptually, all living trusts generally work the same; the actual documents will vary as to language, ease of understanding, and powers.

When should I get a living trust?
You should make an appointment to see an estate-planning attorney or attend a living-trust seminar as soon as possible. There is no advantage to waiting. If you become mentally incapacitated, then you will not be able to set up a trust. You never know when you might

be in an auto accident, plane crash, or have a stroke.

Is my estate plan complete once I have a living trust?
No. There are several things you can do to better your estate; a living trust is just one of them. You should also consider the ancillary documents that are offered, usually at no additional charge, with a living trust; documents such as a pour-over will, durable power of attorney for health care, community-property agreement (if you are married and living in a community property state), a durable general power of attorney, and a living will. For larger estates that include life insurance, an irrevocable life-insurance trust should also be examined.

Estate planning can be an extensive undertaking, but it is well worth the effort. A complete estate plan includes counsel from a life-and-disability-insurance specialist and a financial planner. It is also a good idea to get investment suggestions from your stockbroker.

Do FDIC and SIPC insure accounts listed in the name of a trust?
Yes. FDIC, which insures accounts for up to $100,000, also protects living-trust accounts. The same thing is true with SIPC. The Securities Investor Protection Corporation (SIPC) insures securities accounts for up to $500,000 (up to $100,000 of which can be in cash). Losses due to fraud, negligence, theft, forgery, and embezzlement are protected.

If I name someone else as trustee, do I lose control?
While you are competent, you can hire and fire trustees at any time without reason or justification. This includes getting rid of or substituting family members, a corporate trustee, or bank. After all, it is *your* revocable living trust.

When should my living trust be updated?
It is a good idea to at least review your trust, and probably change it anytime you or your

family experience: (a) a marriage, (b) divorce, (c) separation, (d) death, (e) incapacity, (f) birth, or (g) adoption. If a successor trustee or guardian for a minor child can no longer fill such a role, the person should be replaced. In short, the trust should be changed anytime it no longer does what you want.

Do I need to change my trust if I buy or sell any property?
No. Trust property that is sold is signed off by the trustee(s), you. Purchases made after the trust has been established are done in the name of the trust.

Where should I keep my living trust?
Your attorney should provide you with two copies of your trust, the original and a working copy. The original should be placed in a safe-deposit box or some other place you feel is secure. The "working copy" should be kept in a convenient place so that it can be referred to as needed.

Should burial instructions be included as part of the trust?
No. Things such as burial requests, organ donations, and hopes should not clutter up your trust document. Instead, list these desires on a separate piece of paper. These instructions can then be placed in your living trust *binder.*

Who decides if I later become physically or mentally incapable?
You do when the trust is drawn up. Trust language that you must agree to and sign specifies how many doctors and what kind of doctors need to examine and verify your capacity. You may also list doctors by name, thereby decreasing the chances of some kind of conspiracy.

My spouse lives in a nursing home. Can I set up a trust for both of us?
Yes. As long as your spouse is capable of handling his or her own affairs, you can have him or her join you in a standard trust, A-B

Trust, or A-B-C Trust. If your spouse is incompetent, then you should still look into a living trust for *your* property.

My spouse is not a U.S. citizen. Can we still have a trust?
Yes. The marital deduction may be limited unless you include a "qualified domestic trust," but every other benefit of a living trust and any other ancillary documents remain intact.

Should I use an A-B Trust if I am not married?
Probably Not. An A-B Trust uses the marital deduction as its primary benefit. This deduction is not available to unmarried couples. An A-B Trust would be useful to an unmarried couple for purposes other than estate-tax savings (e.g., to protect the ultimate beneficiaries such as children).

A living trust sounds too good to be true. What's the catch?
There are no catches; and yes, they are as good as they sound. You may experience some minor difficulties in getting property retitled, and you will pay your attorney a fee for setting up the trust. However, this is minor in comparison to the benefits received; benefits that can continue long after you are dead. Keep in mind that you can have someone else retitle your properties, often at no expense. The attorneys' costs may end up being tax deductible.

APPENDIX A

IRS PUBLICATIONS

929	Tax Rules for Children and Dependents
936	Limits on Home Mortgage Interest Deduction
1048	Filing Requirements for Employee Benefit Plans
1041	U.S. Fiduciary Income Tax Return • Schedule D—Capital Gains and Losses • Schedule J—Trust Allocation of an Accumulation Distribution • Schedule K-1—Beneficiary's Share of Income, Deductions, Credits, etc.
1098	Mortgage Interest Statement
1099-B	Statement for Recipients of Proceeds from Broker and Barter Exchange Transactions
1099-DIV	Statement for Recipients of Dividends and Distributions
1099INT	Statement for Recipients of Interest Income
1099MISC	Statement for Recipients of Miscellaneous Income
1099R	Statement for Recipients of Total Distributions From Profit-Sharing, Retirement Plans, Individual Retirement Arrangements, Insurance Contracts, etc.
1099S	Statement for Recipients of Proceeds From Real Estate Transactions
1120	Income Tax Return, S Corporation

APPENDIX B

FEDERAL INCOME-TAX FORMS

Form Number	Title
706	United States Estate Tax Return
709	United States Gift Tax Return
709A	U.S. Short Form Gift Tax Return
1040	U.S. Individual Income Tax Return • Schedule A—Itemized Deductions • Schedule B—Interest and Dividend Income • Schedule C—Profit (Loss) From Business or Profession (Sole Proprietorship) • Schedule D—Capital Gains and Losses • Schedule E—Supplemental Income Schedule • Schedule F—Farm Income and Expenses • Schedule R—Credit for the Elderly and the Permanently and Totally Disabled • Schedule SE—Computation of Social Security Self-Employment Tax
1040A	U.S. Individual Income Tax Return (Short Form)
1040ES	Payment-Voucher for Estimated Tax by Individuals
1040EZ	U.S. Income Tax Return (Short Form for Single Filers With No Dependents)
1040X	Amended U.S. Individual Income Tax Return • Schedule D—Capital Gains and Losses • Schedule K-1—Shareholder's Share of Undistributed Taxable Income, etc.
1310	Statement of Person Claiming Refund Due to a Deceased Taxpayer
2106	Employee Business Expenses
2119	Sale or Exchange of Personal Residence
2120	Underpayment of Estimated Tax by Individuals
2439	Notice to Shareholder of Undistributed Long-Term Capital Gains
2440	Disability Income Exclusion

2441	Credit for Child Care and Dependent Care Expenses
2688	Application for Extension of Time to File
2848	Power of Attorney and Declaration of Representative
3468	Computation of Investment Credit
3559	Alimony or Separate Maintenance Statement
3903	Moving Expenses Adjustment
4137	Computation of Social Security Tax on Unreported Tax Income
4469	Computation of Excess Medicare Tax Credit
4562	Depreciation
4684	Casualties and Thefts
4768	Application for Extension of Time to File U.S. Estate Tax Return and/or Pay Estate Tax
4782	Employee Moving Expense Information
4797	Supplemental Schedule of Gains and Losses
4868	Automatic Extension to File
4952	Investment Interest Expense Deduction
4970	Tax on Accumulation Distribution of Trusts
4972	Special Ten-Year Averaging Method
5329	Return for Individual Retirement Arrangement Taxes
5498	Individual Retirement Arrangement Information
5544	Multiple Recipient Special Ten-Year Averaging
5695	Residential Energy Credits
5884	Job Credit (and WIN Credit Carry-Over)
6251	Alternative Minimum Tax Computation
6252	Computations of Installment Sale Income
8283	Noncash Charitable Contributions
8332	Release of Claim to Exemption for Child of Divorced or Separated Parents
8582	Passive Activity Loss Limitations
8598	Home Mortgage Interest
8606	Nondeductible IRA Contributions, IRA Basis, and Nontaxable IRA Distributions
8615	Computation of Tax for Children Under Age 14 Who Have Investment Income of More than $1,000
8801	Credit for Prior Year Minimum Tax
SSA-1099	Social Security Benefit Statement
W-2	Wage and Tax Statement
W-2c	Statement of Corrected Income and Tax Amounts
W-2P	Statement for Recipients of Annuities, Pensions, Retired Pay, or IRA Payments
W-3	Transmittal of Income and Tax Amounts
W-4	Employee's Withholding Allowance Certificate
W-4P	Withholding Certificate for Pension or Annuity Payments

APPENDIX C

MAILING ADDRESSES FOR TAX RETURNS

Your Location	Mailing Address
Florida, Georgia, South Carolina	Atlanta, GA 39901
New Jersey, New York (New York City and counties of Nassau, Rockland, Suffolk, and Westchester)	Holtsville, NY 00501
Connecticut, Maine, Massachusetts, New Hampshire, New York (all other counties), Rhode Island, Vermont	Andover MA 05501
Illinois, Iowa, Minnesota, Missouri, Wisconsin	Kansas City, MO 64999
Delaware, District of Columbia, Maryland, Pennsylvania, Virginia	Philadelphia, PA 19255
Indiana, Kentucky, Michigan, Ohio, West Virginia	Cincinnati, OH 45999
Kansas, New Mexico, Oklahoma, Texas	Austin, TX 73301
Alaska, Arizona, California (counties of Alpine, Amaor, Butte, Calaveras, Colusa, Contra Costa, Del Norte, El Corado, Glenn, Humboldt, Lake, Lassen, Marin, Mendocino, Modoc, Napa, Nevada, Placer Plumas, Sacramento, San Joaquin, Shasta, Sierra, Siskiyou, Solano, Sonoma, Sutter, Tehema, Trinity, Yolo, and Yuba), Colorado, Idaho, Montana, Nebraska, Nevada, North Dakota, Oregon, South Dakota, Utah, Washington, Wyoming	Ogden, UT 84201
California (all other counties), Hawaii	Fresno, CA 93888
Alabama, Arkansas, Louisiana, Mississippi, North Carolina, Tennessee	Memphis, TN 38501
Foreign country: U.S. citizens and those filing form 2555 or form 4563, even if you have an A.P.O. or F.P.O. address	Philadelphia, PA 19255

A.P.O. or F.P.O. address of:

Miami—Atlanta, GA 39901
New York—Holtsville, NY 00501
San Francisco—Fresno, CA 93888
Seattle—Ogden, UT 84201

APPENDIX D

GIFT AND ESTATE PUBLICATIONS AND FORMS

Publication Number	Title
448	Federal Estate and Gift Taxes
525	Taxable and Nontaxable Income
559	Tax Information for Survivors, Executors, and Administrators
721	Comprehensive Tax Guide to U.S. Civil Service Retirement Benefits
904	Interrelated Computations for Estate and Gift Taxes

Estate and Gift-Tax Return Forms

Form Number	Title
706	U.S. Estate and Generation-Skipping Transfer Tax Return
706-A	U.S. Additional Estate Tax Return
706-B	Generation-Skipping Transfer Tax Return
706CE	Certification of Payment of Foreign Death Tax
706NA	Federal Estate (and Generation-Skipping Transfer) Tax Return for Estate of Nonresident Alien
709	U.S. Gift (and Generation-Skipping Transfer) Tax Return
709-A	U.S. Short Form Gift Tax Return
712	Life Insurance Statement
1041	U.S. Fiduciary Income Tax Return
4351	Interest Computation—Estate Tax Deficiency on Installment Basis

4768	Application for Extension of Time to File U.S. Estate Tax Return and/or Pay Estate Tax
4808	Computation of Credit for Gift Tax (No Credit Allowed for Gifts Made after 12/31/76)
6180	Line Adjustment—Estate Tax

WHAT THE EXECUTOR AND SUCCESSOR TRUSTEE SHOULD DO AT DEATH

YOUR WILL NAMES an executor. This is the person who will handle certain administrative matters. The executor does not serve the same function as your successor trustee. Normally, the executor's responsibilities are nonfinancial. The executor distributes those assets not included in your trust or pour-over will. The executor and the successor trustee are often the same person. If you have not named an executor in your will, the court names one for you. A court-appointed executor is known as an administrator. Listed below are what the executor should do upon someone's death. If there is a living trust, then the successor trustee and executor can share some of these duties.

1. Review the estate-planning documents. Make a note of any funeral instructions or requests to make anatomical gifts.
2. Call the mortuary and make funeral and burial arrangements.
3. Telephone immediate family members, close friends, and the decedent's employer.
4. If the deceased lived alone, make sure the residence is secure. Contact utility companies, the post office, and newspapers to terminate service. Remove valuables and place them in a safe-deposit box or mini warehouse.
5. Get background information about the deceased for the newspaper obituary. This information includes age, place of birth, cause of death, occupation, college degrees, special awards or recognition, survivors' names, and date and place of the funeral service.
6. Contact the attorney who prepared the decedent's will and living trust for helpful instructions on what to do next, who should be contacted, and *who should not be contacted.*
7. Obtain at least six copies of the death certificate from the mortuary; make sure that each is certified. These copies are necessary to transfer property into the names of the beneficiaries. You will need a copy for each asset and/or account.
8. Contact the nearest social security office to learn about the benefits the decedent's family might be entitled to.
9. If the decedent was a veteran, apply for the $250 reimbursement for burial expenses through the Veterans Administration.

10. Contact the decedent's employer, union, and professional group. One of these entities could have special death benefits for their members.

11. Contact credit-card issuers and home lender. The decedent may have owned credit life insurance or a mortgage-insurance policy.

12. Cancel the auto insurance and request a refund for the unused portion.

13. Review all estate-planning documents, recent banking and brokerage-firm statements, stock and bond certificates, real-estate deeds, and insurance policies.

14. Write to all prospective creditors. This list can be compiled by looking at the decedent's correspondence file, mail, signed contracts, and canceled checks. Pay those claims you feel are valid. You may wish to have an attorney help you with this step.

15. A list of all life-insurance policies should be included in the decedent's financial plan or as one of the trust-package documents. Each company should be given a certified copy of the death certificate and request for payment.

16. Have all appreciated property appraised. This may include real estate, securities, and collectibles.

17. Contact the decedent's accountant. State and federal income taxes must be filed for the year in which the death occurred; the surviving spouse may file a joint return for this year. An estate-tax return may also have to be filed and paid. Approximate tax liability should be determined before properties are distributed, thereby limiting the executor's and successor trustee's personal liability to the IRS. If there is an A-B or A-B-C Trust, then a tax-identification number will have to be obtained for the B and C trusts.

18. Read the Letter of Instruction Regarding Personal Property, which will be found with the living-trust documents, and make such distributions accordingly.

19. The successor trustee should request that all titled assets be retitled. Changing the name (ownership) on titled accounts would include contacting the county recorder's office, banks, savings and loan associations, and brokerage firms.

20. Contact the Department of Motor Vehicles so that the decedent's name can be removed as co-owner of any vehicle.

21. Building- or homeowner-policy issuers should be notified so that the decedent is removed as beneficiary.

Summary

An executor is named in your will or pour-over will. This person has the responsibility of watching over any personal property and real estate left outside your trust and not titled as joint tenancy. The executor also is responsible for filing your last income-tax return and possibly an estate-tax return. Income tax and any estate taxes are paid for from cash and other assets in your estate.

The trustee, who is often also the same person you named as executor, is responsible for managing and/or distributing all property titled in the name of your trust. If the trustee and executor are two different persons or institutions, oftentimes each will work with the other in order to make estate settlement as easy as possible.

Checklist of Things to Do

1. Make sure the named executor and trustee understand their respective duties.
2. Tell the executor and trustee where the original trust and will are located.
3. Leave written instructions with your attorney, executor and/or trustee as to which individuals, groups, and companies should be contacted upon your death.

APPENDIX F

LIFE-EXPECTANCY TABLE

Ages				Ages		
Male	Female	Years		Male	Female	Years
59	64	18.9		86	91	5.4
60	65	18.2		87	92	5.1
61	66	17.5		88	93	4.8
62	67	16.9		89	94	4.5
63	68	16.2		90	95	4.2
64	69	15.6		91	96	4.0
65	70	15.0		92	97	3.7
66	71	14.4		93	98	3.5
67	72	13.8		94	99	3.3
68	73	13.2		95	100	3.1
69	74	12.6		96	101	2.9
70	75	12.1		97	102	2.7
71	76	11.6		98	103	2.5
72	77	11.0		99	104	2.3
73	78	10.5		100	105	2.1
74	79	10.1		101	106	1.9
75	80	9.6		102	107	1.7
76	81	9.1		103	108	1.5
77	82	8.7		104	109	1.3
78	83	8.3		105	110	1.2
79	84	7.8		106	111	1.0
80	85	7.5		107	112	.8
81	86	7.1		108	113	.7
82	87	6.7		109	114	.6
83	88	6.3		110	115	.5
84	89	6.0		111	116	.0
85	90	5.7				

GLOSSARY

You may have come across some words that you were either not familiar with or felt needed more explanation. In order to aid your comprehension, this glossary contains definitions that are phrased slightly differently from the way they were in the main text. Also included are terms not used in the main text that you might find helpful when meeting with your attorney, reading other sources, or filling out court forms.

Abate—what happens in a will when the inheritances of one or more persons are reduced in order to pay the estate's debts, probate costs, and taxes.

A-B Trust—a way to provide for your surviving spouse and protect the interests of your children (or other beneficiaries).

Accumulation Trust—a type of trust that does not pay out all of its income until certain conditions occur.

Acknowledgment—a statement made in front of a notary public that a document with your signature was actually signed by you.

Administration—the court-supervised distribution of an estate during probate.

Administrator—the person named by the probate court to represent your estate if there is not a valid will or your will did not name an executor, also referred to as a personal representative.

Affidavit—a statement that is notarized and signed under oath by anyone having personal knowledge of the facts; these statements are used to support facts contained in documents submitted to the court.

Anatomical Gift—a gift of part of your body at death to be used by someone needing that organ or as use in a medical research facility.

Ancillary Probate—an additional probate proceeding in another state; what happens if you own real estate in a state other than where you are domiciled and such property is not in the name of your trust.

Annual Exclusion—the amount you can gift each year per donee without having to file a return or pay gift taxes; $10,000 is the limit for individuals, $20,000 if a married couple makes the gift jointly.

Annuity—set-dollar-amount payments made for a specific period at regular intervals.

Annuity Trust—a type of trust that will pay you a set amount each year while you are alive; the property passes to a charity after your death.

Appraiser—an expert who determines the market or fair value of an asset; the probate court may appoint one or more appraisers to determine the value of an estate for purposes of probate, guardianship, or conservatorship.

Asset—a word used to describe anything that you own, including real estate, life insurance, royalties, jewelry, art, furniture, clothing, automobiles, stocks, bonds, mutual funds, bank accounts, CDs, government securities, gold, silver, and collectibles.

Attestation—what witnesses to a will sign, verifying that you acknowledged that what you were signing was a will and that such signing, as well as those of the witnesses, was done in front of each and every witness.

Backup Trustee—commonly referred to as a successor trustee; a person or entity you would name in your document to manage the trust if the named trustee died, became incompetent, resigned, or was for some other reason unable to serve.

Basis—the price you pay for something adjusted downward for any depreciation taken or upward for fix-up costs; basis is important to know in order to calculate any taxes due when the asset is sold, transferred, gifted, or inherited.

Beneficiaries—the persons and/or organizations who receive trust property (or other property by will) at either the time of your death or at some later date (e.g., when they become an adult, finish college, buy a house, reach age 35).

Bequeath—a legal word used to describe the process of leaving personal property in a will.

Bequest—a gift of property at death; inherited real estate is technically called a *devise* while all other types of assets are called *bequests*.

By Right of Representation—how an asset can be distributed if the intended beneficiary predeceases you; the wording of a trust document or will can specify if the children or other natural heirs of the deceased are to receive an interest in the property upon *your* death.

Bypass Trust—a name sometimes used to describe the B part of an A-B Trust.

Children—the term includes the biological offspring, persons legally adopted, persons born out of wedlock (if the grantor or creator of the will is the mother), persons born out of wedlock if the grantor of the person making a will or trust is a man who has legally acknowledged the child as being his, and stepchildren and foster children if the relationship began while the child was a minor and continues through the parties' joint lifetimes and the "parent" would have adopted the person had it not been for some legal barrier.

Class—one or more beneficiaries, or their heirs, that is described only by status; common examples are "children," "grandchildren," and "issue."

Codicil—A written change or amendment to your will; such a change should be made on a separate piece of paper and signed with the same formalities as your will.

Community Property—property acquired during marriage (salaries, assets, retirement-account contributions, and growth, etc.) is to be equally divided between spouses in the event of divorce or death; the property must have been purchased, transferred, or contributed to while the married couple was living in one of 8 community-property states.

Conditional Bequest—personal property that will be received by someone if something occurs (e.g., "I leave my boat to John if he has finished college by the time of my death, otherwise the boat will go to Mary").

Conservator—the person named to oversee and manage the affairs of an incapacitated person; the appointment can be requested by the person or brought about by court action.

Conservatorship—a court proceeding to appoint the conservator; referred to as a probate guardianship in some states.

Contingent Beneficiary—a person or organization that is entitled to part or all of an estate left by will or trust if the "original" beneficiaries are unable to accept (i.e., they predecease the decedent or refuse to accept).

Corporate Trustee—an entity or organization, such as a bank, savings and loan association, or financial-planning firm, which specializes in managing trusts and/or is listed as a trustee in the trust document.

Corpus—another name for property owned by the trust (titled in the name of the trust).

Cost Basis—what you paid for the personal property or real estate.

Creditor—a person or entity that is owed money or property.

Crummey Letter—named after a person who brought forth what became a landmark case in estate planning; it is a written notification to beneficiaries that a gift has been made to an irrevocable life-insurance trust.

Curtesy—what a husband is entitled to, usually one-third or one-half, of his deceased wife's estate.

Custodian—a person or entity named to manage the financial affairs of a minor; only the custodian has the power to buy, sell, or transfer assets in the minor's account.

Decedent—the person who died.

Deduction—things that cause the value of an estate to be reduced so that estate taxes are eliminated or lessened.

Deed—document that describes a property and its owner.

Deed of Trust—a deed, similar to a mortgage, that gives legal title to real estate in the name of one or more lenders (trustees) as security for a loan.

Descent—property that passes at death.

Devise—an inheritance of real estate or personal property; in short, any asset.

Devisee—the person or organization who receives real estate by a will.

Discharge—the formal ending of an executor's or administrator's duties, which usually occurs at the end of probate.

Disclaimer—the refusal of a gift or inheritance; often done when the initial recipient wants someone else, usually their child, to receive the asset.

Domicile—the state where you are considered to have legal residence.

Donee—a person or entity who receives a gift.

Donor—the person or entity making the gift.

Dower—what a wife is entitled to, usually one-third or one-half, of her deceased husband's estate.

Durable Power of Attorney—a power of attorney that remains valid even if the maker later becomes incompetent.

Durable Power of Attorney for Health Care—the person named to make health-care decisions for you if you are unable to; this power terminates upon revocation or death of its maker—in some states this power must be renewed every 7 years.

Durable Power of Attorney for Finances—the person or entity you name to manage your assets. Like any other durable power, this one also remains in effect even if the person who granted the power (the maker) becomes mentally and/or physically incapacitated.

Encumbrances—something that must be paid off before a property can pass from one owner to another; can include such things as mechanic's liens, court judgments, and loans.

Escheat—when property belonging to the decedent passes to the state owing to a lack of heirs (i.e., no spouse, children, parents, grandparents, brothers, sisters, uncles, aunts, etc.).

Estate—the assets *and* debts left by someone at death.

Estate Planning—a thought-out process of enjoying your assets to the fullest extent possible and leaving what assets remain to your beneficiaries with little or no estate taxes due (and, hopefully, no probate).

Estate Tax—federal and state taxes due based on the net value of one's estate, only a small percentage of estates are subject to this tax, because of the estate-tax exclusion; sometimes called a death, transfer, or inheritance tax.

Executor—the person or entity named in a will or pour-over will to oversee the estate of the deceased until all final distributions are made, taxes paid, and bills settled; sometimes called a personal representative.

Expenses of Administration—costs incurred by the estate's executor or administrator in carrying out the terms of your will or intestate succession.

Fiduciary—person or entity that has a legal duty to act for another's benefit; fiduciaries are common when dealing with estates, trusts, wills, minor children, or incapacitated adults.

Five-Plus-Five Power—a clause that can be included in an A-B Trust that allows the surviving spouse the ability to annually withdraw, for any reason, 5% of the value of the B Trust, or $5,000, whichever is greater.

Flower Bonds—bonds issued over 20 years ago by the U.S. government that pay interest and are designed to be used to pay estate taxes; these types of bonds can still be purchased in the secondary market.

Future Interest—a right to property that can be enforced sometime in the future.

Gain—the difference between the sales price and the adjusted basis.

Generation-Skipping Tax—a large tax on assets that skip a generation and are left instead to grandchildren or great-grandchildren; everyone has a million-dollar exemption from this tax.

Generation-Skipping Trust—a type of trust that is structured so that children are given either nothing or only income for life, with the actual principal passing to grandchildren or great-grandchildren.

Gift Tax—a federal tax on transfers made without fair compensation (a gift or disguised gift) during the donor's life; many states, including California, do not have gift taxes.

Grantor—also known as a trustor or settlor, this is the person who creates the trust.

Grantor Trust—name sometimes used by the IRS to identify a living trust.

Gross Estate—the value of an estate before debts are paid, mortgages subtracted, and funeral costs taken out; this is also the value used to determine probate fees.

Heirs—the persons or organizations who receive assets through intestate succession (when there is no will, an invalid will, or the will does not dispose of all the property and there is not a trust); throughout the book, the words "heirs" and "beneficiaries" are used interchangeably.

Heirs-at-Law—persons entitled to part or all of your estate, owing to your state's laws of intestate succession.

Holographic Will—a will that is completely handwritten; in some states, including California, witnesses are not needed for this type of will.

Incapacitated or Incompetent—two words used interchangeably to refer to the same person: one who is unable to manage his or her own affairs owing to mental or physical conditions that are either temporary or permanent.

Incidents of Ownership—control over a life-insurance policy; this usually means that the policy will be included as part of the decedent's estate if he or she possesses any hint of ownership.

Income—money received from someone or some asset, including rents, royalties, interest, dividends, salary, tips, bonuses, and commissions.

Inherit—receiving property from someone who has died.

Inheritance Tax—sometimes used to describe an estate tax, either on the state or federal level; many states do not have such a tax.

Inter Vivos Trust—a trust that takes effect during the lifetime of its maker. A living trust is a type of inter vivos trust.

Intestate Succession—rules established by your estate to determine who receives property after your death if a valid will and/or trust does not exist.

Inventory—a listing of assets and their respective values that will be needed if your estate is subject to probate or a conservatorship.

Irrevocable Trust—similar to a revocable trust except in two key areas: (1) once signed, an irrevocable trust cannot be revoked or changed and (2) its creation may trigger an immediate gift tax. In this book three of these types of trust were covered: the life-insurance trust, the charitable remainder trust, and the charitable lead trust.

Issue—descendants, including those considered natural, adopted, legitimate, or illegitimate.

Joint Ownership—when two or more persons and/or entities own the same asset; joint tenancy (with rights of survivorship) and tenancy in common are the two most popular forms of joint ownership.

Joint Will—one will, signed by two or more people, usually used by a married couple or two people living together.

Kindred—anyone defined as being one of your relatives.

Lapsed Gift—a inheritance that does not go to the intended beneficiary because he or she has predeceased the trustor or testator.

Legacy—property that passed by will; more commonly referred to as a "bequest" or "devise."

Letters of Administration—document issued by the court giving the court-appointed representative of your estate the power to carry out his or her duties.

Letters Testamentary—document giving your estate's representative the deceased's assets for purposes of distribution.

Life Estate—a gift or inheritance in which the donee is able to use the property during his or her lifetime.

Life-Insurance Trust—an irrevocable trust designed so that your life-insurance premiums are paid by the trust so that the death benefit is not included as part of your estate; this is an estate-planning device.

Living Will—a document stating that you do not want to be kept alive by artificial means if the injury, illness, or condition is terminal; it is not actually a will but a directive instead.

Living Trust—a document that creates a legally recognized entity; you place some or all of your assets in this entity, the trust, and have someone or some entity manage it for the benefit of you, your spouse, children, relatives, friends, and/or organizations (such as a charity, partnership, or corporation).

Marital Deduction—you may gift, will, or transfer an *unlimited* amount of money, real estate, or personal property to your spouse without paying any kind of gift or estate taxes.

Marriage—a legal and tax status conferred on a couple.

Minor Child—a person who is not an adult, thereby generally lacking what is known as "legal capacity" (the ability to enter into a binding contract or sale); in some states a child becomes an adult at age 18, in other states the age is 21.

Mutual Will—two separate wills with substantially identical provisions.

Net Estate Tax Due—taxes due on an estate after credits and deductions have been subtracted.

Net Value—what estate-tax liability is based on (not probate); the value of an estate after all debts, mortgages, burial costs, and other final expenses have been deducted.

Next of Kin—closest living relatives of the decedent.

Notice of Death—notice published and mailed by your estate's representative to creditors and immediate family members.

Nuncupative Will—an oral will that is allowed in some states under special circumstances for very small estates.

Per Capita—a clause that can be included in your will or trust that means if the intended beneficiary predeceases you, his or her share will be equally divided among the other beneficiaries.

Per Stirpes—a clause that can be included in your will or trust that means if the intended beneficiary predeceases you, his or her share will be equally divided among that predeceased's beneficiaries (e.g., you wanted your son to inherit 300 shares of IBM and your personal residence, he dies before you do but he is survived by 3 children, your grandchildren; upon your death each grandchild will get 100 shares of IBM and one-third interest in the house).

Personal Property—everything that is not real estate (real property), including cash, securities, bank accounts, jewelry, art, collections, etc.

Personal Representative—another name for the executor or administrator of an estate.

Petition—a document filed with the court requesting certain action.

Pour-over Will—a section included in a living trust so that all assets not titled in the name of the trust will automatically be "poured over" into the trust and distributed and/or managed according to the general terms of the trust; assets in a pour-over will are subject to possible probate proceedings.

Power of Appointment—giving someone the power to dispose of someone else's property.

Pretermitted Heir—a spouse, child, or grandchild who is not mentioned in a will; in such a case this heir could still be entitled to a certain portion of the decedent's estate.

Probate—a process that validates a will (if there is one). An executor or administrator is appointed, debts and taxes are paid, heirs are identified, and property distributed.

Probate Guardian—a person named by the court who manages the affairs of a minor until the child becomes an adult.

Proving a Will—having the probate court accept a will as being valid; oftentimes, this simply means introducing a properly witnessed and signed will.

Qualified Terminable Interest Property Trust (Q-TIP)—also known as the C Trust in an A-B-C Trust. Property placed in such a trust escapes estate tax when the first spouse dies (but not when the second spouse passes away). The surviving spouse must be entitled to receive all of the income from the C Trust, even though the decedent can control the final distribution and/or management of this trust "from the grave."

Quasi–Community Property—all personal property and real estate located in a community-property state that is owned by a community-property couple but was acquired in a non-community-property state.

Real Property—real estate, land, permanent fixtures (kitchen cabinets, bath fixtures, etc.), and mineral rights.

Remainderman—the person who receives part or all of a trust's assets once the trust is terminated; usually there is nothing left.

Residence—the physical location a person considers to be his or her home; normally, a person can have only one residence for purposes of estate settlement.

Residuary—also referred to as the "residue," this is what is left of an estate after all specified gifts and bequests have been made.

Reversionary Interest—assets that pass on to another person because a condition was either fulfilled or not met.

Revocable Trust—a trust that can be altered, amended, changed, revoked, or terminated at any time while its creator (you) is still alive and competent. The focus of this book is on living trusts, a type of revocable trust.

Right of Representation—occurs when the descendants of a deceased beneficiary equally share what the deceased beneficiary would have received if alive.

Rule Against Perpetuities—a law that requires all trusts to terminate by the time that everyone mentioned in the trust dies, plus 21 years.

Self-Proving Will—a will that allows the court to accept it as valid without further proof; in many states this means a will that was properly witnessed.

Separate Property—all assets that you acquire prior to marriage and those assets acquired by gift or inheritance during marriage.

Settlor—a name for a person who creates a trust; also referred to as trustor, trust maker, or grantor.

Specific Bequest—a specific asset that is to go to a specific beneficiary; if the item is no longer part of the trust or estate at the time it is to be distributed, the beneficiary is out of luck.

Spouse—a husband or wife.

Sprinkling Trust—a provision included in a trust allowing the trustee to distribute trust income and/or principal among different beneficiaries in varying or equal amounts.

State Death (Inheritance) Tax Credit—the amount of any federal estate tax that instead goes to the decedent's state of residency; the estate is not paying anything extra in taxes since the amount owed to the feds is reduced by whatever goes to the state.

Succession—acquiring property not disposed of by will or trust.

Surety Bond—unless waived, a bond required for an executor or administrator before he or she can be actively involved with the estate; the premium for the bond is paid by the estate (you).

Surviving Spouse's Trust—a name sometimes used to refer to the A Trust in an A-B or A-B-C Trust

Taking Against the Will—giving the surviving spouse the option of taking the statutory share of the decedent spouse's estate instead of what has been specified in his or her will; in most of the 42 common-law states, this means that the survivor is entitled to one-third or one-half of such estate.

Tenancy by the Entirety—a type of joint tenancy that can be used only by a married couple; not recognized in all states.

Tenancy in Common—a form of co-ownership wherein each owner has a right to sell, transfer, gift, encumber, or bequeath his or her interest by any means, including a will or living trust; unlike joint tenancy, a tenancy in common has no rights of survivorship.

Testamentary Disposition—property disposed of by will.

Testamentary Trust—a trust that becomes effective when the trustor dies; unlike a living trust, a testamentary trust has no effect while the trustor is alive; it is not a means of avoiding probate.

Testate—someone who dies with a valid will.

Testator—the person who makes a will.

Title—document that proves ownership.

Totten Trust—also known as a "pay-on-death" account; a way to leave a bank account to a beneficiary named when the account was opened—this type of account is not recognized by all banks and can be amended or revoked at any time before the depositor's death.

Transfer Agent—a corporate representative (or employee) who transfers ownership of a corporation's stock and/or bonds from one person to another; transfer agents are used by executors, administrators, trustors, trustees, guardians, and conservators when changing title on a security.

Trust—a fiduciary relationship wherein a person, called the trustor, transfers the title of property from his or her name into the name of the trust; the fiduciary, called a trustee, manages the property for the beneficiary, which may be the trustor, his or her family, friends, relatives, an organization, etc.

Trust Estate—sometimes called the "trust corpus" or "trust res," refers to all property that goes into the trust.

Trust Merger—when the only trustee and sole beneficiary are the same person; the trust ceases to exist at this point since there is no longer a difference between the trustee's legal ownership and the beneficiary's interest.

Trustee—the person and/or entity who has the legal and fiduciary duty to hold, manage, and/or distribute assets within the trust; the trustee's powers are limited by law and the trust document.

Trustor—the person or entity that creates the trust; also referred to as a "grantor" or "settlor."

Unified Credit—the amount an estate can use to offset estate taxes; estate-tax liability on a net estate worth $600,000 is $192,800—this is why the "unified credit" is sometimes referred to as being equal to an equivalent exemption of $600,000 ($1,200,000 if you are married).

Uniform Transfers to Minors Act (UTMA)—very similar to the Uniform Gifts to Minors Act (UGMA). A way to leave property to a minor by appointing a "custodian" to manage the property; an account for a minor without using an attorney or drafting a special document. Can also be used in a will or trust.

Will—a written document that includes the decedent's instructions for the disposition of part or all of his or her estate; a will can be enforced only through the probate court.

Index